DEAR BOYS
World War II Letters from a Woman Back Home

DEAR BOYS

World War II Letters from a Woman Back Home

Back Home

EDITED BY

JUDY BARRETT LITOFF   DAVID C. SMITH

UNIVERSITY PRESS OF MISSISSIPPI
Jackson & London

Print-on-Demand Edition

The paper in this book meets the guidelines for permanence and durability of the Committee on Production Guidelines for Book Longevity of the Council on Library Resources.

Library of Congress Cataloging-in-Publication Data

Somerville, Keith Frazier, 1888-1978.
Dear boys: World War II letters from a woman back home/edited by Judy Barrett Litoff, David C. Smith.
    p.   cm.
"This volume includes excerpts from every 'Dear boys' column written by Mrs. Keith Frazier Somerville and published in the Bolivar commercial between January 15, 1943 and August 31, 1945" —Editor's pref.
Includes bibliographical references (p.   ) and index.
ISBN 978-1-60473-400-3
1. World War, 1939–1945—Mississippi—Bolivar County. 2. World War, 1939–1945—Mississippi—Delta (Region) 3. Bolivar County (Miss.)—Social life and customs. 4. Delta (Miss.: Region)—Social life and customs. I. Litoff, Judy Barrett. II. Smith, David C. (David Clayton), 1929– . III. Title.
D769.M71B657   1991
940.53'7624—dc20

91-16921
CIP

British Library Cataloging-in-Publication data available

*In Memory and in Honor
of Bolivar County Veterans of War*

Contents

Editors' Preface

This volume includes excerpts from every "Dear Boys" column written by Mrs. Keith Frazier Somerville and published in the *Bolivar Commercial* between January 15, 1943 and August 31, 1945. The column frequently contained lengthy paragraphs which listed the names and locations of Bolivar County citizens in the service of their country. Although this information was of great interest to wartime readers, we have chosen to omit some of this detail. We have used ellipses to indicate omissions.

Keith Frazier Somerville was a "creative" speller. We have made every effort to correct misspellings of proper names and places. We apologize for any remaining errors.

We have provided footnotes which identify the many literary allusions, political events, and World War II references found in the column. We hope that readers will be as impressed with the breadth of Mrs. Somerville's knowledge as we are.

Acknowledgments

Individuals from Mississippi to Maine and beyond have generously given of their energy, time, and expertise toward the making of *Dear Boys*. Constance Cameron, Patrick Kelly, and Gretchen McLoughlin of the Hodgson Memorial Library of Bryant College provided yeoman detective work. The reference staff at the Fogler Library of the University of Maine was equally helpful. Ronnie Wise and Jonette Valentine of the Robinson-Carpenter Library of Cleveland, Mississippi took a personal interest in the project. We also wish to thank the staff of the W. R. Roberts Library of Delta State University.

Vivian West, a research assistant at Bryant College, was instrumental in organizing and analyzing the "Dear Boys" columns. Both Bryant College and the University of Maine have supported us in our work with research stipends and sabbatical leaves. Seetha Srinivasan of the University Press of Mississippi provided us with encouragement in the early stages of the project and carefully followed the book through to its completion.

Delta hospitality is world renowned, and we are truly in awe of the warmth and graciousness of the people of the Mississippi Delta. We would like to offer special thanks to Norman C. Van Liew, editor of the *Bolivar Commercial*, and his staff for helping us as we combed through the original pages of the newspaper for the wartime years. Microfilm has great utility, but it in no way replaces the thrill of turning dusty, yellow pages from the past. David "Boo" Ferriss, one of Mrs. Somerville's "Dear Boys," spent part of a memorable afternoon with us discussing baseball, World War II, and life in the Mississippi Delta. Pete Walker of Executive Graphics Corporation took special care in reproducing many of the illustrations which appear in this book. "Judge"

Lucy Somerville Howorth was kind enough to share her personal memories of her sister-in-law and her own work in Washington D.C. during the Depression and World War II.

Although Martha Swain is a Professor of History at Texas Woman's University, everyone who knows her is well aware that she is first and foremost a Mississippian. We want to thank her for taking time from her other research commitments to write the biographical essay about Keith Frazier Somerville. In addition, she read the entire manuscript and offered a number of insightful comments.

The exemplars of Delta hospitality are Keith Somerville Dockery McLean and her husband, Hite. Keith McLean is a true daughter of her wonderful mother. Although we never met Keith Frazier Somerville, we are honored to have known her daughter, Keith Somerville Dockery McLean.

DEAR BOYS
World War II Letters from a Woman Back Home

Cleveland had always been such a good place to live and I guess it had always seemed to be a little isolated from the rest of the world so that anything that happened somewhere else wouldn't affect us. We were just too naive to understand the significance of World War II until the bodies started coming home.

Alma Blaylock Malaby Frazier
quoted in the Centennial Edition
of the *Bolivar Commercial*
June 27, 1986

Introduction

DEAR BOYS: A WARTIME LEGACY

"War has come to all the main streets of Mississippi, and I am more and more convinced each week that with all you grand boys in there enthusiastically pitching, and with all the people at home backing you, victory will certainly be ours."[1] Keith Frazier Somerville expressed this hope soon after she began writing a bi-monthly column, entitled "Dear Boys," which appeared from January 1943 through August 1945, in the *Bolivar Commercial*, a weekly newspaper published in the small Delta town of Cleveland, Bolivar County, Mississippi. Mrs. Somerville, a well-known member of the community and former school teacher, wrote her epistolary column "in the hope that it will give the boys from Cleveland and vicinity who are all over the world an opportunity to keep up with happenings here."[2]

Throughout the wartime years, there was an enormous outpouring of correspondence from all parts of the United States to men and women in the service.[3] Family members and friends often set aside a special time each day to write loved ones stationed far away from home. This flood of mail was supplemented by newsletters written by women's clubs, neighborhood groups, families, businesses, churches, and schools.[4] News columns written in the form of letters were often published in local newspapers. The "Dear Boys" column from Cleveland,

Mississippi, with its mission of sustaining morale as well as insuring that young Americans far away from home were informed of local events, is a significant example of this genre.[5]

The mail and the importance of its rapid and regular delivery was never more poignantly clear than during World War II. Magazine covers, feature and news articles, thousands of advertisements, government posters, greeting cards, advice manuals, novels, short stories, and popular songs all depicted the mail as an important morale builder.[6] Recognizing the important role of the mail in wartime, the Post Office Department reported in 1942 "that frequent and rapid communication with parents, associates, and loved ones strengthens fortitude, enlivens patriotism, makes loneliness endurable, and inspires to even greater devotion the men and women who are carrying on our fight far from home and friends."[7] In fact, there was a 513 percent increase in the volume of mail sent overseas. All told, the United States Post Office handled close to 200 billion pieces of mail between 1940 and 1945. In 1940, about 28 billion items were distributed; by 1945, this figure had risen to 38 billion.[8]

Keith Frazier Somerville was, herself, a prolific wartime letter writer, forwarding the hometown news to many young servicemen and, in turn, hearing from them.[9] When she mentioned to Clifton L. Langford, editor of the *Bolivar Commercial*, that she had been corresponding with many of the local men and women in the service, he suggested, "Why not write a letter now and then to all of them, through the columns of this paper?" As she remarked in her first column, "I jumped at the idea," and "Dear Boys" followed. Mrs. Somerville, who was fifty-four years old at the time, was the ideal person to write such a column. Although she had no boys of her own, or as she said, "all my boys were girls," she knew many of the young people in the service because as a first-grade teacher, "I started a lot of you off in school." As she candidly remarked in her wartime journal, "Honestly, I believe I'm one of the few in town who *could* do it. I know the '400' (and am considered of it!), but I know lots more of the '4 million' from my ten years of teaching the first grade!"[10]

"Dear Boys" was an immediate success. During the early months of 1943, the *Bolivar Commercial* published several enthusiastic letters from local servicemen stationed in Europe, North Africa, and stateside thanking Mrs. Somerville for her column. Their sentiments were probably best summed up by Lt. A.L. Melott who, in a letter which was printed on the front page of the March 12, 1943 issue of the *Bolivar Commercial*, wrote, "I want to tell you how thoroughly I enjoy your write ups in the *Bolivar Commercial* about the lads in the service. Monday is *"Bolivar Commercial Day"* and I look forward to receiving it." The many letters of thanks which continued to arrive throughout the war years were concrete evidence of the importance of the column.[11]

In her first letter, published on January 15, 1943, Keith Somerville set the tone for her column when she told "the boys" how appreciative everyone in Bolivar County was of their contribution to the preservation of freedom in the world. She wrote, "We ARE proud of you, . . . enduring hardships and fighting to preserve [the American way of life]; fighting for Freedom and for us; fighting to keep the rights our forefathers won the hard way, too; fighting to keep liberty in a world, so much of which has been over-run by Hitler and Tojo. . . ." After this stirring beginning, she continued, "Outwardly, life goes on the same here in our little town. People still go to Denton's for a coke, but often they can't get one! Can you feature that? . . . None of us ride to Denton's as much as we used to, with gas rationing on (four gallons don't take you on many joy rides!) so we're all learning to walk."[12] For the next thirty-two months, until the war was over in August 1945, Mrs. Somerville continued to provide information about life in Bolivar County as she also reported on what was happening to local citizens scattered throughout the "four corners of the world."[13]

On the eve of World War II, Cleveland, with a population of 4,100, was a shopping and commercial center for the 67,000 citizens who lived in Bolivar County as well as the county seat of its second judicial district. It was also an educational center as Delta State Teachers College (now Delta State University) had been founded there in 1924. Indeed, Delta State was the alma mater of many young Bolivar County citizens who were summoned to service in the Second World War. Its fall 1940 enrollment of 321 students had dwindled to 153 students by 1943–1944, leaving women to comprise a sizable majority of the remaining student body.[14]

Situated 120 miles south of Memphis, Tennessee, in the heart of the rich alluvial delta plain of the Mississippi River, Cleveland was located in a prime cotton-producing area that the *Bolivar Commercial* described as "one of the richest agricultural sections on earth."[15] Most of the cotton from this area was grown on very large plantations. The owners of these plantations and their families comprised a small planter society which was romanticized, criticized, and mythologized in the writings of William Faulkner, Eudora Welty, and the southern Agrarians. Ironically, however, one of the largest plantations in the Delta at the time of World War II was Delta and Pine Land, a company of British investors which cultivated 38,000 acres of cotton in Bolivar County.[16]

Scattered near and among the plantations of Bolivar County were a number of small towns and hamlets, most with less than a thousand inhabitants. They included Duncan, Alligator, Hushpuckena, Benoit, Pace, Merigold, Shelby, Shaw, and Boyle. The most unusual town in the county was Mound Bayou, one of the few all-black towns in the nation, whose founding in 1887 comprised a unique chapter in Mississippi history. Foremost among its 800 citizens in 1940 was Ben Green, a Harvard-educated lawyer, and the only barrister in Bolivar County who could boast such a degree.[17]

These small Bolivar County towns so familiar to Keith Somerville were very similar to others in the Mississippi Delta country, each usually boasting of a cotton gin, "filling" station, loading platform, and a few brick stores. Farm-to-market roads, many of them unimproved, criss-crossed the country connecting the small settlements or the large plantations that were the center of the cotton culture. Much of the land was tilled by black sharecroppers. In fact, at the outset of the war, 49,000, or 73 percent, of the 67,000 residents of Bolivar County were black. The mechanization of cotton agriculture would not occur until after World War II, and cotton remained a very labor intensive crop, cultivated by this large underclass of black sharecroppers and a few white tenant farmers. Several other ethnic groups, including a small number of Chinese grocers, Jewish businessmen, and Italian farmers, also made their home in Bolivar County.[18] Keith Somerville knew many of these people, and, as with many Bolivar Countians, appreciated the roles that they played in the economic development of the community. Of the diversity represented by Cleveland's citizens, she once wrote, "Our little town, like all of America is a melting pot, and the descendants of all those people are now outstanding good citizens."[19]

Throughout the life of the "Dear Boys" column, Keith Somerville devoted considerable attention to the wartime activities of the various ethnic groups in Bolivar County, often tying her comments to larger issues and world events. When Italian prisoners of war were brought to Bolivar County to pick cotton, she used this occurrence to discuss the impact of the war on local persons of Italian ancestry.[20] The Greek resistance to the Germans was an occasion to discuss Bolivar residents of Greek descent involved in the war effort. Chinese Americans from Mississippi and southerners fighting for China in the American Volunteer Group, "The Flying Tigers," received close attention. Citizens of Polish and Russian descent were also championed. Regardless of the ethnic group under discussion, she nearly always ended on an optimistic note as when on September 24, 1943, she concluded her comments on local Italians in the military by saying, "[We all are] hoping that in the happy days to come when war is no more, that Italy and the United States may ever afterwards live in peace and friendship."[21]

Mrs. Somerville was well informed of events that many other Americans chose to ignore. After recounting the military careers of local Jewish citizens, she made it clear to her readers how she felt about German atrocities directed toward Jews. Referring to reports from the American Jewish Congress in the spring of 1943, she gave horrible details of the massacres of millions of Jews in Poland. She went on to ask, "Why should anyone care whether one is Jew, Gentile, or Catholic? It passeth our understanding truly." She continued by relating an anecdote about Colin Kelly, the Army Air Corps pilot and first well-known hero of the war, whose bombardier was Meyer Levi, a Jew from Brooklyn. She described how another American pilot, when announcing on the radio of his intention to bomb Tokyo, exclaimed that "he was proud to fight for my country where a Jew and an Irish Catholic, the best of buddies, will live in everlasting fame for their heroism." Mrs. Somerville then remarked, "That's our American answer to Nazi intolerance."[22]

"Dear Boys" often discussed the military accomplishments and war related activities of Bolivar County residents of African-American descent. Although Mrs. Somerville used the word "colored" frequently, it was and is obvious that she was a believer in racial tolerance. For example, shortly after the presidential election of 1944, she took the opportunity to chastise the bolting Democratic Mississippi electors who had refused to vote for Franklin Roosevelt because of their great disdain for the New Deal's support for blacks. She told her readers that she had been so "aroused" by this incident that she had sent "protesting letters to all those bolting electors, who, like obnoxious small boys refuse to play when they can't have their way."[23]

Another significant indication of Mrs. Somerville's support for racial tolerance was her visits to the all-black town of Mound Bayou. These visits enabled her to provide a first-hand account of how the black population was aiding the war effort and being affected by the events of the war. In her column of April 23, 1943, following her first visit to Mound Bayou, she stated, "I have told you in recent letters of the contributions being made by the Catholics, Jews, Greeks, and Chinese among us and today I want to tell you what our [N]egroes are doing." She went on to describe the significant role that cotton played in the war effort and how black farmers were engaged in its cultivation. Yet she also noted that "it is not alone in our cotton fields that our Negroes are helping their Uncle Sam. Why up at Mound Bayou during March they bought more War Bonds than either Cleveland or Rosedale!"[24] She was pleased that her Mound Bayou column was published two days before the Memphis *Commercial Appeal* carried a full-page public service announcement, "The Negro and The War." "I beat the *Commercial*," she crowed.[25] Alongside a clipping of the column which she had pasted in her wartime journal, she wrote, "Think I'll have to frame my letter of thanks from the town of Mound Bayou for this letter about the [N]egro soldiers."[26]

She helped Mound Bayou citizens celebrate Abraham Lincoln's birthday during a visit to that town on February 12, 1944. In her next column, she remarked that "Uncle Sam says his colored soldiers are making fine records and it is just as true among our colored friends as among our white that practically every family in Bolivar County can boast at least one service star." In the fall of 1944, she told the story of Annie Tutwiler, a black six star mother, whose children were showing "to the world that all races, creeds, and colors in

America are in there fighting for that victory which today seems almost in sight!"[27]

Perhaps Mrs. Somerville's most extraordinary comments about race relations came after an April 1943 visit to Mound Bayou when she ended her letter to "the boys" with these words:

> . . . in Mound Bayou, Mississippi, I found America dreaming again. Dreaming of the day her sons will come marching home; dreaming of better housing and hospitalization; dreaming of the day when education will really "educate" our farm boys to be made better farmers, proud and happy in their life work, in the dignity of plowing their acres and working with their hands, as the Lord intended 80% of us to do. Dreaming too, of absolute fairness. And here in Bolivar County there are many southern white men and women, descendants of men and women who for 80 years have had their problems close to their hearts, who are dreaming with them that when our boys of all races, creeds and color come home again to peaceful years, we may all work together to make our dreams come true.[28]

Keith Frazier Somerville made many visits to other communities surrounding Cleveland to gather information about their contributions to the war effort. She frequently wrote about the nearby towns and hamlets of Merigold, Rosedale, Duncan, Pace, Shaw, Shelby, and Boyle. With gas rationing in effect, she often "hopped a ride" to neighboring towns, but on one occasion she shamefacedly reported that she had gone "WAY down to Boyle" for a "joy-ride." In actuality, the purpose of this three-mile trip was to glean information for her column. She also circumvented the gasoline shortage by taking a ride on a school bus "on a perfect May morning" so that she could gather news about the whereabouts and activities of the older siblings of the children on the bus.[29]

Mrs. Somerville visited Cleveland High School and attended a club meeting of the Junior Red Cross where the "big 'little sisters'" of the "boys" in the service were packaging hospital supplies for men in combat. She learned that "buddy bags" were made in high school sewing classes, and she further observed that the new knowledge of foods, vitamins, and balanced diets taught in home economic classes helped the war effort by enhancing the health and nutrition of all Americans.[30]

One of the most significant ways in which World War II changed the lives of young people was in the acceleration of romance and marriage. War marriages were frequent, and often one of the partners was no longer the local boyfriend or girlfriend so typical of the prewar era.[31] As Mrs. Somerville roved across the county and related military experiences of Bolivar citizens, she was very aware of the impact of the war on love, marriage, and families. She frequently informed her readers of war marriages celebrated in other areas of the United States, but of local interest because Bolivar County residents were involved.

She also described how war brides had come to Bolivar County to visit and sometimes to live with their parents or in-laws. Many of the recently married women brought their war babies with them, and Mrs. Somerville took special delight in discussing the "Boom in Babies." She noted that "there are a lot of happy grandmothers hereabouts, for the fortunes of war have sent home a bunch of our daughters with their babies."[32]

Her columns often mentioned how the young war brides filled in the days by getting together at "Coca Cola" parties where they shared letters from their husbands, talked of postwar plans, and provided comfort and solace when the inevitable bad news came to one of their number. She complimented the war wives for attending Red Cross knitting classes, rolling bandages for the combat front, and canning and preserving foods.[33] Of course, the spirit of these all female groups diminished as the war dragged on and their members anxiously waited for the return of the young men. For example, Mrs. Somerville reported that "with no boys available," one young bride-to-be found it necessary "to use her red-haired girl cousins for ushers!"[34]

Mrs. Somerville was pleased with the work of Cleveland's hurriedly created United Service Organization (USO). Although she admitted that it "can't equal the Stage Door Canteen in New York," she reported that it was well patronized by the "soldiers watching guard over the thousand Italian prisoners of war who are picking cotton hereabouts." She complimented the hostesses for having "done a bang-up job." In fact, many of the soldiers told her that the Cleveland USO was "the first place they've really met and talked to any Southerners!"[35]

On more than one occasion, Mrs. Somerville noted "how proud we are of our girls, as well as our boys!" She provided detailed news of the local women whose wartime work carried them to widely-scattered locations throughout the world. One young woman was working with the Red Cross in North Africa; another was training in Texas to be a ferry command pilot with the Women's Airforce Service Pilots. Many young Bolivar County women were employed in war plants around the South, and one woman made parts for Flying Fortresses in Inglewood, California. Several young women served their country by joining the WACS and WAVES. In reporting on the new opportunities opening up for women, Mrs. Somerville declared, "Gosh, I wish I were a young girl these days! There are no closed doors for them! They can get out and into the midst of things, and are doing it!"[36]

Keith Somerville was particularly interested in aviation, and she even hinted that she would like to take flying lessons. She reported on dozens of Bolivar County residents who had joined the Army Air Corps while also discussing the potential impact of aviation on the lives of rural Mississippians. She was especially proud of Captain Rowan Thomas of Boyle, Mississippi, and his popular book, *Born in Battle*, which described his experiences as a pilot with the 513th bombardment squadron.[37]

The chronicler of "Dear Boys" was always very careful to describe the local environs so that "homesick" Bolivarians could picture the places, as well as the people, they had left behind. For instance, in one of her earliest columns she described the main street of Cleveland, mentioning nearly every store and shop, and told of how the war was touching the lives of all the shop owners and their families.[38]

Near the end of the war, in February 1945, she returned to Cleveland's main street, again to look at the shops and their owners. This column was prompted by an article in *Liberty*, a widely-circulated magazine of the period, whose author, a returning veteran, had urged letter writers to discuss their small towns in their correspondence. His suggestion for letter writers had included the advice to "tell us what the restaurants have to eat; how many bonds our town bought; the price of things; about the girls working and how they're taking the manpower shortage. In fact tell us how the war is affecting our town!"[39]

Mrs. Somerville's columns were masterpieces in transmitting her sense of the importance of retaining small town American values. Taking the author of the *Liberty* article at his word, she "parked [her] 5 year old Ford in front of Pik-Nik" and started out walking down main street. In her report, she talked of food rationing and how menus at local restaurants had been modified to meet wartime food shortages. She also mentioned that the local grocery store had changed hands during the war period. She even recounted entering the local pool hall in her "wild search" for cigarettes, and although she passed this visit off as "gray hair can go anywhere," the fact that she even thought of entering the pool hall was an indication of the changing times.[40]

While visiting the "5 and 10," she noticed the shortages of the most popular pre-war candies. As she continued down the street, she visited clothing stores, observing prices and noting that civilian clothes were beginning to be made available for returning service personnel. Rationing was still in effect for shoes, as well as for food and gasoline, and she ruefully remarked, "If you go to every store in town, you can eventually get your [shoe] size, tho' I doubt if any of them are half as good as your G. I. issue." Several of the local stores were featuring charts showing comparative buying power between 1918 and 1945. The favorable results in the second war were due, she believed, to rationing and the fact that civilians had done such a good job in holding the line on their purchases.[41]

Further down the street, she observed the service flags and the photographs of the many young people still away. Yet she was also able to report that several persons, who had been discharged because of wounds, sickness or age, were already back home. She assured her readers that, as far as she could see, there would be plenty of jobs for everyone once the war was over. She also reassured her readers that Bolivar County citizens continued to back the war effort. Nearly every family had someone in the service, and she proudly boasted that Cleveland had "gone over the top" in war bond sales and in its acceptance of wartime conditions generally.[42]

She concluded her column about Cleveland's main street by quoting from the author of the *Liberty* article upon his return to his home town: "Suddenly you are home. You belong. You are a part of it. You feel like you have never been gone. You only experience a surge of contentment to find things as you left them. That's the way it is." Mrs. Somerville's response was, "that's the way I hope it is for you already home and will be for each of the others when you come home to stay. We'll be glad to see you all."[43]

Keith Somerville, with her exceptional world-view, was perceptive enough to know that the world was not going to be the same after the war as before. In fact, in many ways she was an advocate of change. Throughout the life of the column, she had provided gentle suggestions about the changes necessary for the postwar world. In the course of the thirty-two months of writing letters to those away from home, she discussed dozens of books and articles which carried a message of tolerance, the need to have a peaceful world, and, toward the end of the war, the promise of the United Nations. Over and over again she provided a glimpse of her vision of what the postwar world might be like.[44]

In her letter of July 2, 1943, for example, with Independence Day uppermost in her mind, she quoted from an article written by Owen Roberts, Justice of the United States Supreme Court, which she had recently read. Roberts had argued that the war had been caused by race prejudice, the lust for national aggrandizement, and weak international law. When peace returned, he hoped that a "daring . . . experiment, in world organization" made up of a "union of the democracies" could be created. Mrs. Somerville then asked her readers, "What do you boys think about it?" She finished her letter with, "Here's wishing a Happy Peaceful future for this war torn world."

As the war approached its end, her homilies about prospects for the postwar world intensified. In January 1945, she referred to the recent writings of James Hilton, who had written a pre-war best seller, *Lost Horizon* (1933), set in a mythical country called Shangri-La, whose name had become symbolic of peaceful existence. She paraphrased Hilton by saying, "1945 will be a year of destiny like 1919, and that to make it so, we must not only fight and work but believe passionately in certain things (like true peace and fairness) and stand up and express our opinions." Three weeks later, she mused about the Russians and the fact that they might enter the war against Japan now that the German and Italian enemies seemed to be close to defeat. She used this occasion to offer, once again, her thoughts about the needs of the postwar world.[45]

In April 1945, she wrote of her intense grief following the death of Franklin Roosevelt and of the small red, white, and blue floral tribute she arranged on her own dining room table. During the seventy-two hours in which she sat beside her radio listening to the news of the death of "the greatest man of our era," she was moved particularly by the comment of a small-town Kentucky newspaper editor, "There's a gold star in the world's window." This column also provided the opportunity for her to analyze the San Francisco conference of the United Nations then underway.[46]

The end of the war in Europe in May 1945 did not bring about the wild celebrations which had marked the close of World War I as there was much remaining to be accomplished. Mrs. Somerville was quick to remind readers that "we are only just half happy" as "we must await the complete surrender of Japan [and] the coming home of all you boys." There was, however, a large interdenominational thanksgiving service in Cleveland to mark the German surrender on the night of V-E Day. As she said, when describing the event, "Multiply our meeting by the hundreds of thousands of hamlets and cities in America, and you can see how many prayers went up on V-E day. Yes, most of us, felt more like praying for the early end of the Japanese war and for an abiding peace than like celebrating." Later in the same column, after suggesting that all eyes should be turned toward the Pacific where the war continued to rage and to San Francisco where the United Nations was meeting, she remarked, "with the horrors of war so close, I believe all nations honestly desire peace more than anything else, and despite differences of opinions, a start has been made."[47]

After the bombs fell on Hiroshima and Nagasaki in August 1945, the war in the Pacific and the Second World War came to an end. Mrs. Somerville wrote in her last column, "It seems almost unbelievable, doesn't it, that Peace has come again to the world? We have lived with war so long—it almost seems forever!" She had learned of the end of the war while in Monteagle, Tennessee, helping to care for her grandchildren. She told her readers of how she had gone to thanksgiving ceremonies and "wept some happy tears and said some prayers." She joined others in ringing the big church bell and even held up her "tiny granddaughters and let them pull the rope, so that in later years they might recall that they had a hand in the jubilation of ushering in peace in our time."

She described, in this column, how the news of the "awe-inspiring and terrifying" atomic bomb had stunned the world. She continued by saying, "Perhaps we have unloosed a Frankenstein, which may eventually destroy us, but it's here, and we should be thankful its secrets were discovered first by a peace loving nation! What if Germany had beaten us to it?"[48]

Keith Frazier Somerville was a most remarkable individual. When reading her "Dear Boys" columns, one is continuously struck by the breadth and depth of coverage given to the many significant and wide-reaching topics she discussed. She perceptively described the important role played by women in the winning of the war. She offered substantial analytical comments about race relations which were uncommon in wartime America, to say nothing of wartime Mississippi. She knew about and informed her readers of Nazi atrocities against Jews at a time when many people in much higher positions avoided the subject. She was proud of the multi-ethnic and multi-faith composition of Bolivar County, and she hoped that the war would provide the opportunity for greater personal and social equality in Bolivar County, in Mississippi, in the United States, and throughout the world. Moreover, she enthusiastically embraced the ideals of the United Nations and was especially concerned that the Soviet Union and the United States remain friends and partners in the postwar era.

After the war was over, the changes Mrs. Somerville predicted and described did not come as fast as she and others might have hoped. Some changes did not come at all. The war however, did change the small town America of Keith Frazier Somerville and her readers, not only in the Mississippi Delta, but everywhere . . . and forever.[49]

Today, on reading Keith Somerville's extraordinary letters to those from Bolivar County "away for the duration," it does not seem too much to suggest that her major legacy to the postwar world were these letters with their gentle description and serenity of outlook that reflected her innate wisdom about the world and Bolivar County in a time of great change and turmoil. Her "Dear Boys" of World War II were certainly better individuals from knowing her and from reading her letters. Keith Frazier Somerville's column was then and remains now a beacon toward the better life we can achieve, if we try.

A version of this essay was published in *The Journal of Mississippi History*. See Judy Barrett Litoff, David C. Smith, and Martha Swain, "'Dear Boys': The Wartime Letters of Mrs. Keith Frazier Somerville, 1943–1945," 52 (May 1990): 77–93. Reprinted courtesy of *The Journal of Mississippi History*.

1. *Bolivar Commercial*, May 7, 1943.

2. *Bolivar Commercial*, January 15, 1943, editorial note announcing the first "Dear Boys" column. Over the past two decades, substantial research on the effect of World War II on the American home front has been undertaken. One of the first historians to recognize the importance of examining the Second World War from the vantage point of those at home was Jim F. Heath, "Domestic America During World War II: Research Opportunities for Historians," *Journal of America History*, 58(1971): 384–414. Useful accounts of the war and its impact on the home front include David Brinkley, *Washington Goes to War* (New York: Alfred A. Knopf, 1988); John Morton Blum, *V Was For Victory: Politics and American Culture During World War II* (New York: Harcourt Brace Jovanovich, 1976); John Costello, *Virtue Under Fire: How World War II Changed Our Social and Sexual Attitudes* (Boston: Little Brown and Co., 1985); Mark Jonathan Harris, Franklin Mitchell, and Steven Schechter, *The Home Front: America During World War II* (New York: G. P. Putnam's Sons, 1984); A.A. Hoehling, *Home Front: U.S.A.* (New York: Thomas Y. Crowell, 1966); Roy Hoopes, *Americans Remember the Home Front - An Oral Narrative* (New York: Hawthorn Books, Inc., 1973); Lee Kennett, *For the Duration: The United States Goes to War: Pearl Harbor - 1942* (New York: Charles Scribner's Sons, 1985); William Kenney, *The Crucial Years, 1940–1945* (New York: McFadden Books, 1962); Richard Kirkendall, *The United States, 1929–1945: Years of Crisis and Change* (New York: McGraw-Hill, 1974); Richard Lingeman, *Don't You Know There's A War On?: The American Home Front, 1941–1945* (New York: G. P. Putnam's Sons, 1970); Geoffrey Perrett, *Days of Sadness, Years of Triumph: The American People, 1939–1945* (New York: Coward, McCann Geoghegan, Inc., 1973); Richard Polenberg, ed., *America At War: The Home Front, 1941–1945* (Englewood Cliffs, New Jersey: Prentice-Hall, Inc., 1968); Richard Polenberg, *War and Society: The United States, 1941–1945* (Philadelphia: J.P. Lippincott Co., 1972); Donald I. Rogers, *Since You Went Away* (New Rochelle, New York: Arlington House, 1973); Archie Satterfield, *The Home Front: An Oral History of the War Years in America, 1941–1945* (Chicago: Playboy Press, 1981); Studs Terkel, *"The Good War": An Oral History of World War II* (New York: Pantheon, 1984); and Allan M. Winkler, *Home Front U.S.A.: America During World War II* (Arlington Heights, Illinois: H. Davidson, 1986).

3. We have collected more than 25,000 letters written by American women during World War II. A selection of these letters appears in *Since You Went Away: World War II Letters from American Women on the Home Front* (New York: Oxford University Press, 1991). For the wartime correspondence of a young southern couple, see Judy Barrett Litoff, David C. Smith, Barbara Wooddall Taylor and Charles E. Taylor, *Miss You: The World War II Letters of Barbara*

Wooddall Taylor and Charles E. Taylor (Athens: University of Georgia Press, 1990). Most published wartime letter collections have been written by men in combat. A good anthology is Annette Tapert, ed., *Lines of Battle: Letters from American Servicemen, 1941–1945* (New York: Times Books, 1987). A few volumes based on letters written by women in uniform are available. One anthology, long out of print, is Alma Lutz, ed., *With Love, Jane: Letters from American Women in the War Fronts* (New York: John Day Company, 1945). A recently published collection of letters by a woman in the WACS is Anne Bosanko Green, *One Woman's War: Letters Home from the Women's Army Corps, 1941–1946* (St. Paul: Minnesota Historical Society Press, 1989).

    4. The Thedford, Nebraska Vicinity Federal Women's Club sent a monthly newsletter to the local "boys" in the service. A reprint of one of these letters appeared in the *Thomas County Herald*, September 8, 1988. A neighborhood newsletter was produced by teenagers living in Glenbrook, Connecticut (personal correspondence to the authors from Ruth B. Hughes of Newburyport, Massachusetts, July 6, 1988). An example of a family newsletter is "Gleanings" by Ruth E. Augustine of Geddes, South Dakota (personal possession of the authors). Factory workers at Firestone Tire and Rubber Company in Akron, Ohio met regularly to write letters to men from the company who were in the service (personal correspondence to the authors from Julia T. Steffen of Westfield, Indiana, May 31, 1988). Management personnel at the Whitin Machine Works in Whitinsville, Massachusetts sent out mimeographed letters to former employees on military duty (Worcester *Sunday Telegram*, January 24, 1988). The Standard Oil Company in Atlanta, Georgia, published a monthly newsletter, "Kysomonique," which was sent to Standard Oil employees in the military. The "Kysomonique" letters are at the Georgia Department of Archives and History in Atlanta. One can read the wartime letters of the Newell Class of the First Presbyterian Church of Wichita, Kansas, in Charles W. Sloan, Jr., ed., "The Newelletters: E. Gail Carpenter Describes Life on the Home Front," *Kansas History*, 11, No. 1–4 (Spring 1988, Summer 1988, Fall 1988, Winter 1988–1989): 54–72, 123–42, 150–69, 243–59. The Baptist, Methodist, and Presbyterian churches of Leland, Mississippi sent mimeographed newsletters to local servicemen and women (Dorothy Love Turk, *Leland, Mississippi: From Hellhole to Beauty Spot* [Leland, MS: Leland Historical Foundation, 1986)], pp. 109–111. Walter Lemke, a journalism professor at the University of Arkansas, published *Uncle Walt's Newsletter* between 1941 and 1946 for his former students in the military. The newsletter is in the special collections of the University of Arkansas Library, Fayetteville. Percy Pratt of Freeport, Maine initiated "Poetry in the News," a weekly newsletter which he sent to Freeport men in the service. The newsletter was sponsored by the Knights of Pythias. Church, school, and community groups aided Pratt in collecting hometown news and addressing the newsletters. At the end of the war, Pratt estimated that he had mailed 52,000 letters to Freeport servicemen stationed around the world (Brunswick *Record*, August 30, 1945). An edition of the newsletters, *On the Square*, was published by Pratt in 1947. The Bryant College Service Club in Providence, Rhode Island sent hundreds of letters to Bryant men and women in the service (Bryant *Ledger*, 1941–1944).

    5. In fact, "Dear Boys" was one of two such endeavors undertaken in Bolivar

County. Mrs. Florence Sillers Ogden of Rosedale wrote a similar column, "My Dear Boys," for the *Bolivar County Democrat*. Two other examples of wartime letter columns are "Reno Review" by Gladys Belknap Rowle, published in the *Nevada State Journal* and "A Letter to the Boys in Service" by "Miss Bobbie" Dodds, published in the Trenton, Tennessee *Herald-Register*.

6. For a detailed examination of the relationship between mail and morale during World War II, see Judy Barrett Litoff and David C. Smith, "'Will He Get My Letter?' Popular Portrayals of Mail and Morale During World War II," *Journal of Popular Culture*, 23(Spring 1990): 21–43.

7. *Annual Report of the Postmaster General, For Fiscal year Ended, June 30, 1942* (Washington, D.C.: Government Printing Office, 1942), p. 3.

8. The *Annual Reports of the Postmaster General*, 1941–1946 (Washington, D.C.: Government Printing Office), provide valuable information, statistical and otherwise, on the importance of the mail during World War II.

9. Many exceptional individuals took it upon themselves to write hundreds, even thousands, of letters to service personnel. These included such people as Dorothy Heath Clary, the "girl next door pin-up" of the U.S.S. *Swordfish*; Molly Carewe, known on her Detroit radio show as "Molly of the Marines;" and Gracie Allen, who distributed bulletin board letters to her mythical brother so well known to pre-war network radio audiences. Another noteworthy correspondent was Mollye Sklut of Wilmington, Delaware. Her letter writing campaign involved writing to 350 men and women, mostly Jewish, in the service. The information on Dorothy Heath Clary is from her letter of September 6, 1988, to the authors and her unpublished thoughts of October 1988, in the possession of the authors. Neal Chapline, *Molly's Boots* (Detroit: Harlow Press, 1983), George Burns, *Gracie: A Love Story* (New York: Putnam's, 1988), pp. 210–211. The personal papers of Mollye Sklut are located at the Historical Society of Delaware in Wilmington.

10. *Bolivar Commercial*, January 15, 1943. Keith Frazier Somerville, 1943 Journal, January 24. Mrs. Somerville had two daughters, Keith and Ashton. School teachers across the United States wrote an untold number of letters to former students in the military. As an example, Mrs. Catherine Manley, a high school art teacher in Clarksdale, Arizona, wrote to about thirty of her former students who were in the armed forces. Personal correspondence with Catherine M. Manley of Prescott, Arizona, May 31, June 22, and September 12, 1988.

11. For examples of these letters of gratitude, see the *Bolivar Commercial*, March 12, 19, 1943.

12. *Bolivar Commercial*, January 15, 1943. In total, forty-five "Dear Boys" columns appeared in the newspaper.

13. *Bolivar Commercial*, February 26, 1943. Very good information about the social, political and economic structure of Bolivar County appears in Linton Weeks, *Cleveland: A Centennial History, 1886–1986* (Cleveland: City of Cleveland, 1985) and the centennial edition of the *Bolivar Commercial*, June 27, 1986.

14. Jack Winton Gunn and Gladys C. Castle, *A Pictorial History of Delta State University* (Jackson: University Press of Mississippi, 1980), p. 57. Weeks, *Cleveland: A Centennial History*, pp. 161–162.

15. This statement appeared in the subscription information section of each issue of the *Bolivar Commercial*.

16. On the origins of the Delta planter class, see Robert L. Brandfon, *Cotton Kingdom of the New South: A History of the Yazoo Mississippi Delta from Reconstruction to the Twentieth Century* (Cambridge: Harvard University Press, 1967). For information on Delta and Pine Land, see the Agricultural section of the centennial edition of the *Bolivar Commercial*, June 27, 1986.

17. For information on the origins and history of Mound Bayou, see Janet Sharp Hermann, *The Pursuit of a Dream* (New York: Oxford University Press, 1981), pp. 219–245 and Neil R. McMillen, *Black Journey: Black Mississippians in the Age of Jim Crow.* (Urbana: University of Illinois Press, 1989), pp. 186–190.

18. Useful information on Bolivar County may be found in Wirt A. Williams, ed., *History of Bolivar County* (Spartanburg, S.C.: The Reprint Company, 1976); Weeks, *Cleveland: A Centennial History*; and, Curt Lamar, ed., *History of Rosedale, Mississippi, 1876–1976* (Spartanburg, S.C.: The Reprint Publishers, 1976). See also, *Mississippi: A Guide to the Magnolia State*, compiled and written by the Federal Writers' Project of the Works Progress Administration, (New York: Viking Press, 1938). For a very good discussion of how agricultural mechanization brought about major changes in the Mississippi Delta, see Nicholas Lemann, *The Promised Land: The Great Black Migration and How it Changed America* (New York: Knopf, 1991).

19. "Just People," *Thinking Back*, unpublished memoir of Keith Frazier Somerville.

20. Information on the POW camps in Bolivar County is included in the "Heritage" section of the centennial edition of the *Bolivar Commercial*, June 27, 1986. See also, Merrill R. Pritchett and William L. Shea, "The Enemy in Mississippi (1943–1946)," *The Journal of Mississippi History*, 41(November 1979): 351–371. For information on Italian immigrants in the Mississippi Delta, see Alfred Holt Stone, "Italian Cotton-Growers in Arkansas," *American Monthly Review of Reviews*, 35(February 1907): 209–213. For a more recent discussion, see Robert L. Branfon, "The End of Immigration to the Cotton Fields," *Mississippi Valley Historical Review*, 50(December 1963): 591–599.

21. *Bolivar Commercial*, January 15, February 26, March 26, August 20, September 24, October 22, 1943. Good information on the Chinese in the Mississippi Delta can be found in James W. Loewen, *The Mississippi Chinese: Between Black and White* (Cambridge, Massachusetts: Harvard University Press, 1971).

22. *Bolivar Commercial*, April 9, 1943.

23. For example, see the *Bolivar Commercial*, January 15, April 23, 1943, January 21, February 25, September 8, September 22, 1944. Mrs. Somerville's comments about the bolting electors occurred in her column of November 10, 1944. For more information on this incident, see Roy H. Ruby, "The Presidential Election of 1944 in Mississippi: The Bolting Electors" (Master's thesis, Mississippi State University, 1966).

24. *Bolivar Commercial*, April 23, 1943. Two good studies on blacks in Mississippi are Janet Sharp Hermann, *The Pursuit of a Dream* (New York: Oxford University Press, 1981) and Neil R. McMillen, *Black Journey: Black Mississippians in the Age of Jim Crow.* (Urbana: University of Illinois Press, 1989).

25. Keith Frazier Somerville, 1943 Journal, April 18, 23, 25. Memphis *Commercial Appeal*, April 25, 1943.

26. Unfortunately, the thank you letter from Mound Bayou was lost.

27. *Bolivar Commercial*, February 25, September 8, 1944.

28. *Bolivar Commercial*, April 23, 1943.

29. *Bolivar Commercial*, February 4, April 9, May 7, May 21, July 30, June 4, 1943, January 16, 1944.

30. *Bolivar Commercial*, February 23, 1945.

31. There were approximately one million more marriages from 1940 to 1943 than would have been expected at prewar rates. Statistical information on the wartime increase in the marriage rate can be found in Karen Anderson, *Wartime Women: Sex Roles, Family Relations, and the Status of Women During World War II* (Westport, Connecticut: Greenwood Press, 1981), pp. 76–79; and D'Ann Campbell, *Women at War with America: Private Lives in a Patriotic Era* (Cambridge: Harvard University Press, 1984), pp. 90–91. Important information on family life during World War II is also included in Susan Hartmann, *The Home Front and Beyond* (Boston: Twayne, 1982), especially chapter 9, "The Unshaken Claim of Family." Contemporary observers frequently wrote about the impact of World War II on family life. See, for example, J.C. Furnas and the Staff of *Ladies' Home Journal, How America Lives* (New York: Henry Holt and Co., 1941); Sidonie Matsner Gruenberg, ed., *The Family in a World at War* (New York: Harper and Brothers, 1942); Reuben Hill and Elise Boulding, *Families Under Stress: Adjustment to the Crises of War, Separation and Reunion* (New York: Harper and Brothers, 1949); Richard Malking, *Marriage, Morals and War* (New York: Arden Books, 1943); Grace Sloan Overton, *Marriage in War and Peace: A Book for Parents and Counselors of Youth* (New York: Abington-Cokesbury Press, 1941); Sylvia Porter, *If War Comes to the American Home: How to Prepare for the Inevitable Adjustment* (New York: Robert M. McBride, 1941); Willard Waller, *War and the Family* (New York: Dryden Press, 1940); Anna W.M. Wolf, *Our Children Face War* (Boston: Houghton Mifflin, 1942); and, Leland Foster Wood and John W. Mullen, eds., *What the American Family Faces* (Chicago: Eugene Hugh Publishers, 1943). In addition, professional journals published a variety of articles on the family in wartime.

32. *Bolivar Commercial*, March 12, 1943, November 10, 1944. Also see December 8, 1944.

33. For example, see the *Bolivar Commercial*, January 29, March 26, June 4, 1943, April 7, September 22, 1944.

34. *Bolivar Commercial*, June 18, 1943, February 9, 1945. For a discussion of the experiences of a war bride from Fairburn, Georgia, see Judy Barrett Litoff and David C. Smith, "Since You Went Away: The World War II Letters of Barbara Wooddall Taylor," *Women's Studies* 17(1990): 249–276, and Litoff, Smith, Taylor, and Taylor, *Miss You*.

35. *Bolivar Commercial*, October 22, 1943.

36. Examples include the *Bolivar Commercial*, January 29, March 12, May 7, May 21, June 4, July 18, August 20, September 3, 1943, January 7, March 17, April 7, August 4, 1944, February 23, 1945. There has been no book-length study of Mississippi women during World War II. A useful monograph on the wartime experiences of women in Alabama is Mary Martha Thomas, *Riveting*

and Rationing in Dixie: Alabama Women in the Second World War (Tuscaloosa: University of Alabama Press, 1987). Other significant studies about American women and World War II include, Karen Tucker Anderson, "Last Hired, First Fired: Black Women Workers During World War II," *Journal of American History*, 69(June 1982): 82–97; Anderson, *Wartime Women*; Alan Clive, "Women Workers in World War II: Michigan as a Test Case," *Labor History*, 20(Winter 1979): 44–72; Campbell, *Women at War with America*; William Chafe, *The American Woman: Her Changing Social, Economic, and Political Roles, 1920–1976* (New York: Oxford University Press, 1972); Sherna B. Gluck, *Rosie the Riveter Revisited: Women, the War and Social Change* (Boston: Twayne 1987); Chester W. Gregory, *Women in Defense Work During World War II: An Analysis of the Labor Problems and Women's Rights* (Jericho, New York: Exposition Press, 1974); Hartmann, *The Home Front and Beyond*; Susan Hartmann, "Prescriptions for Penelope: Literature on Women's Obligations to Returning World War Two Veterans," *Women's Studies* (1978): 223–237; Margaret Randolph Higonnet, Jane Jenson, Sonya Michel, and Margaret Collins Weitz, eds., *Behind the Lines: Gender and the Two World Wars* (New Haven: Yale University Press, 1987); Maureen Honey, *Creating Rosie the Riveter: Class, Gender, and Propaganda During World War II* (Amherst: University of Massachusetts Press, 1984); Maureen Honey, "The Working-Class Woman and Recruitment Propaganda During World War II: Class Differences in the Portrayal of War Work," *Signs*, 8(Summer 1983): 672–687; Sally Van Wagenen Keil, *Those Wonderful Women in Their Flying Machines: The Unknown Heroines of World War II* (New York: Rawson, Wade Publishers, 1979); Amy Kesselman, *Fleeting Opportunities: Women Shipyard Workers in Portland and Vancouver During World War II and Reconversion* (Albany: State University of New York Press, 1990); Ruth Milkman, *Gender at Work: The Dynamics of Job Segregation by Sex During World War II* (Urbana: University of Illinois Press, 1987); Ruth Milkman, "'Redefining Women's Work': The Sexual Division of Labor in the Auto Industry During World War II," *Feminist Studies*, 8(Summer 1982): 337–372; Marc Miller, "Working Women and World War II," *New England Quarterly*, 53(March 1980): 42–61; Leila Rupp, *Mobilizing Women for War: German and American Propaganda, 1939–1945* (Princeton, New Jersey: Princeton University Press, 1978); Paddy Quick, "Rosie the Riveter: Myths and Realities," *Radical America*, 9(July–August 1975): 115–132; Eleanor F. Straub, "Government Policy Toward Civilian Women During World War II" (Ph.D., diss., Emory University, 1973); Eleanor F. Straub, "U.S. Governmental Policy Toward Women During World War II," *Prologue*, 5(Winter 1973): 240–254; Sheila Tobias and Lisa Anderson, "Whatever Happened to Rosie the Riveter?" *Ms.*, June 1973, pp. 92–94; Shelia Tobias and Lisa Anderson, "What Really Happened to Rosie the Riveter? Demobilization and the Female Labor Force, 1944–1947," *MSS Modular Publications*, Module 9,(1974): 1–36; and Joan Ellen Trey, "Women in the War Economy," *Reviews of Radical Political Economy*, 4(July 1972): 40–57.

37. *Bolivar Commercial*, June 18, July 2, October 22, 1943; June 23, July 14, 1944. Rowan T. Thomas, *Born in Battle* (Philadelphia: John C. Winston Co., 1944). Fletcher Pratt, writing for the July 1, 1944 issue of the *Saturday Review of Literature*, described *Born in Battle* as "a kind of microcosm of the war, at least the war in the air, and most of it is told with a surprising energy, freshness and intelligence. . . . among war books this gets an A rating" (p. 19).

38. *Bolivar Commercial*, January 15, 1943.

39. *Bolivar Commercial*, February 23, 1945.

40. Ibid.

41. Ibid.

42. Ibid.

43. Ibid.

44. Discussion of books and articles which address the theme of the postwar world can be found in the *Bolivar Commercial*, August 25, 1944, January 12, February 9, 16, April 27, 1945.

45. *Bolivar Commercial*, January 12, February 9, 1945.

46. *Bolivar Commercial*, April 27, 1945.

47. *Bolivar Commercial*, May 11, 1945.

48. *Bolivar Commercial*, August 31, 1945.

49. A discussion of the impact of World War II on Mississippi may be found in John Ray Skates, "World War II as a Watershed in Mississippi History," *The Journal of Mississippi History*, 37(1975): 135–141. See also chapter eight of Skate's *Mississippi: A Bicentennial History* (New York: W.W. Norton, 1979). For a general discussion of southern reactions to World War II, see Pete Daniel, "Going among Strangers: Southern Reactions to World War II," *Journal of American History*, 77(December 1990): 886–911.

Keith Frazier Somerville
at War and in Peace, 1888–1978

Martha H. Swain

When Keith Frazier Somerville, at the request of a granddaughter, began to write her memoirs of a long life filled with people and events that had spanned nearly three-quarters of a century, she reflected at length about the wars that had occurred in her lifetime.[1] She wrote very affectionately of the many army and navy personnel who had always been among her closest friends. At the same time, she also recalled with equal poignancy the long intervals of peace in her life, first in Tennessee, then in Washington, D.C., and finally in Cleveland, Mississippi, the Delta town that was home for her for more than six decades and home also for the "Dear Boys" to whom she wrote her long letters during World War II.

Anne Keith Frazier was born in Chattanooga on May 14, 1888, to James Beriah and Louise Keith Frazier. One of her earliest childhood memories was of the shudders she felt whenever she visited the Chattanooga home of an eccentric aunt who had covered the expansive walls of her home with frescoes depicting the carnage of the nearby Civil War battlefield of Chickamauga. The older generation of Keiths and Fraziers, the "ancients" as Keith called them, were all Confederates and the occasional reunions of remnants of the "Lost Cause" were grand events in her girlhood.[2]

Some years later she obtained a larger perspective of war when the Spanish-American conflict was part of her milieu. She remembered swinging her baby brother in a hammock while war recruits passed in front of their Chattanooga home, coming and going from Chickamauga Park where they were in training for Cuba. She also remembered that at her tenth birthday party in May 1898, the favors were small glass replicas of the battleship *Maine* filled with candy. The saddest memory of these days was of the funeral processions to the National Cemetery at Chickamauga for those servicemen who were victims of an outbreak of typhoid fever at the camp.[3]

The men on both sides of Keith Frazier's family had distinguished careers in the military, in politics, or in business. Both her grandfathers, Thomas N. Frazier and Alexander Keith, were alumni of Greenville College in Greenville, Tennessee; their graduation suits were made by a local tailor named Andrew Johnson.[4] Successive generations of well-educated Keiths and Fraziers were devotees of literature and learning, and so it was only natural that the four Frazier children were given large doses of Shakespeare, Dickens, and Walter Scott, along with the writings of the major poets of the past. Anne Keith was fascinated by the works of Jules Verne and the stories in the *St. Nicholas* and *Youth's Companion* magazines, which she termed two of the "joys" of her childhood. In fact, when she appeared to devour too many books too rapidly, her mother compelled her to write book reviews to make certain that she absorbed more of what she had read.[5] Later at Hickman High School in Chattanooga, she reveled in her position as editor of the school literary magazine, and she had visions of becoming a novelist.

More consequential than anything else for Keith Frazier in her formative years was the election in 1902 of her father, a railroad attorney by profession, as first, governor of Tennessee and, subsequently, as a United States senator. In the expectation that he would be elected governor and move to the executive mansion in Nashville, James B. Frazier sent Keith ahead to Ward's Seminary, also in Nashville, where soon after she arrived, she threw open the window one morning and called to a newsboy, "Who was elected Governor?" "Frazier, by a big majority," came the reply.[6]

At Ward's, the ebullient Keith made a number of new friends and had a joyous time. In the classroom she excelled at the classics, many of them previously introduced to her by her father. Most of the poetry she also already knew as her mother's "pet" punishment had been to banish her to the parlor to memorize poems. Graduation from Ward's in 1904 was followed by a glorious excursion to the St. Louis World's Fair with her governor father and his staff for the celebrations attendant to "Tennessee Day" at the exposition.[7]

Reelected to the governorship in 1904, James Frazier resigned this office upon his election to the U.S. Senate in March 1905. By the time her family moved to Washington, Keith was at the Castle, an Episcopal seminary for young women at Tarrytown, New York. She had gone there in the fall following her graduation from Ward's. The Castle presented Keith Frazier with memories to last a lifetime. New friends included Mary Brent Smith, the daughter of Governor Hoke Smith of Georgia, and her beloved roommate, Ashton Woodman, for whom she would one day name a daughter. Other new acquaintances came from the army of "K-dets" at nearby West Point, many of whom she met when she accompanied her father on his Board of Visitors inspections of the academy.[8]

The Castle introduced its students to a scholarly regimen and a "modern" curriculum. For example, Keith's reading in a sociology class of a book by Jacob Riis, *How The Other Half Lives* (1890), was followed by a field trip to the tenement section of New York City that left her "shocked and sympathetic." Numerous excursions for concerts, plays, and the opera afforded an opportunity for students at the Castle to enjoy a veritable "Who's Who" of stage notables of the day. She was thrilled when Mark Twain received the Castle girls at his New York home, but was disappointed when the aging John D. Rockefeller only gave them a piece of hard candy when they visited him. Like a later student at the Castle, Clare Booth (Luce), Keith edited the school year book, *The Drawbridge*. As the class valedictorian in 1906, she chose to speak on the topical subject, "The New South."[9]

Scholarship and culture aside, Keith Frazier's most vivid memory of her years at the Castle was her November 1904 trip to Philadelphia in the company of headmistress Cassidy Eliza Mason in order that the senator's daughter could "sponsor," or christen, a new armored cruiser, the U.S.S. *Tennessee*.[10]

A few years later it occurred to her that no organization existed to join together all the young women who had acted as navy "sponsors," and thus she founded a group for that purpose in November 1908. She went about fulfilling her idea by enlisting the aid of the secretary of the navy. She also received the endorsement of President Theodore Roosevelt, who called her venture the latest "launching." In response to her engraved invitation, fourteen women gathered at Washington's Willard Hotel and formed the Society of the Sponsors. Roosevelt, himself, entertained the founders at the White House. Eventually, the group grew to hundreds of members, including wives and daughters of several presidents.[11]

Well into her old age, the periodic gatherings of the Society of the Sponsors of the United States Navy were priority events in Keith Somerville's life. The growing number of women participants swelled her circle of friends and kept alive for her the aura of the United States Navy. The *Tennessee* was part of the armored cruisers that formed the "Great White Fleet" in Theodore Roosevelt's spirited diplomatic program, and she sailed to Europe on a special mission to deliver gold to American citizens stranded there when World War I broke out in August 1914. Renamed the *Memphis* in May 1916, the ship was wrecked the following August by a tidal wave off the coast of Santo Domingo where it was serving as the flagship of the Atlantic fleet during the United States occupation of Haiti and Santo Domingo.[12]

Upon the completion of her studies at the Castle, Keith returned to Washington and the social opportunities open to the daughter of a United States senator, and most especially, to one as attractive and vivacious as she. Within the northwest Washington residential area, where the Fraziers lived, were homes of noted politicians, statesmen, and public figures. Neighbors included the British Ambassador, Lord Bryce; Supreme Court Justice, Rufus W. Peckham; and, the inventor, Alexander Graham Bell. Because Senator Frazier was a member of the Committee on Military Affairs and the Committee on Foreign Relations, it was not uncommon for these prominent neighbors to dine at the Frazier table or for Keith to appear at social events where many notables of the day were present. Her mother, Tennessee-born Louise Keith, was a woman of great beauty and charm. She was adored by her namesake who was delighted to learn that Mrs. William Jennings Bryan had once described Mrs. Frazier as "the wittiest and most brilliant" woman she had met in the entire United States.[13]

Among Keith's most vivid memories of her Washington years were her introduction to President Theodore Roosevelt; the indoor inauguration of William Howard Taft on a snowy day in 1909; Alice Roosevelt's engagement dinner; the Taft's silver wedding anniversary reception; and the White House debut parties of her friends, Edith Roosevelt and Helen Taft. Mrs. Taft wrote that the East Room of the White House was filled, at her daughter's debut ball on December 30, 1910, with young people "clamoring for 'just one more dance' until two o'clock in the morning."[14] For the balls given by the presidential daughters, the music was provided by the U.S. Marine Band. The East Room, Keith was convinced, "was just made for dancing." These were the days of the Turkey Trot, The Castle Walk, Irving Berlin's "Alexander's Rag Time Band," and Franz Lehar's "Merry Widow Waltz." One evening, when the mule-drawn bus used to convey the young women to dances at the Washington Barracks (later Fort McNair) lost a wheel and broke down on the return trip at 3:00 A.M., the military escorts simply "barn-danced" their companions along Pennsylvania Avenue and on to their homes. Keith's own debut parties, held in Washington and Chattanooga, provided further thrills for her as friends came from a number of other states to each affair.[15]

Keith Frazier's years at Washington were also filled with visits to school friends, many of whom lived in the south. In addition, there were numerous houseparties, hosted by the parents of friends in Virginia, Georgia, and Maryland. She fondly recalled the week-long houseparty at the Marietta, Georgia, home of Senator and Mrs. Alexander Stephens Clay, parents of Lucius Clay, one of several friends who later filled the ranks of World War II generals and admirals.[16] What proved to be the most rewarding aspect of those halcyon days was that the bonds of friendship which were forged lasted for more than fifty years. On visits to wartime Washington in the 1940s, for example, she continued to see old friends of an earlier era of peace before two wars had scattered them over the face of the earth.[17]

The Frazier family was not wealthy. In fact, Keith remarked later in her life that her father's savings were exhausted through the cost of maintaining his family in Washington. Yet she met many young men of substantial wealth through her social position. As it turned out, nothing in the way of romance ever came from her friendships with the young scions or with the West Point "K-dets." She was disappointed, in one case, to learn that a young man to whom she was attracted could "talk of nothing but pedigreed dogs."[18] "I was always falling for some attractive guy who didn't know I was there," she confessed in her memoirs, "[and] to be perfectly honest no millionaire was ever bowled over by my charms." Experiences such as these seemed to be her lot in life, even at Monteagle, the residential Chautauqua grounds near Sewanee, Tennessee, a summer mecca for prominent southern families and a matchmaker's paradise. While visiting a Texas friend there, she met a young man from Mississippi whom she "liked very much," but another young woman was wearing his Phi Delta Theta fraternity pin. It was a sore disappointment for Keith to learn that he was claimed by someone else. Yet their paths continued to cross, her luck changed, and to her immense relief the fraternity pin was returned.[19]

Keith's new suitor was Robert Nugent Somerville, a graduate of the University of Mississippi who had moved to Washington to work as secretary to Mississippi Congressman Benjamin Humphrey and to attend law school at George Washington University. The romance developed steadily, hastened along as "Bob" pled his case with boxes of Martha Washington candy and sheet music of the popular songs of the day. It was he who became her choice, much preferred over the more affluent youth who had been the object of her earlier flirtations. "I decided I just preferred my poor Congressman's secretary and would have to forego being rich," was her later comment.[20]

Bob may not have been able to offer Keith Frazier a life of luxury, but he could give her a name well known and widely respected in Mississippi. His grandfather was William L. Nugent, a distinguished Confederate officer; his father, Robert Somerville, was a successful civil engineer; but it was his mother, Nellie Nugent Somerville, who was best known, not only in Mississippi circles, but beyond the state as well. A renowned suffrage and temperance leader, and a prominent club woman and church worker, she became the first woman to be elected to the Mississippi House of Representatives.[21]

Keith Frazier and Robert Somerville were married in a formal ceremony held in her home church in Chattanooga on November 20, 1912. She was 24 and he was 26. Following a honeymoon in Canada, the young couple made their home in Cleveland, Mississippi, for Robert Somerville had recently become a junior partner in a law firm in nearby Rosedale. At first, the new bride was dismayed by the world which greeted her in this small Delta town: an unpaved main street, swarms of mosquitoes, and three months of incessant winter rain that mildewed her trousseau finery as it hung in the closet. When her husband raced from the house one evening, along with other male dinner guests, at the sounds of gunshots, she was seized with fright until she learned that they were responding to the local method of rallying the volunteer fire department. "If I hadn't been married to an exceedingly attractive young man," she later confided in her reminiscences, "I would have run home, wailing." But, she adapted to small-town life. There were, she soon learned, "lots of nice people" in Cleveland.[22]

Among her new acquaintances were the builders of the home that she and Bob began to construct on an elevated plot of land at the edge of town on LeFlore Street. Sitting on the piles of boards for the house, she listened with fascination as one of the workmen told of his experiences in Japan while in the navy. Two huge black walnut trees were the backdrops for the lawn Keith landscaped with flowering shrubs, trellises, and thousands of spring jonquils and iris, as she transformed the one-time cotton patch into her own Eden. However, these beautification efforts had to await town drainage improvements in order that the house would not be marooned by the water that left much of Cleveland flooded by the periodic deluges.[23]

Keith returned to Chattanooga in the spring of 1914 where she gave birth, on May 30, to her first daughter, also named Keith. On that visit, the Fraziers heard a newsboy shouting, "Extra!" Leaning over the house balcony, she learned that "some man" had been "killed in Europe at a place called Sarajevo." This was her first inkling of the beginning of the World War I. Both of her brothers, James Beriah, Jr., and Thomas, became officers during the war, as did her brother-in-law, Abram. Eleven of her Grandmother Keith's grandsons served in the war, but "amazingly all came home safely."[24]

The young Mrs. Somerville's adjustment to life in Cleveland was hastened by a flurry of social and civic activities which she undertook. Her status as wife, mother, and social figure was enhanced with regular contact with other matrons who gathered to assist Mississippi flood victims in 1913 and to answer the call to roll bandages during World War I. The birth of a second daughter, Ashton, in February 1917 further solidified her ties to Cleveland and Bolivar County.

Having founded one quasi-patriotic social and service society, she joined with Mrs. Re Sutherland Johnson, wife of the town mayor, to form the Madame Hodgett Chapter of the Daughters of the American Revolution (DAR) in October 1916. The approximately twenty charter members soon undertook many projects which formed an outlet for Keith Somerville's abundant energies for many decades. Local regent for four terms, she also served as state regent and established seven new DAR chapters. To commemorate local men who lost their lives during World War I, she became involved with a DAR project, spearheaded by her sister-in-law, Eleanor Somerville Shands, to create a Memorial Drive along the barren, three-mile stretch of road between Cleveland and Boyle. The project, begun in 1923, provided for trees which could be purchased for a dollar each to be planted along the drive. Within a few years, a double row of four hundred pin oaks honored the twenty-five Bolivar County men who died in World War I.[25]

While living in Washington, one of the many privileges she had enjoyed as the daughter of a U.S. senator was to have the armloads of books she selected from the open stacks of the Library of Congress delivered to the Frazier home. Finding no source in Cleveland for the books she longed to read, Keith Somerville directed a DAR project to launch a public library. The library project began modestly with donations of books left on the doorsteps of DAR members that were then carried in a one-horse surrey to a receiving room at the local Methodist Church. When the DAR "library" outgrew this location, Bolivar County supervisors responded by providing space for the library in the court house. Early financial support came from a variety of fund raising events sponsored by the intrepid library organizers: whist parties, luncheons, auctions, and even a "society circus" held in the Somerville front yard. The circus had as its main attraction a Roman chariot race with four of the "town fathers" dressed in sheets for togas, mounted on tiny wooden kiddiecars. Until the end of her life, the Cleveland Library provided Mrs.

Somerville with more hours of pleasure than any other community institution.[26]

Her active community service notwithstanding, Keith Somerville's family remained the primary focus of her life. The 1920s were busy years as the two daughters entered school and took up many activities of their own. The older Somervilles remained busy themselves—she with her civic work and a kindergarten which she established in her home and he with Rotary International, the Mississippi and American Bar Associations, and alumni functions of Phi Delta Theta. "Someone has said that the great American sport is neither baseball nor football, but conventions," Keith once mused, and she attended many such events with her husband. "I loved being married to Bob for we were very congenial," she added.[27]

Compatibility and common interests helped the Somervilles weather the difficulties that came with the Depression and their near financial ruin which resulted from the failure of the Clarksdale bank for which Robert Somerville, as a director, was fiscally accountable. Keith's worries were exacerbated in 1929 when Bob was struck by an automobile, and he was forced to remain in Campbell's Clinic in Memphis for nearly a year, healing from complicated bone fractures. As the couple was "flat broke [and with] almost no law business, for when times are hard few people start lawsuits," Keith turned to paid employment herself. For ten years, from 1929 to 1939, she taught a first-grade class. She found immense satisfaction with the added income which did so much to help with the college expenses for their daughters, Keith, who attended the University of Mississippi, and Ashton, who was a student at Louisiana State University.[28]

With daughters whose high school and college years came in the decade that preceded World War II, Keith's children and their friends were squarely in the middle of the generation that would be called to service after 1940. In the prewar years, Keith Somerville had become acquainted with many Bolivar County young people who attended the tea dances, buffet suppers, and other events that comprised the social life of well-to-do and middle-class citizens of the Mississippi Delta. She also knew many other families and their circumstances. She had, after all, been an active force in the community ever since she arrived as a bride nearly thirty years earlier, and she had taught hundreds of local youngsters in her decade in the classroom.[29]

Keith Somerville kept scrapbooks all of her life. She created one during the Spanish-American War, while still a child, and she later kept what she termed a "Literary Digest" of World War I. Early in 1942, she began to paste newspaper clippings, cartoons, photographs, articles from magazines, and poems which chronicled the events of the Second World War into a notebook. Alongside these gleanings from the press, she kept a journal that recounted her own emotions of disbelief and horror over the early setbacks suffered by the Allies and her deep concern for the local men whom she knew were in the thick of the fighting.

In April 1942, Keith traveled by bus to Chattanooga to visit her mother as the older woman's health and mind were failing. Mrs. Frazier, on hearing of the victories of the Axis powers, told her daughter, "we better pack up the silver." On November 20, 1942, her thirtieth wedding anniversary, she was back in Chattanooga for her mother's funeral. Having lost her father on Easter Sunday, 1937, she was immensely saddened to realize that this era of her life had now ended. Going through her mother's possessions after the funeral, all "freighted with memories," was the saddest task she ever had to perform.[30]

During her April 1942 bus trip from Memphis to Cleveland, Keith Somerville had found herself surrounded by servicemen. She was delighted to find that they were "more interested in a gray haired grandmother," than all of the "pretty girls aboard." Yet she was grateful to be home again on LeFlore Street, home to "my nice husband and my *peaceful* life" and to her yard filled with spring flowers, out in full array, "a picture for Country Life."[31]

Alternating the grim war news with items about local men in training or missing in action at the front, Keith wrote in her journal in August 1942, "I'd give my life—so willingly—if I could just help." The newspapers which she, like most Americans, read so avidly for the war news, informed her of just how she could assist the war cause. She spent a September afternoon "hunting up scrap metal" and the next day the government "junk man" came to collect the 208 pounds she had accumulated. She even decided to give up her brass bed and also to sacrifice her prized seventy-pound brass porthole from the U.S.S. *Tennessee*. "I'd like to feel that I am sending a torpedo toward Germany or Japan," she told a reporter from the Memphis *Commercial Appeal* after she delivered the keepsake to Mayor Walter Chandler. Meanwhile, she began to roll surgical bandages for the Red Cross, proud that her increasing output had become "an achievement record."[32]

"Poor Russia is having a terrible time," she began her entry on September 20, 1942. She was conscience-stricken that in Cleveland life went on pretty much the same as always. She remarked to her journal in a minatory way, "this town doesn't know there's war on." There were too many parties where the food was too lavish. "We shouldn't have them," she wrote in her journal. She could, however, justify the simple "Coca-Cola" parties which she and her friends gave for the brides-to-be of young men leaving for the war. She received one invitation to a bridal party which read, "Seated Tea. War Rations."[33]

Throughout the war years, Keith Somerville diligently practiced conservation. She did a great deal of mending "so as to be more patriotic and make things last for the duration." She also curtailed food consumption beyond the limits imposed by rationing, although New Year's dinner on January 1, 1943, consisted of "the usual cornbread-greens-sweet potatoes-buttermilk." When she and her husband brought two servicemen home to a meal a fortnight later, in which the meat dish was their "Christmas sausage," the cook, Charity Bass, was mortified and scoffed that this was no dinner to be served to guests. Life in the Somerville household was simple and the holidays subdued in this time of great sacrifice around the world. For example, she spent Christmas Day 1943 before the fireplace "listening to carols and the overseas broadcasts from the boys, from the four corners of the globe, from subs underseas, battleships, and in the air, and even from several hundred American boys singing carols from Bethlehem . . . all very inspiring."[34]

Keith Somerville's journal provides a vivid description of the many changes which occurred in wartime life. New songs flooded the airways that continuously beamed the war news into her home. She noted in December 1942 that "now playing is 'Rosie the Riveter.'" Whatever lift she may have received from this song was dashed the next day when she burst into tears upon receiving "A Christmas

Greeting from the Middle East," sent by V-Mail, from Captain Rowan Thomas, an Army Air Corps officer from neighboring Boyle who was stationed somewhere in Africa. She could recall happier times when he had been her younger daughter's beau. But now, as the year came to an end, "more than 1 million Yanks [are] fighting on foreign soil."[35]

Less than a month later, in January 1943, Keith Somerville began her "Dear Boys" column for the *Bolivar Commercial.*[36] Preparing the columns consumed much time, but the gratitude expressed by her readers from all over the world was sufficient recompense for the labor involved. "If only one or two boys a week enjoy them, it's well worth my time and work," she wrote in her journal. Writing the letters, correcting the proofs, and addressing the newspapers became "almost a full time job." Anxious that her Christmas 1943 letter reach as many servicemen as possible, she spent two full weeks work obtaining the addresses and writing them on the newspaper wrappers. "Mr. Langford [the editor of the *Bolivar Commercial*] said he'd send one to every boy whose address I could get," she was pleased to note. Mild remonstrances at home over the extent of this activity caused her to write in her journal, "Bob wishes . . . I could see dust, etc., more. . . . I'm not lazy, but honestly I am so much more interested in this than in everlasting sweeping and dusting."[37]

The "Dear Boys" columns eventually took precedence over writing entries in her journal which, at the beginning of 1943, had filled the Sunday afternoon hour in which she had always written her mother. Indeed, Keith Somerville's absorption in the war affected her entire household. The war maps she hung all over the house spread even onto the walls in the bathroom. "Now I have to stand in the tub to follow the African campaigns and we even go so far to conduct guests into the Maproom!" wrote Keith, not too long after she styled herself a "pencil-packing Mama!"[38]

Early in 1943, Joe Rice Dockery, the husband of the younger Keith Somerville, was sworn into the Coast Guard as an officer. His commission left the older woman wishing that she were "young enough to be a WAC or a WAVE or a SPAR"[39] After Joe Dockery's family joined him at his assignment on the Gulf Coast, the Robert Somervilles paid periodic visits to their own service family, first in Mobile and later in New Orleans. Ashton Somerville's marriage to

George Mason Ingram, then a budget officer with the Tennessee Valley Authority and later an officer in the United States Navy, found her during the war years near Knoxville, where Mrs. Somerville spent a portion of the summer of 1943. Subsequent visits piqued her interest in the secretive "Project X" underway at nearby Oak Ridge.[40]

Often apologetic that she could not devote even more time to the war effort, Keith realized in early 1943 that her mother's death the previous November had caused her to be unaware of the great Russian offensive. She felt guilty because she was almost as excited in the spring of 1943 by the first blooms of her iris garden as she was by the news from Tunis and Bizerte.[41] While reflecting upon her own perceived lack of sacrifice for the war effort at the beginning of 1944, she was contrite: "I wrote 3 of my friends the other nite who have lost loved sons—yet I have given so little, just written a few letters, made a few bandages, done without a little less coffee and gas and sugar than I could have used and bought a few [war savings] stamps. God help me to do more this year." Becoming county Red Cross chairwoman, making surgical dressings, taking her turn as USO hostess at the American Legion hut, *and* writing her "Dear Boys" column consumed so much time that her 1944 journal consists mostly of extensive newspaper clippings about the advances of the Allied forces on the European and Pacific fronts, with only brief items about her life and wartime Cleveland.[42] She apparently made no effort to keep her journal in 1945, although she continued to produce her columns, now often filled with the promises of peace, the United Nations, and her visions of what the postwar world might be like.[43]

Keith Somerville's postwar life was that of a widow. Robert Somerville died unexpectedly, at the age of 60, on June 20, 1946, from a cerebral hemorrhage while attending a meeting of the state bar association in Jackson.[44] Once she had recovered from the initial shock of her husband's death, she devoted much time to her daughters and their families. Ashton's husband, George Ingram, became an officer in the U.S. State Department, and his assignments to Vienna and Helsinki led to lengthy visits by Mrs. Somerville. At the age of seventy-nine, she sailed from Mobile to Finland as the single passenger aboard a Finnish freighter.[45] An earlier trip to Scotland to probe into her Scottish ancestry was vital to her genealogical study of the Keith line and that of others for whom she compiled family histories. She was proud that her comprehensive family tree and intensive family research won special praise from the Virginia Historical Society. Equally gratifying was the fact that the proceeds from the sale of the family genealogy financed her trip to Scotland.[46]

Mrs. Somerville also collaborated with a friend from the Navy Sponsors to compile a volume, *Ships of the Navy and Their Sponsors*, published by the United States Naval Institute in 1952.[47] She still had an entree into official Washington since her brother, James Beriah Frazier, Jr., served as congressman from Tennessee from 1949 to 1963. Her visits to him were occasions in which she could relive an earlier era. During a 1961 visit, she calculated that she had attended "15 luncheons, 5 teas, and 5 dinners."[48] In 1963, the Frazier circle was broken again when her sister, Louise, died shortly before she was to visit Keith in Cleveland. Three years later her beloved roommate at the Castle, Ashton Woodman Renier, also died after a long illness.[49]

Mingled with these sad events of her declining years were also many pleasures. She continued to consume books voraciously, usually at the rate of one a night. She wrote many reviews for the local paper about books which dealt with a plethora of intellectual topics. She also shared her reading interests with her favorite in-law, Lucy Somerville Howorth, the family's career woman, now retired after twenty-five years of public service in Washington.[50] In addition, there still were anniversary reunions with the Society of the Sponsors in Washington, the fiftieth in 1958, and then the sixtieth a decade later. In 1964, Edward L. Beach, Jr., was in Memphis to share the honors with her when they dedicated a plaque to the survivors of the *Memphis* whose colors he had raised on his own ship, the U.S.S. *Triton*, the first nuclear-powered submarine. Its undersea circumnavigation of the globe combined for Keith the marvels of the Jules Verne fantasies of her childhood with the realization that Verne's fantasy had come true, even though the *Triton* sailed less than 20,000 leagues on her trip under the sea.[51]

"Old age is a mess," Keith growled at the age of seventy-six. It was "definitely not the blessing it is cracked up to be." Her later memoirs sadly reveal the way in which aging robbed her of her earlier ability to be interested in all that went on about her. At times she was insomniac, depressed that she had so little vitality, and petulant whenever she was alone. She vacillated between being very thankful for the full life she had lived and for the devotion of her family, and being resentful that her friends had gone, leaving her to ebb out her life alone. She worried endlessly about mundane matters—"dead car batteries, electric short circuits, [and] frozen water pipes." At the same time, she was very much aware of the courtesies of townspeople, "often doing nice things for me, like calling me from the library to say they are saving me a book I would like, bringing me salt-rising bread on a cold rainy day, [and] hunting thru boxes of keys for one which would open my car trunk." To the last she remained candid to others and honest with herself, frankly confessing that "one can't fill one's days and endless nights being grateful hard as one tries." Simply put, Keith Frazier Somerville did not "enjoy aging."[52]

In 1964, as Keith thought back over the four wars through which she had lived, she concluded, "I had just as soon not be here for the 5th one."[53] Unfortunately, she did not get her wish as she also lived through the Vietnam War. Too old now to do more than worry and read books about "that country where we are fighting such a controversial war," she was relieved in 1969 when the husband of her granddaughter, Keith Dockery Derbes, returned safely from a stint in Saigon. She was also gratified when another granddaughter, Ashton Ingram, joined the Peace Corps, and she cherished her long letters from Nepal.[54]

Keith Frazier Somerville died at the age of ninety on December 23, 1978.[55] It had been more than thirty years since she had written her "victory" letter to the "Dear Boys." In the interim, she had had many opportunities to contemplate whether the world after the war was as good as the young people to whom she addressed her letters had hoped it would be.

Reprinting Keith Somerville's perceptive, warm, and humane letters gives historical visibility to countless young Mississippians who were, in the final analysis, little different from those who lived Anywhere, U.S.A. To peer into the soul of Bolivar Countians at war and to perceive their love of family and community and visions of a world at peace is to gain a fuller understanding of a major epic in

United States history and its effect upon those citizens whose names rarely appear in standard accounts of World War II.

1. At about the age of seventy, Keith Somerville began typing two manuscripts: "Thinking Back" and "Random Thoughts." "Thinking Back" contains essays on a variety of subjects, such as "Girlhood," "Washington Memories," and "People I Have Known." It is unpaginated and unbound as is the second volume, "Random Thoughts," a diary-style journal in which Mrs. Somerville recorded her views about aspects of her life, contemporary affairs, and the books that she had read. Some of the entries are dated, but a majority are not. Both manuscripts are in the possession of her daughter, Keith Dockery McLean, Cleveland, Mississippi. The author bas a photocopy. See also, Mellie Virginia Bolen, "Anne Keith Frazier Somerville, 1887–1978: Socialite, Activist, and Diarist," (M.A. thesis, Delta State University, 1979).

2. "Kith and Kin," in "Thinking Back."

3. "Random Thoughts," (undated).

4. "Kith and Kin," in "Thinking Back."

5. "Childhood," in "Thinking Back."

6. "Girlhood," in "Thinking Back"; "James B. Frazier," *National Cyclopedia*, XXVIII (New York: James T. White, 1940), pp. 106–107; *Biographical Directory of the American Congress, 1774–1971* (Washington: G.P.O., 1971) p. 968.

7. "Girlhood," in "Thinking Back."

8. "Washington Memories," in "Thinking Back."

9. "Introduction," "Girlhood," in "Thinking Back;" "Random Thoughts" (April 1, 1960). According to a biographer, the two happiest years of Luce's life were spent at the Castle (1917–1919). The beadmistress, described as a feminist with progressive ideas, provided a setting for Clare Booth that was "a wonderfully exciting little world." Alden Hatch, *Ambassador Extraordinary*, (New York: Henry Holt, 1956) p. 41.

10. "Girlhood," in "Thinking Back." The new ship, the "latest in a fleet of powerful cruisers," was featured in a cover story in *Scientific American*, 94(March 17, 1906): 230–31.

11. Keith Frazier to Dear Girls, circa 1908, in Somerville file, Bolivar County Citizens File, Robinson-Carpenter Library, Cleveland, Mississippi. "Mrs. Keith Somerville," *Bolivar Commercial*, June 30, 1976.

12. Edward L. Beach, *The Wreck of the Memphis*, (New York: Holt: Rinehart and Winston, 1966.) pp. 303–304. In 1959, the surviving crew and widows formed a commemorative unit known as The Survivors Association of the United States Armored Cruiser *Memphis* that rivalled the "Sponsors" for the affection of and a place in the reveries of an aging Keith Somerville. She remained close to commander Edward L. Beach, the son of the commander of the vessel at the time of its destruction, for many years. Two mementos of the *Tennessee* came to be among Keith's most cherished treasures. One was the neck of the christening bottle, mounted on silver by Tiffany's, and the other was an inscribed brass porthole from the ship which was sent to her by Congressman Lemuel Padgett, chairman of the House Naval Affairs Committee, following the loss of her beloved vessel. "Girlhood," in "Thinking Back;" "My Treasures," in "Random Thoughts;" New York *Times*, August 30, 1916. For more information on the

Tennessee, see Robert A. Hart, *The Great White Fleet: Its Voyage Around the World, 1907–1909* (Boston: Little Brown, 1965), p. 177.

13. Quoted in Keith Frazier Somerville, 1942 Journal, November 30. Newspaper obituaries and editorials at the death of the elder Mrs. Frazier praised her as "half [her husband's] noted career." *Chattanooga Times*, November 19, 1942.

14. "Washington Memories," in "Thinking Back;" Mrs. William Howard Taft, *Recollections of Full Years* (New York: Dodd, Mead & Co., 1914), p. 391.

15. "Introduction," "Washington Memories," in "Thinking Back."

16. Frank Clay, who was the same age as Keith Somerville, was one of her favorite West Point "K-dets." Some insight into Clay family life in Marietta, Georgia may be found in Jean Edward Smith, *Lucius D. Clay: An American Life* (New York: Henry Holt, 1990), pp. 25–30.

17. "Girlhood," in "Thinking Back."

18. "Random Thoughts" (undated).

19. "Girlhood," "Washington Memories," in "Thinking Back." In Frank C. Waldrop, ed., *Mountain Voices: The Centennial History of the Monteagle Sunday School Assembly* (Nashville: Parthenon Press, 1982), pp. 346–347, Bob is described as "one of the favorite beaux at the Assembly."

20. "Random Thoughts" (undated).

21. On the Somerville family, see William M. Cash and Lucy Somerville Howorth, eds., *My Dear Nellie; The Civil War Letters of William L. Nugent to Eleanor Smith Nugent* (Jackson: University Press of Mississippi, 1977), pp. 3–6, 237–243, and Mary L. Merideth, "The Mississippi Woman's Rights Movement, 1889–1923: The Leadership Role of Nellie Nugent Somerville and Greenville in Suffrage Reform," (M.A. thesis, Delta State University, 1974). A biographical sketch of Nellie Nugent Somerville appears in Barbara Sicherman and Carol Hurd Green, ed., *Notable American Women: The Modern Period* (Cambridge, Mass.: Harvard University Press, 1980), pp. 654–656.

22. "Married Life," in "Thinking Back."

23. Statements by Keith Frazier Somerville and Keith Somerville Dockery, County Citizen File, Robinson-Carpenter Library, Cleveland, Mississippi.

24. "Married Life," in "Thinking Back;" "Random Thoughts" (undated).

25. Keith Somerville, "Thumbnail Sketch of My Life," Bolivar County Citizen File, Robinson-Carpenter Library, Cleveland, Mississippi. Linton Weeks, *Cleveland: A Centennial History, 1886–1986*, (Cleveland: City of Cleveland, 1985), pp. 105, 214.

26. "I See All," *Bolivar Commercial*, August 24, 1961; "Start of the Cleveland Public Library," "Random Thoughts." Mary Lee Beal, "Public Libraries Since 1900," in Margaret Peebles and J.B. Howell, ed., *A History of Mississippi Libraries* (Montgomery, Alabama: Paragon Press, 1975), pp. 79–80. Other library founders included Mrs. E. J. Nott, Mrs. R. P. Walt, and Mrs. A. W. Shands.

27. "Random Thoughts," (undated).

28. "Random Thoughts," (undated).

29. "Random Thoughts," (December 1959).

30. Keith Frazier Somerville, 1942 Journal, April 9, 19, November 19, 20.

31. Keith Frazier Somerville, 1942 Journal, April 11.

32. Keith Frazier Somerville, 1942 Journal, August 5, September 6, 7, 16, 22, 25, October 16, 1942. Quotation from Memphis *Commercial Appeal*, October 16, 1942.

33. Keith Frazier Somerville, 1942 Journal, September 16, 17, 20; 1943 Journal, February 28.

34. Keith Frazier Somerville, 1943 Journal, January 1, 10, December 25.

35. Keith Frazier Somerville, 1942 Journal, December 10, 11. 12.

36. A bound scrapbook of the columns is located in the Mississippi Department of Archives and History, Jackson, Mississippi.

37. *Bolivar Commercial*, January 15, 1943; Keith Frazier Somerville, 1943 Journal, December 17; 1944 Journal, January 1.

38. Keith Frazier Somerville, 1943 Journal, January 1, February 7, November 11. "Pistol Packing Mama" was a hit song of the day.

39. Keith Frazier Somerville, 1943 Journal, February 21. For six months prior to joining the Coast Guard, Joe Rice Dockery had served as a "dollar a year man" with the Office of Defense Supply Corporation in Washington, D.C.

40. Keith Frazier Somerville, 1943 Journal, October 10; *Bolivar Commercial*, November 10, 1944.

41. Keith Frazier Somerville, 1943 Journal, January 10, May 9.

42. Keith Frazier Somerville, 1943 Journal, February 7, 14, June 20; 1944 Journal, January 1, 30.

43. *Bolivar Commercial*, August 25, 1944; January 12, February 9, 16, April 12, 1945.

44. Memphis *Commercial Appeal*, June 30, 1946.

45. "Scandinavia at Seventy-nine," in "Random Thoughts."

46. The Library of Congress catalogue, c. 1947, described the Keith Family Tree.

47. Keith F. Somerville and Harriett W. B. Smith, *Ships of the Navy and Their Sponsors*, III, (Annapolis: United States Naval Institute, 1952).

48. For information on J. B. Frazier, see *Biographical Directory of the American Congress, 1774–1971* (Washington: G.P.O., 1971), p. 968; "Random Thoughts," May 14, 1961.

49. "Random Thoughts," January 1964; March 20, 1966.

50. Lucy Somerville Howorth (1895–) had been a member of the Mississippi House of Representatives before becoming a member of the Board of Veterans Appeals in Washington, D.C. in 1934. She was subsequently a General Counsel, War Claims Commission, the first woman to fill that position. She returned to Cleveland in 1957. See Joanne V. Hawks, "Like Mother, Like Daughter: Nellie Nugent Somerville and Lucy Somerville Howorth," *The Journal of Mississippi*, 45(May 1983): 116–123.

51. "Random Thoughts," May 11, 22, 1960; January 16, 1967, and several undated entries; "My Treasures," in "Random Thoughts;" Memphis *Commercial Appeal*, August 28, 1944; New York *Times*, May 11, 1960 (on the *Triton*); Beach, *Wreck of the Memphis*, p. 303. In 1968, at the age of eighty, she spoke for the last time to The Survivors Association of the United States Armored Cruiser *Memphis*.

52. "Random Thoughts," January 1963 and undated entries.

53. "Random Thoughts," January 1964. She must have included the Korean Conflict in her count, but she made no reference to it in her random musings.

54. "Random Thoughts," July 30, 1968; August 23, 1969.

55. Memphis *Commercial Appeal*, December 24, 1978.

1

WAR HAS COME TO ALL THE MAIN STREETS OF MISSISSIPPI

January 1943—May 1943

January 15, 1943

Dear Boys:

I have been reading for weeks, with such interest, a delightful continued letter which my friend, Florence Sillers Ogden, has been writing in the Rosedale paper to the boys in the service from the other side of Bolivar County.[1] Through it I have gleaned a knowledge of the whereabouts of many of the boys we used to see at Delta dances, basketball tournaments, football games, and the like. We stay-at-homes are all so interested in hearing about you! When I mentioned to the editor that I'd been writing personal letters to some of you, he said, "Why not write a letter now and then to all of them, through the columns of this paper? It might reach some of those whose addresses you do not have."[2]

Of course, I jumped at the idea because, as you know, tho' I

---

1. Florence Sillers Ogden wrote a weekly "Dear Boys" column for the *Bolivar Democrat* from 1941–1945. A four-volume scrapbook of these letters is at the Rosedale, Mississippi Public Library.

2. Clifton L. Langford was the editor of the *Bolivar Commercial* throughout the war. For Langford's announcement about Mrs. Somerville's "Dear Boys" column, see the *Bolivar Commercial*, January 15, 1943.

haven't any boys of my own (all my boys were girls!), I've always enjoyed other people's boys tremendously! And somehow, because I started a lot of you off in school, I feel that you're part "my boys," and that I, like your mothers, am privileged to be proud of you! For we ARE proud of you, scattered "from Greenland's icy mountains to India's coral strand" and at many an in-between station![3] Just the sight of the flags waving on our Cleveland streets (which used to mean, perhaps, only a barbecue in Wade's Grove on July 4th, or a bank holiday on Washington's or Lee's birthday) now brings a lump to our throats and a feeling of exultation that our boys so thoroughly believe in "the American way" of life that they are away enduring hardships and fighting to preserve it; fighting for Freedom and for us; fighting to keep the rights our forefathers won the hard way, too; fighting to keep liberty in the world, so much of which has been overrun by Hitler and Tojo, who do NOT believe in Liberty for ANY people, not even their own! I wonder if any of you heard the radio program on New Year's Eve, when the light atop the Statue of Liberty in New York harbor was flashed on for a moment three times (Morse code for the letter V—V for Victory) as a symbol to the submerged peoples of the world that the light of Liberty was still burning in America? With your help, dear boys, we'll always keep that light burning. This land of ours will always be "the land of the free and the home of the brave." You have a job to do, and you're doing it magnificently. For that, each of us thanks you!

Outwardly, life goes on the same here in our little town. People still go to Denton's for a coke, but often they can't get one![4] Can you feature that? Perhaps Melvin Shuler and Charles Collins of those "fighting Marines" may have met sometime over there in the Pacific

3. Mrs. Somerville taught first grade in the local public schools from 1929–1941. School teachers across the United States wrote an untold number of letters to former students in the military. As an example, Mrs. Catherine Manley, a high school art teacher in Clarksdale, Arizona, wrote to about thirty of her former students who were in the armed forces. Personal correspondence with Catherine M. Manley of Prescott, Arizona, May 31, June 22, and September 12, 1988.

4. Denton's is the headquarters of a local dairy in Cleveland. During the 1930s and 1940s, it featured a popular soda fountain serviced with "car hops." As Bolivar County men departed for the military, young women replaced them as "car hops."

fighting area and talked about it, and about how funny it must seem to have girls "jumping cars" there, and driving the milk truck! Charlie's young brother, Lamar, is one of the few males left working there, and he's hoping the draft will get him soon! Capt. Joe Denton, by the way, is now stationed at Gainesville, Texas, and Marian and the baby are with him.

None of us ride to Denton's as much as we used to, with gas rationing on (four gallons don't take you on many joy rides!), so we're all learning to walk![5] I bought a pair of shoes the other day which I was assured was just what the W.A.V.E.S. were billowing about it![6] (You knew, didn't you, that Leona Dakin Dannenberg was one of those "hi-rollers" and was recently commissioned an officer in the Navy? And that Mary Shands is now working in the Naval Intelligence down in New Orleans?)

As I waited for the train to pass at the depot crossing, I counted 122 tank cars of gasoline going north. The railroads are "Keeping 'em rolling" to "Keep 'em flying, and doing a grand job of it." There are no "empties" on our sidings now! Did you see that amusing cartoon of the big engine pulling a long train of "dining car restaurants" (labeled "Al's Diner," "Good Eats," "Home Cooking Aboard," etc.) with the caption—"The railroads are buying back all the rolling stock they can find"? You'd think we were a big city, so many trains go through daily (loaded with supplies, gas, and troops), but none of them stop at our little "crossroad-of-America." They just keep on rolling toward Berlin and Tokyo!

When the train finally passed, I walked on over by John Ward's drug store and missed Jane Floyd's pretty face among the girls working there. That good-looking aviator down at the Greenville Air Base (Jack Sawyer) took one of our loveliest girls when he flew away with her! We all enjoyed your letter, John, from far across the Pacific, and talked of it at the Surgical Dressing class.[7] Your firsthand

5. Nationwide gas rationing went into effect on December 1, 1942.

6. The WAVES (Women Accepted for Volunteer Emergency Service) was the woman's component of the U.S. Navy. It was established on July 30, 1942.

7. Mrs. Somerville was an active member of the local Surgical Dressing Class which rolled bandages for the war effort. The women who attended these classes regularly provided Mrs. Somerville with news for her column. The *Bolivar Commercial* often carried news of the activities of the local Surgical Dressing Class.

knowledge of the need for our dressings, after the Jap[anese] had been around, inspired us all to do extra folds! It made me, and I imagine lots of others, ashamed that we hadn't done more! Mrs. Eustis, Mrs. Bobb, and Mrs. Hyman, those grand unpaid workers who are always on the job, doubtless [were thinking] . . . of their boys as they inspected our work. (Harold Eustis has been commanding a colored company in North Carolina.[8] Billy Bobb writes it's cold out at Camp Leonard Wood, Missouri, but I'll wager he's not finding it as cold as some of you are having it in Alaska, Northern Ireland, or Iceland! Jerome Hyman just turned nineteen, is still at William and Mary College in Virginia, but his mother imagines the eighteen to twenty draft will take him from his studies ere long.)

On across the street at their drug store, Mrs. Owen told me of Marian Alice, with her husband, Lt. Ben Perkins, way out at Camp Adair, Corvallis, Oregon. Marian Alice, I hear, is ambitious to be a W.A.C. when friend-husband goes overseas.[9]

In Kamien's for a spool of thread, I heard of I.A. [Kamien, Jr.] now transferred from Camp Pickett, Virginia to Camp Walters, Texas.[10] That is where Bernell Simmons . . . got his commission. He and I.A. just changed locations, for he is now at Camp Pickett.

Bertram Wade is not carrying the mail anymore, but he's handling it just the same—at Embarkation Post Office, Seattle, Washington, and Kline Bedwell is Battalion Postmaster at Camp Barkley, Texas. They're out to win this war at the Post Office—to "stamp out" the dictators in more ways than one! Mrs. Hill's grandson, Ed, is a paratrooper up in North Carolina, and Graham (at Ft. Sill, Oklaho-

---

8. Throughout most of World War II, black servicepeople were concentrated in segregated units which were usually commanded by white officers. Two recent articles on this subject are David Brion Davis, "World War II and Memory," *Journal of American History* 77(September 1990): 580–587 and John Hope Franklin, "Their War and Mine," *Journal of American History,* 77(September 1990): 576–579. The standard source is Ulysses Grant Lee, *The United States Army in World War II: Special Studies: The Employment of Negro Troops* (Washington, D.C.: Government Printing Office, 1966).

9. The Women's Army Auxiliary Corps (WAAC) was established on May 14, 1942. Within a year, it became an integral part of the U.S. Army and was renamed the Women's Army Corps (WAC).

10. Kamien's, a dry goods store in Cleveland, was founded at the turn of the twentieth century by I.A. Kamien, Sr.

ma) expects to get his commission next month—before he is nineteen! And Aviation Cadet William Buckley is due to get his wings this week "away down in Georgia." (Wife Clarice's mother is proudly wearing some gold wings he sent as a gift to his swell mother-in-law! Nice going, Bill! Besides being proud of her son-in-law, Mary Kelly is also quite justly pleased that "Sonny" is now physical instructor in jumping. Sgt. George, his red head and his contagious grin is, you may have guessed, a paratrooper, also in Florida.) Now even the Post Office janitor, Amzie Moore, is in the service—a sergeant out in Phoenix, Arizona![11] The ones left there are working overtime—often far into the night—to get your letters to you! They're some of America's "unsung heroes."[12]

Speaking of mail, you just ought to see those mothers with two sons in Uncle Sam's Army! They simply live for mail! There's Lois Hardee, working at O.P.A. and thinking of Ben, down at Camp Shelby, Mississippi and of Norman, flying somewhere over the Pacific, and between times making a priceless war scrapbook.[13] One treasured feature of it is the wonderful picture of Norman and a friend in their plane, which appeared in the New York *Times* feature section last summer, as well as in a lot of other papers over the country. Norman writes, "I'm getting a good sun tan. You'd think I was spending a season at Miami . . . things are going swell for me. We live in a tent on a hill and really have a big time fighting over the merits of our favorite towns and states." Here's hoping Lt. Hardee still thinks Cleveland and Mississippi are "tops!" . . .

I talked to Mrs. Pleasant the other day and was so interested to

11. After the war, Amzie Moore (1911–1982) became a leader in the Mississippi National Association for the Advancement of Colored People and was very active in voter registration efforts. Robert Moses, the Student Nonviolent Coordinating Committee leader, described Moore in August 1960 as "the best I've met yet." For information on Moore's role in the civil rights movement, see Taylor Branch, *Parting the Waters: America in the King Years, 1954–1963* (New York: Simon and Schuster, 1988), pp. 330–31, 345, 486–7, 492–3, 559–60, 635, 712. The quote from Robert Moses appears on p. 330.

12. For a discussion of the mail and its delivery during World War II, see Judy Barrett Litoff and David C. Smith, "'Will He Get My Letter?': Popular Portrayals of Mail and Morale During World War II," *Journal of Popular Culture*, 23(Spring 1990): 23–45.

13. The OPA was the Office of Price Administration, a wartime federal agency charged with the responsibility of setting prices to help control inflation.

hear about her boys. Bobbie isn't exactly in the service, but he's serving Uncle Sam all right, as the pilot of a big commercial plane (Chicago and Southern Airlines—between Houston and Memphis). What with priorities, practically no-one but generals and admirals and war workers can ride on planes these days. (Personally, I haven't gotten in the habit yet, so it hasn't bothered me any. But I am crazy to learn to fly! I can't bear the idea of any grandchildren saying, in future years, "Grandmother is SO old fashioned! She can't even pilot a plane!") Did you know Bobbie had gotten married? (To that attractive Elizabeth Cornell, who used to be Dugas Shand's secretary.) And the War Department has just notified Mrs. Pleasant that her ever happy Cecil (who got his wings and aviation training in California and Arizona) "has arrived safely at his destination." This is notice to the enemy: "Watch out—a live wire is on the way!" . . .

In the Modern Store, we miss the smiling face of Ralph Y. Joe, now at Camp Lee, Virginia.[14] A lot of our friends of Chinese descent are in there helping their Uncle Sam! B.M. John, Ernest Joe, Jack Wong, and Louis Joe left only last week, while Chester Joe and Jack Chow have been in several months. Wee L. Wong has been a year in the Army and is now a corporal at Ft. Knox, Kentucky. We Southerners like the Chinese people. I heard one of Gen. Chennault's officers say, on the radio, that practically all the famed "Flying Tigers" who have pitched so successful "for quite a spell" for Chiang Kai-Shek are from the South. You know, the General himself is from Louisiana and several of his family are now doing war work in our state. . . . [15]

Because in this, our land of cotton, all of us have many colored friends, some of you may be interested to know that Tab Block's son, Fox, was here the other day from Camp Pickett, Virginia, and that Charles Rivers, who enlisted in the Navy two years ago and was at Pearl Harbor, drove in just before Christmas. He's gone back now, "ready to lay on to any Jap[anese] he meets!" O.D. Sterling, who

14. The Modern Store was one of the few grocery stores in Cleveland. Most of Cleveland's grocery stores were owned and operated by Chinese families.

15. General Claire Chennault (1890–1958) founded and commanded the very well-known American Volunteer Group (AVG) in China, commonly referred to as the "Flying Tigers." Chiang Kai-Shek (1887–1975) was the president of China and Allied Supreme Commander of the China Theatre of Operations.

grew up on Pearl Street, Cleveland, was not so fortunate, for life ended for him at Pearl Harbor. Sgt. Ed Hilley has been way up in Alaska working on the northern end of the now completed new Alaskan highway. It is rumored that Ed is one of our most successful crapshooters and has picked up so many gold nuggets that he's bought enough government bonds to buy a spot of land here after the war! T.A. Reed, who was principal of the colored school at Pace, is now a sergeant in the Quartermaster's Department up at Wilmington, North Carolina. You know each of them had big tales to tell—just as each of you has! What a saga of adventure would be the combined experiences of Bolivar County's heroes!

We missed you all during this past holiday season. Even the streets didn't look supremely happy without all you boys and without the brilliantly lighted little Christmas trees which, in other years, have made of our little town a beauty spot. But "When the lights are on again, all over the world, and the boys are home again, all over the world" (as the popular song goes), then Christmas will be Christmas right, and we'll celebrate in true Delta fashion—tea dance and all![16]

Best of luck to each of you, and may 1943 be a victorious year to you, and to the lovers of liberty everywhere.

Sincerely,
Keith Frazier Somerville

January 29, 1943

Dear Boys:

The last time I wrote you, I was telling about some of the two-star mothers, but today I'm going to introduce you to a few of the three-star mothers![17] One of the happiest of these last week was Mrs.

---

16. This is a reference to the 1942 song, "When the Lights Go On Again (All Over the World)," made popular by Vaughn Monroe and his orchestra. Tea dances, with live orchestras, were annual Christmas afternoon events. Invitations were sent to guests who lived as far as fifty miles away.

17. Small flags and banners, with blue stars on a white field, appeared in front windows across the United States. The blue stars indicated that a person from that house was in the service. Gold stars indicated that a person had been killed in action. Group flags were commonplace in businesses, churches, synagogues, schools, and lodges.

A.E. Lorance, because that charming Lt. Lorance of the Navy ("Snooks" to you, "Gene" to his girls, and "Lt. (J.G.) A.E." to the Navy) blew in all unexpectedly. He's been in the Navy, you know, since 1940. When most of the rest of us were apathetic about the war, he was part of the North Atlantic Patrol and Convoy, delivering lend-lease material to England and helping prepare for what the Navy, at least, knew was in the offing.[18] He's been all over the Pacific, too, most of the time on our aircraft carriers. A month ago he was sent to Norfolk, and his visit home was just a stopover, en route back to the Pacific. "Snooks," despite the fact that he's SO attractive that I longed to have my face lifted, my hair blonded, and to be eighteen again, is the most modest person alive, and if it hadn't been for his proud mother, I'd never have learned that he had six stars on his service ribbon (battles he's been in) and that he is eligible for six out of the seven medals which have been given Navy men in this war! One of these medals is from England, another from Australia! An optimistic note he sounded I'll pass on to you—the fact that the Jap[anese] flyers today aren't nearly as reckless nor as good as they were at first. Then they'd fly straight at the ships, in formations of a dozen or more, and come down close enough for the men on shipboard to see their features and see them thumb their noses at our boys. (Of course, just before our gunners got them for the impudence!) He said they were suicide flyers all right, bound to drop their bombs if they all died in the attempt, but that today's flyers are nowhere nearly so anxious to get killed! I wish I had space to tell you all the interesting things he told me! One advantage in gray hair is that I could rush boldly over to call on him! If I'd been young and gay and giddy, I'd have had to stay at home, twirling my thumbs, praying that he'd remember me and might accidentally phone! He wouldn't want me to "tell all" anyway, so I'll say nothing more except to tell you where Mrs. Lorance's other two boys are. Sgt. Cecil is an instructor in Radio Communications at Ft. Sill, Oklahoma, and Harold is in the Coast Artillery (Anti-Aircraft) at Burbank, California....

Mrs. J.T. Crawford also has three fine sons in the service of their

18. The Lend-Lease Act was passed by Congress in March 1941. By the time the war ended, $50 billion worth of war materials had been provided to the Allies by this act.

country. I was lucky enough to be allowed to read a most interesting letter from Bertram the other day. He's been in the Navy seven years, during which time he has studied and equipped himself to be a dentist and a pharmacist. After the war he hopes to be a dentist in California, where wife Dolly is now living with her father. Bertram writes hopefully from French Morocco, Northwest Africa—"This is only my personal opinion, but I think this war will be over soon. Gen. Rommel and his African Army is about wiped out, the Germans aren't doing so well in Russia either, and we are winning in the Solomons, too.[19] I don't see how they can beat us. Of course we've lost some ships, but we can build others easier than the Jap[anese] or Germans. We spent some time in Casablanca, a beautiful place, full of Arabs. The men wear robes and caps called fez. The women wear veils, leaving only their eyes showing. Many of them come in from the great Sahara desert to buy things. Some live here and own shops where they sell leather goods. The French here are a very decent sort, but the girls have bum looking legs. All their food is rationed and soap is practically non-existent." Another of the Crawford boys, SSGT Carl, when last heard from, was at Camp Pickett, Virginia, while Sgt. Louis is down at Camp Shelby.

Lots of things are changed, besides time, by this war. Graduations, for instance, used always to come in June, but next week life is really "commencing" for a bunch of our boys, home now from "State," diplomas in hand, to tarry only a short time among us.[20]

Robert Smith signed up while in college for the Armored Force, Leon Young for the Air Corps, William O. Williford for the Marines, and Charles House for the Navy. A "glad hand" for each of you with an extra special clasp for Robert, because I KNOW it was only yesterday since he was a chubby little boy in my room!

Another of my favorite "chillun," Lt. Kimball Glassco, Jr., who also graduated from "State" last summer right into the Army (Fort Benning, Georgia), is now stationed at Austin, Texas. En route,

19. General Erwin Rommel (1891–1944), nicknamed the "Desert Fox," commanded the Afrika Corps from February 1941 until British forces stopped him in Egypt late in 1942. He then had to withdraw to the German bridgehead in Tunis. In March 1943, Hitler ordered Rommel to return to Germany.

20. "State" is Mississippi State College, now Mississippi State University, in Starkville, Mississippi.

you'll probably remember, he stopped here and took unto himself a wife, lovely Nell Busby, and she is in Texas with him. Nell says she's gotten to be "a pretty good cook." I'm proud of you girls, too! So many of you have packed away your evening dresses and donned aprons and are making grand wives! And the rest of you have all gotten yourselves jobs![21]

I went to church (Methodist) the other Sunday, and I want to tell you about our new preacher, J.M. Bradley. He's a "grand old man" and preaches like a bishop! Standing beside the huge American flag in the pulpit and telling us he'd been "drafted, too, for the duration" (seventy-two is a bit over the draft age, but he was on the retired list and was called back into service because so many of the younger preachers have gone to be chaplains), he preached of "the faith of our fathers," faith in the future, faith in the principles for which our flag stands. His sermon was an inspiration to all of us who sometime falter in our own faith. He had us all stand a moment in silent prayer for you boys away fighting, or getting ready to fight, our battles for us. Lovely Jeannette Kelso, in her choir vestments was, I'm sure, breathing a prayer for Richard (still at Keesler Field, though expecting to be moved soon). Mrs. "Emma" Smith's pleas must have been for flying Capt. Milton (in charge at Eglin Field, Florida); for Robert, soon to leave for Ft. Knox, Kentucky; and for Clarence, in Marine Reserves at Delta State.[22] (She's almost a three-star mother, herself!) Mr. Nowell, doubtless remembering the temptations which beset him in his long ago Navy days, I surmise, sent up a prayer for his friendly Jack, now like his father before him serving his country (up

21. For an examination of the experiences of World War II war brides, see Judy Barrett Litoff and David C. Smith, "Since You Went Away: The World War II Letters of Barbara Wooddall Taylor," *Women's Studies*, 17(1990): 249–76. The proportion of women who were employed increased from 25 percent at the beginning of the war to 36 percent at the war's end—an increase greater than that of the previous four decades. A pioneering study about the life of a service wife on the move is Barbara Klaw, *Camp Follower: The Story of a Soldier's Wife* (New York: Random House, 1943). Two good contemporary accounts of women war workers are Augusta M. Clawson, *Shipyard Diary of a Woman Welder* (New York: Penguin Books, 1944) and Josephine Von Miklos, *I Took a War Job* (New York: Simon and Schuster, 1943).

22. Delta State Teachers College (now Delta State University) is located in Cleveland. It was the alma mater of many of the young Bolivar Countians who were summoned to service.

at Pittsburgh now). Mrs. Lalla Mitchell, who always beautifies the church for us, must, I'm convinced, have sent up beautiful prayers for Capt. Ben, now stationed at historic Fort Sam Houston, Texas, and the Nances doubtless had handsome Dick (now in the hospital at Camp Leonard Wood, Missouri, after an operation), in their minds. . . .

Speaking of preachers, I imagine you've all heard that "Brother Eavenson" of the Baptist Church is now at the Chaplain's School at Harvard. Brother Eavenson of the welcoming smile and the ever ready sympathy, who wasn't just the Baptists' preacher, but everybody's! You probably don't remember it, but when my daughter, Ashton, was married, our Methodist preacher was taken ill suddenly. Who was to marry her? Should we send away for another Methodist preacher? "Not at all," said the bride. "I'll ask my friend, Brother Eavenson, to marry us." And she did and he did. "The first time he ever married anyone in a Methodist Church," he said. That he can "Praise the Lord and Pass the Ammunition" we have no doubt, but he'll also pass out many a friendly, comforting word to the lucky soldiers he ministers to. . . . [23]

I heard the other day of one of our colored friends who had "heard the call" to preach since he'd been in the Army. Warren Robertson, now serving in Arizona, used to be a "fun box for everybody, always laughing and mocking the preachers," yet he preached three sermons on Christmas day, and the soldiers liked his sermons so well they gave him three big collections! [24] Warren writes, "This is a swell place out here. The mountains are all around me. It's cold on the mountains where the snow is, but it's warm in the valley where I am. The clouds sometimes come down to the top of the mountains and rest on them." Perhaps Warren "lifted up his eyes to the hills" and there received his inspiration to preach!

Levi Anderson was the only colored man saved when his ship went down in the Pacific, but he's now on another one! A little thing like a

23. "Praise the Lord and Pass the Ammunition" was a popular World War II song based on an event which supposedly took place during the Japanese attack on Pearl Harbor in which a Navy chaplain passed ammunition to an anti-aircraft gun after members of the gun crew were wounded.

24. Fort Huachuca, Arizona, was a military installation where many black troops were trained.

sinking ship can't down the fighting spirit of our boys! Black and white alike, they're ready to "be up and at 'em" again.

You remember the Cockrell boys, of course. Richard, recently home to rest up a bit after his strenuous experiences, was also on one of those ships the Jap[anese] got, but he's at an Atlantic port now, awaiting return to the sea. Better luck this time, "Hot." His brother, Corp. William E., is now at the Air Base, Pyote, Texas. . . .

Oh, yes, and I MUST tell you about the Hytkens boys. Max was for some months out at Cheyenne, Wyoming, but now he's at Omaha (Quartermaster's Department). Ens. Robert, for quite a while at Indianapolis after making several short cruises, is now also at an Atlantic port, likely to go "sailing, sailing, over the deep blue sea" ere long.[25] I ran into Robert one day last fall in the lobby of the Peabody and was overcome (even at my advanced age) by how wonderful and moving-picture-y he looked in his uniform![26] You may have deduced from this letter that I'm allergic to uniforms! They do things to my heart!

You know David Cohn, the Greenville author, said the Delta begins in the lobby of the Peabody.[27] Which reminds me, if you want an interesting book to read, try to get ahold of *The Good Old Days* by this same Cohn.[28] He took the Sears, Roebuck catalogs for fifty years and wrote delightfully of the changes the years have brought in things advertised in them. It makes a history of how life here in America has changed in the past half a century. We can't even imagine what will be advertised fifty years from now! But anyway, you boys who have been "raised up" seeing that bulky volume about the house would enjoy the book as much as I did, I'm sure. I read somewhere that during the last war, the head of Sears made a trip to Europe, carrying three packing cases as his only luggage. "What's in

---

25. This is, most likely, a reference to the nineteenth-century song, "Sailing," by Godfrey Marks. The chorus includes the words, "Sailing, Sailing over the bounding main;/For many a Stormy wind shall blow ere Jack comes home again."

26. The Peabody Hotel is in Memphis, Tennessee.

27. David Cohn (1896–1960) was a writer and satirist from Greenville, Mississippi. In his autobiography, Cohn stated, "The Mississippi Delta begins in the lobby of the Peabody Hotel in Memphis and ends on Catfish Row in Vicksburg." *Where I Was Born and Raised* (Boston: Houghton Mifflin, 1948), p. 12.

28. David Cohn, *The Good Old Days* (New York: Simon and Schuster, 1940).

them?" he was asked. "Sears, Roebuck catalogs to be distributed to the hospitals, so the boys can look over them and cease being homesick," was the reply. So if you need an antidote for a yearning within you for turnip greens and cornbread and home and mother, then I recommend this book.

Our Uncle Sam doesn't like for us to talk about the weather, but I don't think he'd mind if I tell you we've been having our usual unpredictable kind lately.[29] The first weeks of this month were March-in-January, and we'd about decided that the God-of-the-Harvest, taking note of America's avowed intention of trying to feed the starving world, was smiling down on our winter turnip patches! Then came (of all things!) snow, and icicles on the yellow jonquils in my yard. We won't fuss about it, though, for we all know that cold will kill the boll weevil, don't we? Our weather drives the Yankee boys in our Mississippi camps crazy, but it means home to us, and by tomorrow we'll probably be going about in shirt sleeves again!

Goodbye for this time and every good wish for each of you.

Sincerely,
Keith Frazier Somerville,

February 12, 1943

Dear Boys:

By the time this letter reaches you it will be Valentine's Day. I can't send you any red candy hearts or lace edged missives, but you know St. Valentino, who started all this business several hundred years ago, was a letter writer! And I CAN send you news of Cleveland's own Valentine (Carman Epton—another of my "chillun"), who is now somewhere in Hawaii. An artist like Epton (did you ever see the wonderfully lifelike bust he made of his father?) couldn't but be impressed with the beauty of the Pacific islands and the lovely moonlight nights, but he writes, "It's different in a lot of ways from home. For instance, going barefoot in the middle of town is something I never saw grown people doing before."...

I couldn't get that far from home, but I did use up some of my

---

29. Public discussion of the weather was discouraged because it was felt that such information could be useful to the enemy.

precious gas going WAY down to Boyle one day.[30] I was glad one of our state traffic cops in his big white car didn't see and arrest me for going on a joy ride, as I see from the papers they're doing up East. If he'd known how much joy I got out of hearing all about you boys who have gone to war, he'd have been justified in doing so!

Mrs. V.W. Thomas told me much about Capt. Rowan, pilot in the Air Corps, who was recently given a medal "in recognition of meritorious service in participation in aerial flights of one hundred hours in pursuit of enemy bombardment." Rowan has been in the Middle East for the past ten months. Before that he was in the Far East. He says that now he's seen the entire world! You remember he went to Europe on a freighter one summer while he was in college. And here's a secret. He has kept a diary ever since the first day he went into training for the Air Corps and is writing a book about his experiences. I hope he has it published, for that is one book I'd certainly like to read....[31] Dropped by Garfinkel's and was lucky enough to find "Buddy" (Bernard) home from Millington, Tennessee where he's a storekeeper in the disbursing end.[32] He looks almost as cherubic in his Navy uniform as he used to look in his sailor suits when the twins came to kindergarten to me![33] Had you heard about Leona? She and "Sonny" Gordon got married Sunday up at the Peabody! After finishing up at Chanute Field, Illinois (in weather-forecasting), Sgt. Norman was ordered to Key Field in Meridian, Mississippi and as he had a three day leave, Leona, her mother, and a few friends met him in Memphis and they had the wedding there. Though the groom is a Charleston lad, a lot of you will remember when he went to Delta State.

Lt. A.L. Melott, after graduating from the M.P. School at Oglethrope, Georgia is really "seeing America first," riding all the time on swank

30. Boyle is three miles south of Cleveland.

31. The book, *Born in Battle* (Philadelphia: John C. Winston Co., 1944), based on Captain Thomas's diary was very well received. Fletcher Pratt, writing for the July 1, 1944, issue of the *Saturday Review of Literature*, described the book as "a kind of microcosm of the war, at least the war in the air, and most of it is told with a surprising energy, freshness, and intelligence . . . among war books this gets an A rating" (p. 19).

32. Garfinkel's was a small mercantile store in the center of Cleveland.

33. During the 1920s, Mrs. Somerville established the first kindergarten in Cleveland in her home.

trains and watching out for soldiers on leave. He's sent home a bunch of autographs of interesting people he's met in his travels, among them Orson Welles, and "Catherine, the trumpet player" with the All-Girl Orchestra on the Hour of Charm program.[34]

From North Africa comes word of Sgt. George Woolfolk, who writes that his boat ride over was uneventful as far as action was concerned: that he's living in one of the larger towns and seeing amazing sights. He reports that the Arab customs were his first interest but that "their living conditions are terrible," and that he imagines they must have many deaths due to that fact. Like Rowan, he is impressed with the backwardness of the people whose "dwellings remind you of pictures of Bible days."

Oscar Crutchfield expects to get his wings soon at Maxwell Field, Alabama, and A.T. Janis and Sydney Mayo are Marines, now at the destroyer base in San Diego, California. Dick Alexander is there, too, while his brother, Bill, Jr., is down at Camp Shelby, Mississippi. The three Boozer boys have all taken to the air. Lt. James, you may remember, was attached to a mapping group way up in the wilds of Alaska last summer where he had no haircut for two months, no shave for seven weeks, no hot water at all, and saw no girls save an occasional, uninteresting Eskimo! He's now at Salt Lake City. Lt. George W. recently transferred to the Air Corps, is now taking pre-flight training at Long Beach, California, and Bob is an Aviation Cadet pilot at Kelly Field, San Antonio, Texas.

Over at the Walls, I learned that Bobbie, who is with the F.B.I., is now connected with the Washington office. He's been in since 1940, long before Pearl Harbor, so he's one of the tried and trusted "old men," since J. Edgar Hoover has recruited so many of the nation's finest since then to combat the Gestapo and the Jap[anese] Secret Service.[35] They're doing it, too! Hardly a paper we pick up but notes that the F.B.I. has broken up a spy ring! Those F.B.I. men have to be quick on the trigger, mentally and physically, and we're proud that

34. Orson Welles (1911–1982) actor and movie director; the Hour of Charm was a popular, weekly radio program which featured Phil Spitalny and his All-Girl Orchestra.

35. J. Edgar Hoover (1895–1972) was the first director of the Federal Bureau of Investigation.

one of our boys is one of that fine group who are doing so much toward helping us win this war. . . .

I've been telling you in recent letters about two and three star mothers, but listen—Mrs. Monroe Steed is a five-star mother and her sixth son, James, is rarin' to go! Beside these six, she has three more sons at home! To have nine sons must be wonderful, but to have all those patriotic sons—well, that's something! I know she's the proudest mother in Bolivar County! The Steeds live out east of Boyle and Mr. Steed is a brother of "Pete" in the City Barber Shop (Cleveland), well known to many of you. All five of the Steed boys volunteered! The Axis nations thought we were soft and wouldn't fight, but we fooled 'em, didn't we? Three of them are sergeants now—Sgt. Edward, Camp Wallace, Texas, Sgt. Carlee, Ft. Benning, Georgia, and Sgt. Bernice, Camp Shelby. Dewitt is at Camp Barkley, Texas, and Estell at Camp Crowder, Missouri. Our congratulations to Mr. and Mrs. Steed! There was a pacifist song people were singing a few years ago, "I Didn't Raise My Boy To Be A Soldier."[36] Of course they didn't, for we are a peace loving nation, but they certainly reared them with the right principles and a love for their country!

The same is true of Mr. and Mrs. Whit Lamberson, who have four sons who are soldiers. Capt. O.B. and Sgt. John W. left here two years ago with the National Guard, and both are now at Camp Shelby, while E.C. and Bob Frank who joined the Marines last summer now are somewhere across the Pacific.

Mr. and Mrs. Jim Browning also have four sons in uniform. Sgt. Durwood (National Guard, too) is at Camp Shelby; the other three are in the Navy; Toy in Panama; Otto and James in the Pacific fighting area. I know F.D.R. is no prouder of his four sons in the service than they are of theirs! And we're all proud with them!

Mr. and Mrs. R. H. Creekmore, too, have every right to be very proud of their five sons, who have all placed their names on the roll of those aiding their country. Three of them are in the Army: Sgt. Lyle J. (Air Base Headquarters, Morrison Field, Florida); Pvt. Rufus (air mechanic at Walterbone, South Carolina); Pvt. Lester (Radio Training School, Sioux Falls, South Dakota). In addition to these,

---

36. "I Didn't Raise My Boy To Be A Soldier" was a very popular, but controversial, ballad of 1915 which opposed U.S. entry into World War I.

Richmond is making anti-aircraft guns in Chicago, and Hardy worked for many months in the shipyards, Houston, Texas, till his eye was injured and he was forced to stop work temporarily, but he expects to return soon.

Evan Chapman writes from Ft. Crankrit, California of shooting big guns on the mountains near there (Coast Artillery) and making eighty-six in marksmanship! And Lt. Paul Goforth (another National Guarder) is now up in South Carolina. Orville Jaquith is in the Navy, training at Camp Perry, Virginia. Since he graduated at Keesler Field, Rufus Pitts has been at Midland, Texas. (Did you know he and that cute Nell Jones are going to be married?)...

Did you know Dick Peeples was a "Seabee?"[37] Bet you don't know what THAT is! I didn't, but it means he's in the construction end of the Navy. He's a petty officer now stationed at historic Williamsburg (Camp Perry) and wife Willie is teaching in Greenville.

Lt. Lawson Magruder, 3rd, is now at Camp Rucker, Alabama, a member of the 7th Corps Testing Team. He comes of a long line of "fighting Magruders," for grandfather, Maj. Lawson, was an officer in the Civil War, and uncle, Capt. Carey, is now in charge of the Naval Training Station at Newport, Rhode Island. Another uncle, Adm. Pickett Magruder, was one of the heroes of World War I. Mary Ann and their small daughter are now at Augusta, Georgia (near Lawson's home base, Camp Gordon). Father Lawson served three years with Coast Artillery—uncles, Maj. Edmund and Lt. S.S (U.S.N.), were casualties of the last war, while their brother, Sgt. Maxwell, served twenty-eight months in France. Some family to live up to, young Lawson, but we're betting on you to do it!

One of Boyle's favorite sons, Capt. Buck Lemons, is at home now in that good looking R.A.F. uniform, with gold U.S.A. on his sleeve.[38] And has HE had experiences! You all remember when he was dusting

37. Seabees was the *nom de guerre* of special U.S. Navy construction battalions. These units were composed of persons with experience in road and bridge construction. The Seabees played an important role in building roads and air fields, often while battles ranged around them.

38. Prior to the summer of 1942, three Eagle Squadrons, made up of U.S. citizens, were part of the British Royal Air Force (RAF). The nationality of Americans who served with the RAF was indicated by a gold U.S.A. emblem worn on the left sleeve. In September 1942, the Eagle Squadrons were transferred to the U.S. 8th Air Force.

cotton all over the Delta, don't you? Well, he joined the R.A.F. down in Florida, trained a bit up in Canada, and arrived in England in March 1941, nine months before Pearl Harbor. They received him with open arms, and he was asked everywhere if he and the 225 Americans with him were the first contingent of American soldiers, and were terribly disappointed to find he'd come "on his own." The London *Standard* of April 28, 1941 contained his picture with several other Americans and a write-up about the [crop] "Dusters" who did such dangerous flying in the U.S.A., [who] had joined up to help and were "fighting mad" over the sights in bombed London.[39] Buck saw plenty of "sights," for his job was flying "replacements" to bases all over England, Scotland, the Orkneys, and other spots. When a plane failed to return to its base, they'd phone his outfit, and they'd fly them another. During his two years in England, he has flown thirty-nine types of planes, including Liberators and Flying Fortresses.[40] Speaking of rationing there, he said the people were allowed sixty-six clothing points for an entire year, a suit taking up twenty-seven, socks three, hat six, tie two—and everything else in proportion. Yes, he's eaten the powdered eggs Lend-Lease is sending over. Mostly they're awful, grainy like cornbread, but one little cafe, run by an American, made omelets of them which were really good. He's not too optimistic about the war ending soon. He says, with his delight- ful smile, "There'll be plenty more fun before it's over!" Having done his bit for England, Buck is back to help in his own land now and leaves soon to test bombers for Henry Ford in Detroit.

There are lots more Boyle heroes, but this is all I have space for today. Emerson says war has one virtue: "It breaks up the old horizon and we see through the rifts a wider vista."[41] You globe- trotting "Yanks" are certainly opening up vistas to us here at home!

Thanks for that and for all the bigger things you're doing for us!

Sincerely,

Keith Frazier Somerville,

39. Crop dusting was dangerous because flights occurred at very low altitudes.

40. Liberators and Flying Fortresses were famous types of World War II bombing aircraft. The Liberator was a B-24 and the Flying Fortress was a B-17.

41. On several occasions, Ralph Waldo Emerson (1803–1882) expressed views somewhat similar to the one cited by Mrs. Somerville. However, we have been unable to locate this particular quotation.

February 26, 1943

Dear Boys:

Conserve this and conserve that, the papers caution us daily! Keep your house at sixty-five, don't waste fuel or matches—so we're conserving here at home! At my house, it's almost like a cartoon I saw of a crowded kitchen, where besides the stove and ice box, they also had an entire living room set and three beds! The caption read, "We just kept cutting off one room after another till here we are!"[42]

In the line of conservation, I went in to Barbati's Shoe Shop the other day and was reminded of an experience I had in Washington a few years ago.[43] One night I broke the heel off a shoe. The next morning I walked miles trying to get it fixed, but everyone was too busy to bother with such a little job! When I finally found a man who would stop and mend it, he charged me a dollar for this job! Now I've always loved Washington, where I spent a number of my happy girlhood years, but I fairly snorted that day—"Cities! You can have 'em! I'm glad I live in a nice little, sleepy Southern town, where people can take time to be obliging!" Why if I'd been at home, I'd have gone straight to Mr. Barbati, and he would have laid aside whatever he was doing, tacked this on in a jiffy, and handed it back with his everpresent smile. If I'd asked, "What do I owe you, Mr. Barbati?" the chances are he'd have shaken his head, still smiling and said, "Not a thing—it didn't take a minute!" I've often wondered how Papa Barbati ever raised all that fine, big family of his, for he's SO generous with his time! I think they must have been raised on the goodwill of the entire community! And now three of his boys are in the Army. Sgt. Monte (Mario) is with the Air Force down at Victoria, Texas; Lawrence at Camp Shelby; and Sgt. Joe at Camp Claiborne,

42. Throughout the wartime period, civilians were urged to limit their consumption of scarce items and to be conservative in their use of items which had military value. Some twenty-five programs of conservation were proposed to civilians, including the better use of fuel oil, salvaging metal scrap and waste paper, and saving household grease. Special campaigns were mounted to salvage rarer metals such as lead and tin.

43. Shoes were rationed during World War II because of the scarcity of rubber and military needs for leather. Shoe repair shops experienced a brisk trade. Many shoe conservation measures, such as resoling, had begun during the Depression and were familiar to the population.

Louisiana. (I wonder if you ever knew, Joe, that you were once one of this "teacher's pets?")

I've never been to Sunny Italy, but I've thought sometime that perhaps there must be something about it like our Delta, for so many people of Italian descent have settled and thrived here.[44] I once heard Mr. Charlie Scott of Rosedale say that nowhere in the world had he ever seen a sunset comparable to ours except in Italy. Remember how our sun goes down like a big red ball and seems to actually rest for awhile on the ground before dissolving into a gorgeous rainbow of colors that lasts and lasts, changing its hues momentarily, getting more vivid, then paling into pastel tints, till it finally fades into the soft grays of twilight? (It's then that the mockingbirds and mosquitoes and bullfrogs come out!) I'm sure you've all admired our sunsets, going home from school or work or out in the cotton fields. They are incomparably beautiful, aren't they?

Among our friends of Italian ancestry, there's Joe Feduccio, who has quit his lawyer-ing and gone into soldiering. He's now at the Station Hospital (medical detachment) at Brookley Field, Alabama. And up at Vanderbilt University, C. P. Brocato, a senior in the Naval Reserves, is making straight A's in navigation—which bodes well for his commission come June. He's good in other lines, too, for he was recently initiated into one of the Honor Societies. Anthony, in the Army Reserves at State, is not far behind his brother in collegiate records. I'm proud of you, my "chillun!"

Then there are the Fioranellis. Of course none of us can ever forget Nazarena (Ned)! What a picture he made in his little dress

44. Around 1907–1908, Bolivar County began to experience the first significant influx of Italian families into the area. See Joseph E. Rocconi, "My Memoirs," the unpublished autobiography of an Italian immigrant who settled in Bolivar County in the early twentieth century, available in the Robinson-Carpenter Library in Cleveland, Mississippi. An early examination of Italian immigrants in the Mississippi Delta is Alfred Holt Stone, "Italian Cotton-Growers in Arkansas," *American Monthly Review of Reviews*, 35(February 1907): 209–213. For a more recent discussion, see Robert L. Branfon, "The End of Immigration to the Cotton Fields," *Mississippi Valley Historical Review*, 50(December 1963): 591–599.

Mrs. Somerville made no reference to an earlier, much less happy, period among Italian immigrants in the Mississippi and Arkansas Delta when their treatment by planters led to federal investigations of peonage charges.

suit, and what a perfect orchestra leader of the Kiddie Band he was at the age of eight! Now he's down at Keesler Field in Biloxi and doubtless his sense of rhythm is helping him locate what's wrong in airplanes! Brother Armando is up at Camp Davis, North Carolina, and he doesn't like the way they dance up there! No, "Mando," they don't "get hot" like we do anywhere else! All our young people agree that there never have been dances in any place to equal ours! Maybe it's because the "Blues" were really born here in Cleveland on a night long ago when Handy's band was playing for a dance, and he was suddenly inspired to "swing it"![45] Mando wishes for a kodak that would picture all the sights, "like us sleeping in pup-tents with frost everywhere, or a plane diving down while we practice shooting at it, or tanks crawling up to our dug-outs. But it's not like Mississippi," he complains. "I wouldn't give two cents for the whole state of North Carolina!" Attaboy, Mando! We all agree that "there's no place like home," and that Mississippi is SOME state!

Three of the Ronconis are in the service, too. Aldo V. is in Hawaii and loves everything about it. "I have never seen so many people go to church," he writes. "I go to Mass each Sunday at the beautiful Cathedral." Richard is at Maxey Field, Texas, and Julio at Camp Leonard Wood, Missouri. Charles Camise is also at Camp Maxey, working in the office there, and much pleased with his job. Others of Italian descent, hereabout, now serving in the Army include Tony Dangelo, Victor Ferri, and Joseph Eusepi—while the Christopher Columbus Club of Shaw boasts that thirty-five of their members are

45. Handy is a reference to the famous Blues musician, W. C. Handy (1873–1958). In his autobiography, *Father of the Blues* (New York: Macmillan Co., 1941), pp. 76–77, Handy credits Cleveland with being the "Home of the Blues." Charley Patton (1887–1934), an early Blues master, worked at the nearby plantation of Will Dockery. Will Dockery's son, Joe Rice Dockery, was married to Mrs. Somerville's oldest daughter, Keith. Of course, many different towns claim to be "the home of the blues." There are also many versions of "the birth of the blues." Useful books include David Evans, *Big Road Blues* (Berkeley: University of California Press, 1982), Samuel Charters, *The Country Blues* (New York: Rinehart and Co., 1959), Paul Oliver, *Blues Fell This Morning* (New York: Horizon Press, 1960), Le Roi Jones, *Blues People: Negro Music in White America* (New York: William Morrow, 1963), and Robert M. W. Dixon and John Godrich, *Recording the Blues* (New York: Stein and Day, 1970). The first copyright song with the word "blues" in the title is "Dallas Blues," published in March 1912 in Oklahoma City, Oklahoma.

in uniform! I know Father Rotondo is proud of his flock! His eyes grow more sparkling and his smile more gleaming when he speaks of them and of the pride he feels that many members of "The Church of our Lady of Victories" will help bring Victory eventually to the Allied cause, "for right is on our side," he affirms. You know the good Father was born in Rome, Italy, though he left there when he was only eleven, and his happiest memories are not of Rome, but of Bruges, Belgium, when he was a student of the University there. His eyes cloud as he wonders sadly of the fate of his many friends there, now under Nazi rule.

All these friends of ours may have had Italian ancestors, but they don't agree with Dictator Mussolini or his Axis partners, it's plain to be seen. I knew Mussolini didn't have the right idea years ago when he instituted that silly idea about making the Italian people vote! But here in America we feel that voting is a privilege and not something to be forced on us, and the freedom of choice is ONE of the things you boys are fighting to preserve.

But we can't all have the glory of wearing a uniform, much as we'd all like to! Some of us must be "the man behind the man behind the gun," so I thought that today you'd like to have some news about your friends who are working to supply you with the sinews of war, and the housing facilities necessary for that eleven million force F.D.R. is so rapidly assembling.[46] They are a patriotic group, too, many of them with members of their families on the far flung battlefields of the world, and are just as anxious for this war to end in Victory as you or I. Quite recently, up in Memphis at the Firestone plant, there was a strike, deplored by all of us. How we would all like to see disputes, controversies, and cessation of work wiped out! But it wouldn't be fair, would it, for us to pick out that specific incident (or others like it) as a sample of what is being done by all labor? . . . [47] [Captain Eddie] Rickenbacker told California airplane workers, "If you could only understand what our boys are doing in those hell holes in the Pacific and on the burning sands of Africa, that

46. In total, approximately sixteen million persons served in the armed forces of the United States during World War II.

47. In 1941, labor union leaders endorsed an informal "no strike" pledge. Although strikes did occur in war-related industries, labor, for the most part, lived up to the spirit of the "no strike" pledge.

your way of life may be preserved, you would not worry about eight hour days of overtime. Don't let our boys come back and plague you for having failed in your obligation on the home front."[48] Bolivar County men won't, Capt. Eddie, they won't let you down, Boys! "Most of the workers are patriotic," says [Hans Von] Kaltenborn, my favorite commentator, "it only remains to see whether their leaders are!"[49] So here's to our friends on the Labor front.

Jessie Tatum has been in four states this past year, installing plumbing in camps. His last one was Camp Sibert (Attalla, Alabama) but he says the prettiest camp he ever saw is Camp Hood (Killeen, Texas), the tank destroyer camp, up on those "table-top" mountains. His brother, Roy, has been at Camp Tysen, Paris, Tennessee. Jake Collins, Jr., has been working in the government hospital in Memphis, and Raymond Howard at Millington. Tal Lawrence is working in a shipyard in Charleston, South Carolina; Joe Howard in the Mobile, Alabama shipyards; Les Poe at Ocean Springs, Mississippi shipyards; and Manky Thomas (a brother of Capt. Rowan Thomas) at the shipyards in Brunswick, Georgia.[50]

A lot of our men have been helping to finish up Camp McCain, one of our home state camps between Winona and Grenada. Carl Funchess was engineer inspector there and Louis Wilson has been there, too. So has "Beau" Walker (concrete inspector) and Douglas Johnson (Marjorie Ward's husband and a former Clarksdale contractor), while Marjorie, smart girl, worked in the same office with her husband. Bobbie Sterritt is now making airplane parts for the Bendix Washing Machine Company. His technical knowledge, gained up in Indiana, is standing him in good stead, for he is rising rapidly and

48. Captain Eddie Rickenbacker (1890–1973) was a World War I flying ace. During the Second World War, he served as a special representative of the U.S. Secretary of War and, while on an inspection trip in 1942, was stranded on a raft in the Pacific Ocean for twenty-three days before being rescued. Rickenbacker wrote an account of his adventures, *Seven Came Through* (New York: Doubleday Doran, 1943).

49. Hans Von Kaltenborn (1875–1965) was a well-known radio broadcaster of the period who became even more famous when he announced the wrong winner in the presidential election between Harry Truman and Thomas Dewey in 1948. His memoirs, *Fifty Fabulous Years: 1900–1950* (New York: Putnam, 1950), provide a good look at the first half of the twentieth century.

50. The Census Bureau estimated that 15,300,000 civilians moved during the war, over half of them across state lines.

I'm sure is one reason why those 5000 planes a month are rolling off the assembly lines here in the U.S.A.! Bobbie got a pretty wife up in Indiana, too, and she and his two little girls are in South Bend with him. Curtis Poe is making air planes in Akron, Ohio and so is Shirley Wingate (while her husband, Leo, formerly with the Mississippi Power and Light Company, trains for the Air Corps at Yale.) "Snag" McLellan is a draftsman for the huge Vultee airplane plant in Nashville (wife, Eleanor Lyon, who "snagged" one of our best beaux, is with him there). Cannon Dawkins (Boyle), a graduate of the William. R. Moore School of Technology, is also a draftsman—at the Fisher Aircraft Company in Memphis.

Ted Reade, until recently with a company making airplanes in New York, is now with the Whitehead Rubber Company in Trenton, New Jersey. Dick Beard has been in Arkansas (El Dorado Air Base). Mr. Richardson, too, has been in Arkansas nine months, working on the arsenal plant at Pine Bluff. His son, Sgt. Andrew, is still up at Chanute Field, Illinois, where he's been a technical instructor for two years. You knew, didn't you, that Andrew married one of those delightful Yankee girls, Margaret Collins, from Decatur, Illinois? Tough luck on our home town gals, all you boys being stationed so far from home, and us with no camp at all! Son James is now attending school at the American Television Laboratories in Chicago (after Delta State and the Radio School at State). "F.B.I. men are all about and everything is very hush-hush," he writes, but terribly interesting we gather from his letters. He and Billy Cobb (Catherine Moore's husband) are studying hard but finding time to get a thrill out of the sights of the big city. (I've heard it called "the Mississippians' idea of Heaven!") They're learning, too, the Signal Corps Song—"V for Victory, U for Unity, L for Liberty, the Signal Corps for me— Uncle Sam's eyes and ears of the war. Be it in the air or on the ground. We'll signal to you the world around. Radio voice or vision. Keep sending is our tradition!" Even Sister Fay is helping on the home front, in the busy telephone office. Others working with Father Richardson on the Pine Bluff arsenal plant included two of the McKnights, Lloyd and John Bingham, Ruth and Rufus Griffin, and Harry Morrison. . . .

There are so many doing war work that the editor wouldn't have space for any other news if I mentioned all of them! But I just wanted you boys to know that all of us are backing you up, each in our own way. Together we'll win this war! "You in your small corner, and I in mine"—only most of you are in such big corners—the "Four Corners of the World"! That little Sunday school song we used to sing likened us to "candles, shining in the night with a clear pure light"—the light of Liberty again! Our combined rays will, we know, one day illumine the darkened world. Till that happy day, we'll all try to keep our individual candles lit and burning brightly!

Goodbye for this time,
Keith Frazier Somerville

March, 12, 1943

Dear Boys:

After I mentioned in a recent letter that girls were working at Denton's, one of you boys wrote in "What girls?" So here they are, and a fine job they're doing according to Mr. Williams.... Making sandwiches, Denton-burgers, and coffee, there's Ruby Renfro, with a smile and a friendly greeting for everyone. Even Mr. Denton, when he blows in from Shelby, kids her about her rationed coffee! I know her brother, Sgt. Charles, got a big kick out of seeing her there when he was home on furlough. You know he trained at Shepherd Field, Texas and San Diego, California, and is now at the combat cruising school at Smyrna, Tennessee. Helping Ruby is that cute Juanita McArthur and lovely, blonde Virginia Ivy (who married Robert Holloway last January 7th when he was home on leave. He's a staff sergeant up at Camp Sutton, North Carolina). In the back of the plant are three Mrs.—Dorothy Genola Lewis, Elizabeth Murray and Dorris Houston Robbins. Pretty Dorris, in slacks, is making ice cream and Brownies-on-a-stick, carrying on bravely while husband (Frank Robbins) is away off on an island in the Pacific. Writes Frank, "I picked some wild pineapples, lemons, and bananas the other day! Boy, it seems funny to pick those kinds of fruits! I've been out after bark a couple of days lately. We use it for thatching. We ran across a native village where they live very primitive like, in bamboo huts with grass roofs. All their cooking is done outside in open fireplaces. You may have seen how they do it in the movies. The children run around naked, and the adults nearly so. The only language we could make out they spoke was French, so as one of the fellows with us spoke that, we were able to talk to them. All of it is very interesting, except that I wish I wasn't here. That's the only trouble." Well, Frank, Dorris and the rest of us wish you were in Cleveland, too, and we're all looking forward to the day when Johnnie (and Frank and Robert and Charles and all you boys!) come marching home again! Meanwhile the gals will keep on working, with Mrs. Christine Burdine Poe driving Denton's milk truck.

Have you heard about the Boom in Babies?[51] A magazine article says the war isn't responsible; that it started way back in 1936. Nevertheless a bunch of our servicemen are new fathers! "Jimmie" Newman (Lt. James V.) from out Pace way was home from Keesler Field not long ago for the arrival of his wee daughter, and "Pete" Gammil (Lt. Tom L.) flew home to Skene from Phoenix, Arizona with his month old twins, a four pound girl and a five pound boy! Naturally his wife (Frances Foster of Greenwood, a Delta State girl) came along to show the home folks their treasures! John Hugh McDonald, Jr., aged two months, plans on taking a trip himself soon, when father, John Hugh, arrives from Camp Lee, Virginia (Quartermaster's Corps), and takes his wife (Laura Katherine Sledge) and young son back with him. Laura Eustis Fenne, her cute Lola, and young son (also two months old) are visiting with her mother while Capt. Fred is at Ft. Leavenworth, Kansas. And a sure "proud papa" is Ralph Collins Reed, home from Camp Pendleton (the biggest Marine camp of all, at Oceanside, California) to visit with his son and wife (Lorraine Ruscoe). We all know about the bravery of the "fighting Marines," but tho' Ralph probably will be steel against the Jap[anese], I'll wager he'll be but putty in the hands of that adorable babe!

Here's hoping when these proud fathers returned to their posts, they didn't take off any of the babies' equipment, for I see from *Time* that soldiers up at Ft. Belvoir, Virginia, are using diapers to clean rifles, polish mess kits, dust shoes, and pad the inside of helmets! Maybe that accounts for the shortage! Did you hear that amusing

---

51. During the early years of the war, the birth rate climbed from 2.4 million births in 1939 to 3.1 million births in 1943. Many of these births were "good-bye babies."

radio program the other nite when a younger soldier-father was made to put a diaper on a doll and describe the proceedings in military terms! Here's how he managed—"Attention, members of the Wet-Panzier division! Attack in the rear, flanking movement: pincer movements." Which took care of that operation nicely, don't you think?

I notice there are a lot of girl babies, but that's good, for they say that unless there are enough girls born to replace grandma, the population will go "floo-ey" by 1980. I have three granddaughters to replace me, so I won't worry about that just now, with all I have to bother about (like trying to figure out point rationing and what's become of Hitler's blatant voice)! Leland Stowe, war correspondent, thinks it likely his madness has caught up with him, and the Russian defeats have landed him in a straight-jacket. But former ambassador to Russia, Joseph Davies, still thinks he may be dead.[52] However, I fear "Hitler's Children" have been so educated that even his permanent disappearance wouldn't stop them—nothing but your guns can!

But I'm rambling away from babies and there are dozens more of them, many more than I can even mention today. Mrs. Fleming now has a little granddaughter, too, baby Marion (named for father and grandfather, the two David Marions). Corp. D.M. was home from the Coast (Gulfport) for the young lady's arrival. She's sure to be lovely if she looks like either her mother or her daddy's beautiful sister, Laurette, who was one of Cleveland's most attractive girls.

Another adorable baby whose father hasn't yet seen her is Mary Alice Walton. Her father, SSGT John H., after many months in England, is now in Africa, working day and night, he reports. His last letter spoke of receiving her first picture, so I know with that with him, he'll feel that he has more than ever to fight for!...

But back to our babies again—Neely Woodrow Yarborough, now at the gunnery base, Camp Cambell, Kentucky, and his wife (Nellie Green) are proud of their son, Clois, who made his appearance at the hospital one day last December. About the same time appeared

52. Leland Stowe (1899–   ) was a war correspondent for the Chicago *Daily News* and a news analyst for the American Broadcasting Corporation during World War II. Joseph Davies (1876–1958) was the U.S. Ambassador to the Soviet Union from 1936–1938. His book, *Mission to Moscow* (New York: Simon and Schuster, 1941), and a paperback edition with a new epilogue (New York: Pocketbooks, 1943), were best sellers.

young Oscar Melton Gillespie, whose father, Oscar, is now stationed at Las Vegas, Nevada. And Ens. Robert Cain was here only the other day from New Orleans for his first wedding anniversary and the birth next day of his little daughter, Clarina Hallam. Ens. Earl Fortenberry (old Delta State boy, who formerly coached at Ruleville and is now training at Harvard) is also the father of a tiny daughter.

Besides the ensigns who belong to the biggest club in the world, "the order of fatherhood,"... there are a lot more ensigns among you boys from "this neck of the woods." Ens. Bill Carr is now somewhere in the Pacific, but not long ago on shore leave in California, while walking on the beach one night near Los Angeles, guess who he saw throwing stones at the sea gulls? Why, Wood Smith, who is a "Seabee." Whenever two Bolivar Countyites run into each other, it's cause for a celebration, isn't it?...

Ens. W.T. Woods, Jr., (Smoky) is now in the electrical department, Bureau of Ships, in Washington and he and Margaret are living in Arlington, Virginia. Nice, isn't it, for if they get too homesick for "the deep South" they can stroll down to "Marse Robert" E. Lee's home and breathe in a bit of it.

Ens. "Bill" Ballard, who trained over a year ago on the old "Prairie State" up New York way (along with Ens. Robert Hytken, now in New Orleans) has recently been transferred from the cruiser he's been on to one of the newest and biggest battleships in the Atlantic. The cause? Because even till yet he gets so very seasick on the small ships! Why that poor boy has lost sixty pounds (from one hundred eighty down to one hundred twenty pounds) just from that!

Ens. Wirt Williams, on a destroyer in the Atlantic, says everyone gets seasick sometimes on those small ships when they run into storms, but he has one consolation, his higher-up officers get worse seasick than he does! Lt. Comdr. Schwab of the Navy Medical Corps says sixty per cent of men in the Navy are subject to that malady! Tough luck, me lads! But despite their some-time discomfort and their all-time dangers, all the sailor boys seem to love the Navy.

We know they're ensigns, and we know how wonderful they look in their Navy blues, but we wonder sometime just what kind of a job they're doing nowadays. Like the little poem I read, "Twinkle, twinkle, little star, How I wonder what you are, Shining on an ensign's sleeve, Tell me which I may believe. Tell me, as you glisten bright, On a shoulder gleaming white, Does he pace a warship's decks, Or O.K. a pile of checks? Does he answer Battle Stations, Or letters headed Press Relations?..."

Lt. (J.G.) Lanier Pratt is taking an intensive course in naval communications at Harvard. Ella Fountain, his charming wife, was here awhile back but she's now gone back to Duke (Durham, North Carolina) to shut up their home and decide what to do with herself for the duration. Professor Young tells me that Leon is enjoying his stay at Yale, where he is an Aviation Cadet.[53] He will finish his course in aeronautical engineering about July 1st. Mr. C.V. Casady, who has been stationed up at Camp Eustis, Virginia, has been released for physical disabilities and is home again. He may not be quite up to Army standards as far as strength goes, but he looks well and his wife says he's quite "A-1" for her!

Our colored friends are working hard these days, too, helping Uncle Sam. There's Harrison Matthews, across the Pacific, who writes, "Don't worry about me. I am over the sea but I am all right. Pray for me."... And Pvt. Jacy Carlisle, out at Ft. Huachuca, Arizona, writing my Charity, says: "Hello, Queen Mother—I am doing like you told me. I pray every nite before I go to bed and I'm doing my best in the Army. I like it fine in this camp run by [N]egroes. Its a beautiful place to be."[54]

Hereabouts this month everybody has been scratching around trying to get taxes paid. Lord Birkenhead says the only thing not taxed in England is Hope![55] "Hope," says Lin Yutang in his *Wisdom of China and India*, "is like a road in the country: there never was a road, but when many people walk on it the road comes into existence."[56] We're all treading along the same path these days, aren't we?

Yours, with Hope for the future,
Keith Frazier Somerville

53. Professor Young is Albert Leon Young, a member of the original faculty of Delta State Teachers College.

54. Charity Bass worked as a cook and housekeeper for Mrs. Somerville.

55. Lord Birkenhead (Frederick Winston Furneaux Smith) (1907–1975) was the son of the British statesman, Frederick Edwin Smith (1872–1930), the first holder of the earldom who, as lord chancellor, helped to negotiate the Anglo-Irish Treaty of 1921.

56. Lin Yutang (1895–1976), a Chinese philosopher, compiled the widely read *Wisdom of China and India* (New York: Random House, 1942).

March 26, 1943

Dear Boys:

Angelo Patri, eminent educator, says "love is still the ruling power in the world."[57] Now that we are called upon to shoulder arms for the protection of all we hold dear, we are not denying love, we are affirming its truth. We are certain, sure and proud in the faith that love will prevail, that we are serving to guard the things we love, the love that destroys evil. Love of country, love of home, and love of a maid for a man: it's evident all around us everywhere these days. One of the clever M.S.C.W. girls, writing in their monthly magazine about "The Army As I See It" says, "Marriage is frowned upon in this Army. At least the married Army frowns upon the marriage of the unmarried Army. This is all very confusing to me, but I am not supposed to marry the unmarried Army, who is always up town or on its way there, and which prefers street corners to store aisles."[58] But despite those supposed frowns, marriage goes on all about us, and so many of our girls have been War Brides.[59] The latest one is that sweet Carolyn McLean who, last Friday, married Ens. Webb De Loach, formerly of Greenwood, now of the Naval base at Pensacola. He has rented a house near there, and Carolyn has joined that big group of hometown girls whose husbands are in the service. Every time we turn the dial on the radio we hear "this ring I wear, shows how much I care" or "to be perfectly candid, my heart has been branded. I'm saving myself for Philadelphia." That's their spirit, boys, all of them, whether they are the lucky few who are, for the present, with their husbands, or the many who, because of jobs or babies, housing facilities, or because you are overseas, are here at home for the duration. I run into this latter group everywhere, and while they are all lonesome, they're all terribly proud of their husbands! I've told you of some of them

57. Angelo Patri (1876–1965) was a well-respected educator and author. One of his best-known books was *Talks to Mothers* (New York: D. Appleton and Co., 1923).

58. M.S.C.W. is Mississippi State College for Women, now Mississippi University for Women, in Columbus, Mississippi.

59. An almost continuous discussion of the pros and cons of wartime marriages took place throughout the United States during the war years. In actuality, there were one million more marriages between 1940 and 1943 than would have been expected at prewar rates.

before, will tell you of others later, but here's news about a few for today.

Camille McLean, after maid of honoring for sister, Carolyn, in an American beauty frock and looking still war-bride-y and American beautiful herself, is due to rejoin Lt. Bill Boyd, her spouse, at Ft. Benning, Georgia soon.

Margaret Pleasants, Bobbie's wife, will soon join him in Detroit, where he, after years of flying commercial planes, is now testing airplanes for Henry Ford and Uncle Sam.

"Dot" Robinson is with Corp. "Bunny" Carpenter in Memphis now. He is in the Quartermaster's Corps. Had you heard that Dot's brother, Jimmie T., went down to Jackson last week and passed all tests for the Air Corps? He's back at Ole Miss now, impatiently awaiting his call.[60]

Peggy Wiggins is with her husband, Capt. R.G. Grant, at Camp Breckenridge, Kentucky. Peggy Jr., aged two months, has already begun life as a much feted young lady with much attention and many gifts, among the latter being a $25 war bond from her daddy's company and a gold bracelet from the colonel of his regiment.

Marie Lewis, with little four year old Eddie Jr. and his two precious little sisters, has taken a house near her parents to be here while her husband is away. He's in Africa now and Marie was happy over a recent letter (after not hearing for a month) which reported him safe, tho' admitting he'd "been thru a lot of hell" lately. I hear that at Port Lyautey, Morocco, our boys have put up a sign which reads—"Los Angeles—City Limits." But Lt. Todd's African thoughts are, I'm sure, more often of Cleveland, Mississippi!

Margaret Love Shuler and her three adorable little daughters are home, too, with her mother, while husband, Hugh Gary, is attending an Air Corps school in Denver where he's been stationed since Thanksgiving. Her wee-ist daughter, five months old, bears the lovely name of Sharon James and will doubtless, like her beautiful mother, be one of the Delta belles of the future.

Margaret Thomas and her husband, Corp. E.J. Thompson, were here last weekend from Hattiesburg and a welcome sight they were to the Dakins and Mother Willis. My mouth waters at the thought of

60. Ole Miss is the University of Mississippi in Oxford, Mississippi.

the good eats they probably had, for Willis is a super cook, and I bet even with rationing she managed a perfect cake for such beloved guests!

You knew, didn't you, that our blonde beauty, Miriam Gibert, left her Rosedale teaching last Christmas and went up to Ithaca, New York and got married to Ens. Shelby Roberts of the Coast Guard, who was training at Cornell at the time? Well, he's stationed in New York City now and Miriam has an apartment there, but she expects to get home sometime during the coming summer to share all her interesting experiences with us here at home.

I'm rather Coast Guard minded myself these days since my Keith's husband is now Lt. (J.G.) Joe Rice Dockery of that branch. He's studying anti-aircraft gunnery at Shell Beach, near New Orleans at present, before going to Mobile as a Beach Patrol Officer. Keith and her two baby daughters are out on the plantation, but she paid him a visit last week, and says New Orleans has a hysterical atmosphere of wartime gaiety, with twenty service men and women to one civilian, and Arnaud's, Galatoire's, and Antoine's jammed with them.[61] So many are on leave or passing thru and making merry that it gives a gala aspect to the city, as tho it was Carnival time and no-one working! But she found that was only on the surface: that there is hard work aplenty going on thereabouts. Passing that Coast Guard Cutter, *Campbell*, that single handed sank a German sub and fought off five others in a twelve hour battle protecting a convoy, brought to her a realization that the Coast Guard is protecting other things beside our coasts these days and is, in wartime, truly a part of the Navy.[62]

Eleanette Shands, with her two little sons, Hunter Jr. and Robert, arrived today for a visit home while her husband, Lt. Hunter Leake, is taking an advanced naval training course in New York City. Lucy Aldridge's husband, Lt. Mike Carr, is ferrying planes overseas now. I

61. Arnaud's, Galatoire's, and Antoine's are well-known restaurants in New Orleans.

62. The U.S.C.G. cutter *Campbell* formed part of the protection for Convoy ON 166 which crossed the Atlantic in February 1943. The *Campbell* shelled and then rammed the submarine, U606, after which the cutter had to be towed home. This convoy, which took a tremendous beating, was under attack during the latter part of February 1943.

saw them uptown one day on his last leave and tho't what a very handsome couple they made.

Dehlia Ray Liddel, one of our war brides, is home just now too, for a visit, but she's been with Louis (Lt. Hallam) in Savannah most of the time since their marriage. He was here for a flying visit the other day from De Riddle, Louisiana, where he's now on maneuvers.

Betsy Nelson, with her small son, Bob, has been living lately at Vincennes, Indiana near husband, Randal R. Craft, who by this time has probably gotten his wings at George Field, Illinois. He took his early training at Walnut Ridge, Arkansas (Betsy lived then at Blytheville), but his graduation has been delayed several weeks by bad flying weather. Her younger brother, Carl Reid, a yeoman, 2nd class in the Coast Guard, has just been transferred from Key West to Pigeon Key, Florida, a lone island with not a woman on it, not even a S.P.A.R.![63] He'll be home about June, tho', after a year in the service, and doubtless will find the hometown girls more attractive than ever due to that fact!

Rose Engleberg is now back in Dugas Shand's [law] office, while husband, Harold Sabin, is with the Air Corps in the personnel office at Atlantic City. Spring in the Boardwalk's swank hostelries used to be where only multi-millionaires were found, but Uncle Sam knows nothing is too good for you boys! Rose's sister, Dorothy, now in Ben Mitchell's [accounting] office, is lucky enough to have her husband, E.B. Howard, close, for he's stationed at the Greenville airbase.

Louise Sanders is working for the Mississippi Power and Light Company, while Corp. James Bryant Reid, her husband, is at San Angelo, Texas. He's served there with the ground Air Corps for the past seven months.

To me all you boys are heroes, but we get an extra thrill when we hear that some of you are so outstandingly heroic that you've been decorated for bravery. So when, in one week, the papers carried the announcement that two boys from our little community had been so honored, we fairly "busted" with pride. "Miss Sydney" (Roby) and ex-mayor Corinne (McLemore) were beaming over the fact that way

63. The SPARS was the woman's component of the U.S. Coast Guard Reserve. It was established on November 23, 1942 and demobilized in 1946. The acronym stood for the Coast Guard motto, "*Semper Paratus*—Always Ready."

out in India, Burch Williams was given the Distinguished Flying Cross.[64] That's his third decoration, for he already has the Purple Heart (injured in action over the Burma airdrome last July) and the Air Medal.[65] You know Lt. Burch has been in India about a year, serving under [General Claire] Cheneault at Chung-King and in India. Around February 1st he was transferred to another bombing squadron deeper in India.

And we were all excited over the announcement in the Memphis *Commercial Appeal* that "Sgt. James Gates of Cleveland, Mississippi had been decorated for distinguished bravery in the Solomons, receiving the Silver Star."[66] Personally, I was much perturbed over us having another special hero, and me not even knowing him! But on inquiry I find he really is a Shaw boy, tho' his parents, Mr. and Mrs. J.F. Gates, did move from Shaw here, and remained for a short time before going on to Memphis last November. He's been in the service three years and did spend his last leave here, and he is a Bolivar County hero, so we can all "point with pride."

Boys, we all rejoice together here at home and we all worry together. So the whole town has been so sad with Mr. and Mrs. D.C. Beavers over hearing from the War Department that Earl was missing in action. But now we're all rejoicing with them over news that he is a prisoner of war (either of the Germans or Italians). Maybe that isn't exactly cause for happiness, but it is to that smiling mother with three sons in the service and another who has just been called and given an A1 rating! When I went to see her she was feeding her three hundred chickens (some almost big enough to eat) and her little two year old grandson, Billy, was helping her! "Earl sent me some money when he was at Camp Miles Standish, Taunton, Massachusetts (his last letter came from there January 19th) and told me to buy anything I wanted with it. I bought a brooder and

---

64. The Distinguished Flying Cross is awarded to any person in any capacity with the armed forces who has performed a heroic or extraordinary act while participating in aerial flight.

65. The Purple Heart is awarded to persons serving in the armed forces who are wounded in action against the enemy. The Air Medal is awarded for meritorious achievement while in flight against an armed enemy.

66. The Silver Star is awarded to persons in the armed forces for conspicuous gallantry while in action.

chicken-run and it has helped me alot in these last dark days to have something to keep me busy," she told me. "Earl went from Camp Shelby to Camp Croft, South Carolina, then to Ft. Slocum, New York before going to Taunton. We didn't know he was overseas till we got word he was missing. You know I have another son in North Africa, Tech. Sgt. Dennis C., with the Signal Corps Battallion. We hear from him often and he says he knows all about what running into fox holes means and the excitement of riding a jeep along the front lines." A third son is Staff Sgt. Clarence W. who is a technical air plane mechanic, teaching three classes daily at Moody Field, Valdosta, Georgia. And now Truman S., working in a defense plant as a welder down at Mobile, has just gotten his call! And their sister, Elaine, is cashier of the Officers' Club at Camp McCain, Mississippi. Now what do you think of the patriotism of that family! And with it all, Mother Beavers isn't crying a bit! Far from it! "Of course I'm proud of my boys! They're a fine lot and they're doing their duty," she says. When I see mothers with her spirit, boys (and most of your mothers are like that), then I'm proud myself and I know what gives you boys the courage you all are showing! God bless American mothers, as they say "God bless our boys!"

Lt. John Wiley Erwin is now flight commander of the 402 Bombing Squadron at Davis Monthan Field, Arizona. You remember he was one of the first of you boys to "get into the scrap," leaving here in November 1941 to join the Canadian Air Force. Up at Fingal, Ontario, he trained Canadian flyers in their combat school. That he made good there is proved by the wonderful letters of recommendation they gave him when he "returned to the States" to join our Air Corps, as well as by the very lovely wife he married up there (Lenor Petree of London, Ontario, Canada). She's with him at Tucson, where he's now giving our flyers the same strenuous training in nite flying and bomb dropping (over desert and mountains) that he gave to our Canadian friends. Ever so often he takes a group of them down to Alamagordo, New Mexico to "finish them up"—the sand there, underfoot, in their eyes and ears, is, I imagine, a good preparation for what they may run into in Africa. We were proud of you, John Wiley, when you first got in to help the brave English, fighting then against such odds, and we're proud now that one of our own boys is so well equipped to speed up our own war effort. . . .

Sgt. Jack Houston is in India with the Air Corps. He's a gunner, too, and I'm betting he's good, for he took training practically all over the U.S. map: Florida, Tennessee, New Mexico, and Idaho! When he was home just before Christmas his description of interesting places he'd seen sounded just like the American travelogues we used to hear in the Chapel of Cleveland High! And now he's seeing "fur places." "After seeing lots of South America, Africa and Arabia," writes Jack, "we've arrived in India. The trip as a whole was very interesting. It's hot during the day but cold at night. In fact, my winter flying clothes come in handy as cover. It's so hot in the daytime they have to feed hens chipped ice to keep them from laying hard boiled eggs!" For thirty-two cents a week, he gets a flunky to make bunks, sweep, shine shoes, and do odds and ends! But that doesn't make a very big dent in his salary, so he has asked his mother to be custodian of most of it, as, with picture shows and amusements provided, he has little to spend it on, so he's asked her to buy him a bond every month! And, though he probably wouldn't want me to mention it, when his young brother, Ralph, now a junior in hi school wrote him about the class rings they were hoping to get, he wrote back, "if you hold your mouth right talking to Mom she might use some of my money to buy your ring for you! Write me how you make out!" What a nice, nice brother to have, but I always knew you were like that, Jack!

Another of the Houston boys, Sgt. Frederick, is now at Camp Gruber, Oklahoma. He used to work in the bakery here, and in one in Jackson, so it's no wonder he's such a good cook that he's constantly being congratulated on the grand meals he serves! Lucky girl is "Choo" (his wife, now working in Memphis). Most of us have to worry along with husbands who can't even fry an egg, much less bake a cake.

Lt. Claude Milstead has traveled overseas now with an armored division, after getting his commission at Ft. Benning, Georgia and tank training at Ft. Knox, Kentucky and Camp Sutton, North Carolina. His brother, Corp. James, was home for ten days recently and much pleased because, after finishing his course in "paratrooping" (excuse me if I coin a word!) at Camp Byrd, Texas and Ft. Benning, he has now at Benning been transferred to the academic regiment to train men in rifle shooting. You always did like to hunt, didn't you, James? So gunning for the enemy will be right up your alley! I hope you boys don't hold it against me that I sometime used to yell lustily at you and warn you not to shoot my mocking birds when you were practicing with your BB guns down in the tangle of honeysuckles on the bayou bank in my front yard! That was my mistake! For what is a bird or two against training a perfect shot? But how was I to know we'd need good "shooters" soon?

I'm continually impressed with how many sets of brothers there are in this war! Up at the Post Office Cafe the other night, I heard of another pair, George and Mike Ballas. Sgt. George has been stationed at Ft. Bragg, North Carolina, and "Mike" in South Carolina.[67] Though Thermopylae fell finally before the Nazi onrush, the world stood with hats off for months at the bravery of the Greek nation, so I know our Americanized Greek brothers will do well their part wherever they are sent.[68] So will "Mike" (Michael L.) Carouso. He's a naturalized Greek who volunteered in 1941 to serve the land of his adoption and now is serving on a subchaser (last heard from at Dutch Harbor) and probably helping shoot torpedoes at the Jap[anese] in lieu of pool balls! Do you know those gallant Greeks are still fighting on in Athens?[69] A recent item carried the news of one "Maj. Jean Tsigantes, patriot," who, when Gestapo agents closed in on his house and ordered him to surrender, killed three and wounded many others with his revolver before they finally got him! The Greeks are said to have had the greatest imagination in the world and to have made the greatest use of it. Today's most fertile field for the imagination is in the movies, so we're not surprised that one of the big-wigs in Hollywood is Spyros Skouras, born in Greece.[70] When he

67. The Post Office Cafe was in Cleveland.

68. Thermophylae, which was the scene of a famous battle in 480 B.C. where the Spartans under Leonidas withstood the Persians to the last man, was the site of another battle during World War II. British rear guard units held off the advancing Germans for several days in April 1941, allowing British and Greek troops to escape.

69. Following the fall of Greece in late April 1941, resistance to German forces continued. However, the underground political life of Greece was complicated. One group of resistance fighters supported the return of the monarchy, a second, more liberal group, supported a republican state, and a third group, the communists, wanted a government which they could control. All three groups mustered secret armies to fight the Germans and each other.

70. Spyros Skouros (1893–1971) was president of Twentieth Century-Fox Film Corporation.

first arrived in America, he, too, like the Ballas boys, worked in a Greek restaurant (in St. Louis). The proprietor, he said, hired him on condition that within a week he'd memorize all the words of the "Star Spangled Banner." He did, and has never forgotten them. How few of us can say as much. Now Skouras, at the top of the ladder, entertained the King of Greece and the heads of the Greek relief societies recently. We still have success stories like that in this, our land of freedom and opportunity, and it peps us up no end to hear of them! Among you boys who have left Bolivar County and are seeing the world are probably some, who when the war is over, will go elsewhere to live: boys who will conquer not only the Jap[anese] and the Germans, but someday the world of finance, or letters, or the cinema, or become naval or military heads! Among my girlhood friends today, for example, there are eleven generals and two admirals, but when I first knew them in school and colleges, they were just nice boys like you, never dreaming that one day they'd be appearing on the covers of *Life* or *Time*. Fibber McGee, on the radio last week, ordered a horoscope to tell him about what the future held for him. If I weren't as skeptical as Molly was about such things, I'd wish for one that could tell me which of you boys, thirty years from now, would be met at the train with a brass band![71]

But why speculate on that, when we know we'll bring out all our brass bands for the Delta "Yanks" of World War II when you come home, and we know it won't be any thirty years before we do it either! We're all praying that that day may come soon!

Goodbye and good luck,
Keith Frazier Somerville

April 9, 1943

Dear Boys:

Remember all the delightfully silly things you used to do and say in hi school days? How well I remember my silly, salad days! Well, I think your young brothers and sisters have us all beat! They go about

---

71. Fibber McGee and Molly was the name of a popular radio program which ran from 1935 until 1952.

asking each other moron questions and telling moron jokes.[72] This is the way they go—"Had you heard about the little moron who punched his eyes out so he could have a blind date? Did you hear about the moron who stayed up all night studying for a blood test? And about the little moron who cut off his arms to wear a sleeveless sweater? And the little moron who went to the lumber company to see his draft board? Or the one who went into the florist to buy a defense plant? And those who killed their parents so they could attend the orphan's picnic? And the one who went into the closet to change his mind? Or the one who took his nose apart to see it run? And the little moron who drank ten coca-colas and burped 7-up"?

The stories go like this. A little moron got on a street car and didn't pay. "Why?" asked the conductor. "I'm crime and crime don't pay," replied the moron. A little moron walked thru the red light. "Why did you do that?" asked the cop. "I'm time and time marches on!" was the answer. A moron called another at 3 a.m.: first moron, "I hope I didn't wake you up." Second moron, "That's O.K., I had to get up anyway to answer the phone." Another: first moron, "Where's my hat?" Second moron, "On your head." First moron, "Funny, I didn't feel it." Second moron, "Course not. It's not a felt hat."

And some one told me about the daughter of one of our dignified and erudite Delta State professors who came into her father's study one nite, sticking out her tongue and making awful faces. "What am I, father?" she asked. "I don't know," he replied, "but you look like a moron," which perfect answer reduced her to paroxysms of laughter!

Aren't they priceless and isn't it marvelous to feel that way in times like these that try men's souls! I don't imagine that in Nazi Germany any young people feel like joking, but thank heaven, ours still do! That up-bubbling of youth that knows only safety and laughter may not be one of the Four Freedoms, but it's something we'd all fight to preserve, wouldn't we, Boys?[73]

72. "Little Moron" jokes and stories flourished throughout the United States during 1942 and 1943.

73. The Four Freedoms were described by President Franklin D. Roosevelt (1882–1945) in his annual message to the U.S. Congress on January 6, 1941. They included freedom of speech and expression, freedom of religion, freedom from want, and freedom from fear. The Four Freedoms came to symbolize the reasons for which the Allies were fighting the Second World War. Norman Rockwell painted four pictures depicting the ideals of the Four Freedoms.

One day last week (a lovely spring day with jonquils and redbud blooming on every side), I drove up to Merigold to get news of our boys there. In the drug store hangs a big service chart with one hundred thirty-eight names on it, and Merigold is proud indeed of all her sons! Four of them have recently gotten their wings: Lt. James Strawbridge (Randolph Field); Lt. Henry Jones (Columbus); Lt. James Oran Thomas (Georgia); and Lt. Carl Bailey (Brooks Field, Texas). There are three of those Bailey boys in the service now. Sgt. Jordon W. is with the Marines in the Pacific and writes that he and his buddies "are firing no poor volleys at the Jap[anese]." (That goes without saying! They're Marines, aren't they?) And his brother, Doyle, is at Camp Young, California.

Another set of three brothers are the Robertson boys. I do wish you could see their pictures in their Navy uniforms, all laughing and all so young and attractive! For that matter, their mother is laughing and attractive, too, and as she greeted me in brown slacks and a yellow blouse, she looked much too young to be a three star mother, with another son, Glenn, almost old enough to sing "Anchors Away" too! Paul Jr., has been in the Navy two years and is now at Pearl Harbor; Owen, a yeoman, 2nd Class, is now at Philadelphia; and John Rogers is . . . [in training] at Norman, Oklahoma. Those boys come naturally by their love of the sea, for their maternal grandfather, John Johnson, was born and spent his boyhood in a little fishing village near Stockholm, Sweden, and sailed before the mast for many years prior to becoming naturalized and settling in Merigold.

Enlisting at the same time with John Rogers were three other Merigold boys: Hubert Mullins, Vernon Springer, and Van Hallman. They not only enlisted together, but took "boot training" together and now are all four attending the Aviation Ordinance School at Norman, Oklahoma. Mrs. Hallman and Mrs. Mullins are just back from a trip to see the boys and report that it was quite worth the inconvenience of wartime travel just to see that the boys really are all happy and well and "not just writing that home." Mrs. Hallman is making a wonderful scrapbook about Merigold boys who have gone to war. The most prized pages contains a hand tinted, real lace-edged Valentine which reads—"You who are always so understanding will know the love that's in my heart today," and son, Van, had added, "And I mean every word of it!" But while primarily it is

Van's book, it has pages devoted to the rest of Merigold's sons. . . .

Dr. Wynne's boys have certainly been around! Lt. Jack, who graduated from the Texas Dental College at Houston, has been in the Navy two years now, during which time he served at Corpus Christi, Boston Navy Yard, Iceland (thirteen months), and is now at the Naval Hospital, Bainbridge, Maryland. His brother, Capt. Monroe, got his wings at Kelly Field and has been in the Army two years. He used to fly for American Airlines and was one of their "million-milers," so we know he's good: so good, in fact, that he's now with the Army Transport Command and flies huge cargos here and there and everywhere: to Greenland, Iceland, and "over the waters." Just now he's engaged in the hazardous task of trying to rescue one of his buddies and his huge cargo plane which fell on a frozen lake in the Canadian wilds. With more than a score of searching planes, Capt. Wynne scoured the countryside and finally located his friend, and because of his flying ability, the general gave him the rescue job. A huge snowstorm has intervened since the last feeble radio call for help was heard, so it will be some job. He wrote that the plan was to equip the plane with skis. We're all hoping that his mission is successful and that the rescue work won't be too late.

Everyone in the country has been so distressed with Mr. and Mrs. Frank Wynne over the news that their son, Frank, an aerial gunner, is missing in action in the Pacific. And all of us, like his brave mother, are hoping that she'll hear from him one of these days; that perhaps he may be on one of the small islands near where he was last heard from (reputedly peopled by friendly natives), or a prisoner of the Jap[anese].[74] Out at Keith's the other night, I heard, over shortwave, a broadcast from Berlin, featuring our boys who had been taken prisoners in Africa.[75] I believe it would have broken my heart

74. Frank Wynne of Merigold was a Japanese prisoner of war from January 1943 until August 1945. For additional information see, "Frank Wynne Reported Safe—Missing a Year," *Bolivar Commercial*, February 18, 1944.

75. Keith is Mrs. Somerville's daughter, Keith Somerville Dockery. Many people listened to shortwave broadcasts during the war as a way of obtaining additional information about wartime events. The general role of radio in wartime is discussed in Sherman H. Dryer, *Radio in Wartime* (New York: Greenberg, 1942). The story of wartime radio from the point of view of the participants is told by Edward M. Kirby and Jack C. Harris in *Star-Spangled Radio* (Chicago: Ziff-Davis, 1948).

had I heard any of your voices (I wept anyway!). They all said, "If anyone listening in lives near, tell Mom I'm a prisoner, but I'm all right." There were only two southern boys, but I had my paper and pencil ready. Because a friend of mine, Mrs. Oscar Spears (her husband is an Admiral now, but he used to be one of my hometown boys with whom I had dates and went dancing long ago), wrote to me that the night her son spoke from Tokyo, a prisoner of the Jap[anese], many people notified her, tho' she didn't hear the broadcast herself. She, by the way, is another of the many brave mothers I know, for she has another son who is still missing in the Pacific, and now her third and youngest son is in the Navy, too....

To us in this section with so many Jewish friends, the news recently given out by the American Jewish Congress, that two million of their race had been massacred last year in Poland alone where they were rounded up, stripped of their clothes for Nazi use, and killed by machine guns, lethal gas, electricity, or hunger, was a shocking tragic story.[76] In his last speech to Nazi members, Hitler reiterated his prophecy, "This struggle will end with the extinction of Jewry." (But you boys won't let it end that way, will you? Even tho' the Nazis are doing their worst!) Why in one town (Otwak, Poland), they massacred every Jewish man, woman, and child. Starting at midnight, the slaughter lasted eight hours. We, with our intense feeling about the Four Freedoms, of which freedom of worship is such an important one, simply can't take it in. "Why," we ask ourselves in our American tolerance, "should anyone care whether one is Jew, Gentile, or Catholic?" It passeth our understanding truly. I heard a radio program recently that made me want to weep and cheer at the same time. It was the young bombardier, on Ginny Simms' program, who asked permission to put in a long distance call to a man he didn't know: to the father of Meyer Levi in Brooklyn.[77] (Meyer, you probably haven't forgotten, was Colin Kelly's bombardier.)[78] "I just want

76. The American Jewish Congress was first assembled in Philadelphia in 1918. During the 1930s, it emerged as a leading force in the anti-Nazi movement and in efforts to aid the victims of Hitlerism.

77. Ginny Simms (1916–   ) was a singer with the Kay Kyser orchestra, and this is, most likely, a reference to the long-running radio show, Kay Kyser's Kollege of Musical Knowledge, which used a musical quiz format.

78. Colin Kelly (1915–1941) was an Army Air Corps pilot and one of the first heroes of the war. His bombardier was Meyer Levi, a Jew from Brooklyn.

to tell him that I'm on my way to Tokyo and I'll drop some bombs for Meyer, and that I am proud to fight for my country where a Jew and an Irish Catholic, the best of buddies, will live in everlasting fame for their heroism." That's our American answer to the Nazi intolerance!...

But how far I've wandered from the lovely little town of Merigold! And I know you're dying to hear what's become of Claire and Dr. McHardy. Well, they're living up near Boston at Westover Field, Chicopee, Massachusetts, and "young doc" is thriving on Army life and getting to be quite a man! And Claire's brother, Bill Michie, recently "rendered distinguished service as a ground crewman with a heavy bomber in India." Additionally, he's buying bonds, too. Keeping 'em flying from both ends!

Then there are the Lee boys. Charles Stanley is at a Naval training school for electricians at the University of Minnesota, and his brother, Jimmie, is a Navy radio man at Lake Charles, Louisiana. Their father, too, was in the service for awhile, but he was let out for physical disabilities. And had you heard that Lt. Bentley Leverett, a retired Naval officer, is back again and that he and his wife are now at Seattle? Also, lest the man cop all the glory, it will soon be Lt. Janice T. Williams of the W.A.C.S! Curtis Seawright, his wife, and daughter, Nancy Lee, are at Shepherd's Field, Texas, and J.T. and Mary Anna (Pemble) Davis are now "camping" near Salt Lake City. Sgt. Tommy Craddock (Army Air Corps) is doing patrol duty in the Atlantic and keeping a weather eye out for those Axis subs. Maybe he helped O. P. Gant (Navy) who was with the first group who landed troops in Africa! In the Merigold post office, my old friend "Miss Lucy" (Mrs. Henry Park) told me she'd just had a cable from son, Kirk, an Army radio man in the South Pacific, that all was well with him, and that her young grandson, Henry Park Hiter (an honor student both at Merigold Hi and at Ole Miss), has now been in the Army Air Corps for five weeks.

Charles Coffman, one of the brave Marines who held Guadalcanal so long, is now recuperating in Australia from a wound the Jap[anese] inflicted.[79] Sgt. John McGovern, another Marine, is now at Quantico,

79. Guadalcanal, north of Australia, is the largest of the Solomon Islands. Allied forces landed there on August 7, 1942 to repel Japanese advances. Bloody battles both on land and sea followed as both sides attempted to reinforce their men. The battles in and around Guadalcanal lasted until February 9, 1943. Casualties were very heavy. An important book is Richard Tregaskis, *Guadalcanal Diary* (New York: Random House, 1943).

Virginia. James Jacks and Roy Prewitt are out in the Pacific, too, and so, it is believed, is Donald Kealhofer. (A recent wire from him from California reported his imminent departure for unknown parts.) His brother, John, is an airplane mechanic with the Lockhead Vegas Airplant, Burbank, California. And Dan Smith was home last week from Tampa, Florida (Air Corps) on a sad mission for his father's funeral. Elmer Adams is just out of the Coast Guard hospital, while his brother, Quenton, is in Philadelphia. Quenton writes that he's "sure the Army will either make or kill him!"

Well, you boys will have to do our fighting for us, but I want you to know that behind each of you are the people of your town and county. New York's "little flower" is not more famous in his state than is our "Merigold" within the confines of Bolivar County![80] For from Merigold comes T.W. Waldrop, the efficient Chairman of Bolivar County War Savings Committee, who has practically given up his own business to transact Uncle Sam's. He anticipates no trouble raising the next quotas of over $300,000, and though he feels that as yet not many sacrificial dollars have gone into War Bonds, he has faith that if it becomes necessary to fill our quotas, then the home folks will cheerfully sacrifice. Mr. Waldrop has received outstanding support from citizens of Merigold, whose large buying gave the drive its original impetus, and the good work goes on, for during March, Merigold was one of the three highest towns in the county for bond buying.

From Merigold, too, comes Mrs. Albert Smith, County Chairman of Women at War. With her happy smile and enthusiasm, it is no wonder that her bond drive is being crowned with the success that always accompanies her efforts along any line. Margaret is one of those wonderful people who is always ready to help anyone, be it Uncle Sam or a friend! It is to her, by the way, that I am indebted for much of the news contained in this letter, and I know you'll all join me in thanks to her for taking time out from her "driving" to help me gather news for you about your friends.[81]

---

80. "Little Flower" was a nickname for Fiorello H. La Guardia (1882–1947), the mayor of New York City from 1934–1945.

81. Bolivar Countians, like citizens throughout the United States, readily volunteered their time and services to the war effort by joining war bond drives, salvage committees, war savings committees, Red Cross knitting classes, and surgical dressing groups.

From Merigold, too, comes our High Sheriff, Ed Rayner, and his lovely wife, both ever ready with a helping hand for every good cause. In their lovely new home, our gracious sheriff-ess told me of her Victory live-at-home program. Meat, butter, and canned goods rationing mean nothing in her life, for she has chickens, cows, and a grand garden as an added attraction to her new home. Has anyone written you about that beautiful house? Well, you boys have something to look forward to, for I'm sure that big living room, library, and game room (grand for dancing!) will welcome many a returning hero! Yes, of course—Carolyn and Bettye Sue, those attractive daughters, will be part of the welcoming committee!

If all the little flower-towns (Magnolia, Rosedale, and the rest) in our beautiful flowering State are sprouting Patriotism like Merigold, we have no reason to doubt that one day the whole world will bloom again into a beautiful garden of Peace! Our Merigolds will encourage and help the tulips of Holland and the fleur-de-lis of France to blossom again. When "the winter of our discontent" is over, then the world will everywhere be as lovely and peaceful as I found it this week in charming Merigold![82]

Till that flowering time, good luck and "happy landings" to each of you.

Sincerely,
Keith Frazier Somerville

April 23, 1943

Dear Boys:

"Regardless of race, creed, or color," said our founding fathers, and it is regardless of race, creed, or color that you boys are fighting this war: a war we didn't want, but which was thrust upon us by the treachery of Japan at the very moment we were treating with them in the hope of maintaining peace. I have told you in recent letters of the contributions being made by the Catholics, Jews, Greeks, and Chinese among us, and today I want to tell you what our [N]egroes

82. "The winter of our discontent" is from the opening lines of *King Richard the Third,* "Now is the winter of our discontent/Made glorious summer by this sun of York."

are doing.[83] They, you know, constitute a large proportion of our population. The approximate figures in our county are, I believe, around 18,000 white people to 49,000 [N]egroes. We are all well aware that much of the success of our economic life is dependent on them. "Git up mule, go on plowing," says the now popular song, and the mule and the tractor, both steered by our colored men are on the move these lovely spring days to assure us of an adequate cotton crop to provide us with the weapons of war. Cotton, you know, is second only to steel, as a vital weapon. One bale of short-staple cotton . . . will provide smokeless powder for 20,440 rounds of machine gun ammunition, 100,000 rounds of rifle ammunition, or eighty-five rounds of heavy tank ammunition. In addition to that, cotton linters also make plastics for war plane windows, cockpit enclosures, cargo and flame chutes, rayon, X-ray and photographic films, fabric coatings, and replacements for metal parts. Moreover, a bale of cotton produces 900 pounds of seed, yielding 140 pounds of vegetable oil for food, 200 pounds of meal for livestock, and 240 pounds of hulls for roughage and chemical use. Our 1942 cotton crop supplied enough oil to furnish the total fat requirements for an army of 7,500,000 and a navy of 1,500,000, plus for 42,000,000 civilians. Yes, our cotton is truly America's Number One War Crop![84]

But it is not alone in our cotton fields that our [N]egroes are helping their Uncle Sam. Why up at Mound Bayou during March they bought more War Bonds than either Cleveland or Rosedale![85] Some of them, it is true, have in past months cashed in on those bonds soon after purchase, but that, I have been told, is because some of them have not properly understood the value of lending their earnings for the "duration" of the war (to help shorten the conflict), or, because of the overemphasis placed on the fact that

83. In an era in which racism was widespread and segregation was commonplace, it is remarkable that Mrs. Somerville provided so much information about the contributions of African-American citizens of Bolivar County to the war effort.

84. For additional information on the role of cotton during World War II, see James H. Street, *The New Revolution in the Cotton Economy* (Chapel Hill: University of North Carolina Press, 1957), chapter 4, "World War II Shakes up the Enterprise."

85. Mound Bayou is an all-black town located nine miles north of Cleveland, founded by ex-slaves in 1887.

bonds can be cashed in after sixty days, have felt it obligatory to do so.

The draft board refuses to tell how many of our colored boys have gone into the armed forces, but we all known there are thousands of them from Bolivar County, and many additional hundreds have volunteered.[86] I've told you of some of the local ones, but I haven't scratched the surface. There's Harry (Fox) Block, a sergeant up at Langley Field, who is trying to get into an officer's training camp, and we who know him are sure he'd make a good officer, for like his father before him, he has "getting along sense" and the capacity to deal alike with all kinds of people. And there's Mose Jefferson (Carrie's boy) who is now in Africa, and Sam Lee, out in the Pacific (Quartermaster's Corps). And there's LeRoy Bufkin in the Navy (Atlantic) and Willie Strong at Ft. Huachuca, Arizona—that camp I've told you of before where so many of our [N]egro soldiers are happily located. Amzie Moore, from the post office, was home last week from there. Also on leave was Clarence Wilson, who used to be at the Memphis *Press-Scimitar* before he took up insurance. He's

---

86. Mrs. Somerville is focusing on a significant World War II issue. The Selective Service law specifically forbade draft boards from using racial descriptions or racial evidence as they filled their draft quotas. Because the military was racially segregated, however, persons were selected for service only as space became available for training. As there were only a limited number of training spaces for blacks, this meant that blacks were usually drafted at a different schedule than were whites. General Lewis B. Hershey (1893–1977), the Director of the Selective Service System, refused to allow local draft boards to determine the racial makeup of individuals, and draft boards were instructed to accept an individual's view as to which race he considered himself. Of the 32.4 million persons who registered for the draft during World War II, 3.4 million were classified as black. In total, 1,074,083 blacks were inducted and an additional 80,637 enlisted. Blacks, who comprised 10.6 percent of the population according to the 1940 census, made up about 10.7 percent of all inductions. Largely because of the efforts of Lewis Hershey, blacks did not fight in World War II in undue proportion to the white population. For good material on this issue see, George Q. Flynn, *Lewis B. Hershey: Mr. Selective Service* (Chapel Hill: University of North Carolina Press, 1985). For a brief discussion of the treatment of blacks by draft boards in the Mississippi Delta, see Pete Daniel, "Going among Strangers: Southern Reactions to World War II," *Journal of American History*, 77(December 1990): 891 and James C. Cobb, "'Somebody Done Nailed Us on the Cross': Federal Farm and Welfare Policy and the Civil Rights Movement in the Mississippi Delta," *Journal of American History*, 77(December 1990): 916.

now at Camp Rucker, Alabama, and was proudly wearing a sharp shooter's medal. John Davis, Jr. was home, too, from Sacramento, California (Aviation Corps) and L.K. Braxton from Camp Shelby. Seab Sterling is at Lowry Field, Denver and Chatman Grimes at Ft. Jackson, South Carolina.

Last Sunday I went up to Mound Bayou, the town which has interested me so much for the past quarter of a century. Mound Bayou, as you all know, is entirely a [N]egro town. Its mayor is Ben A. Green, who received his early education in the public school of Mound Bayou... receiving his B.A. at Fisk University, Nashville (1909) and his law degree from the Harvard Law School in 1914. Following this, he volunteered in World War I and served in France in the Judge Advocate Department. In 1919, he was elected mayor of Mound Bayou, founded by his father, Ben Green, and his cousin, Isaiah T. Montgomery, who with eighteen friends bought land from the... railroad in 1887 and started the town. Both Green and Montgomery were ex-slaves of the Davis family and spent their boyhood days at "The Briars," Davis Bend, near Natchez. Isaiah was the dreamer and Ben Green the business man. Together they succeeded in their venture, which in 1937, celebrated its fiftieth anniversary....

I learned from the fathers and mothers I met in Mayor Green's office that a lot of people at Mound Bayou, as elsewhere in our county, have more than one son in the service. There are three Glass boys: Otis (home this past week from Texas); Winston (in Arkansas); and Thurston (in Indiana).

Gilbert Thompson is somewhere across the Pacific, and his brother, Ward, is at Camp Davis, South Carolina. Ward was called while attending Southern College in Louisiana, and is now taking radio mechanical training.[87] Greenley Pressly was also attending Southern when he got his call and is also at Camp Davis. James Thomas Hayes, Jr. was at Alcorn College (Army Reserve) when the Army called and sent him to the officers training camp at Ft. Benning, Georgia.[88] He writes his father that it is little different there from

87. Southern College is Southern University and Agricultural and Mechanical College at Baton Rouge, Louisiana, founded in 1880.
88. Alcorn College, now Alcorn State University, is in Lorman, Mississippi.

college, that he likes it a lot, and that there's "a grand bunch" there. Another pair of brothers are SSGT Nicholas L. Tharp, at Patago Park, Phoenix, Arizona and John, with a labor battalion at Los Angeles, California. Two more brothers are the Baines—Corp. Calvin in Africa and Sgt. Fred at Camp Robinson, Arkansas. And Paul Gant is at Camp Davis, North Carolina and his brother, Jonas Claude, out west, and the younger brother, Card, has just passed his physical and is awaiting his call.

Sgt. Rayford Dillon is in Australia with the Army engineers and his brother, Cornelius, is in the hospital at Jefferson Barracks, Missouri, suffering with his eyes. His mother has been worried about him, but not worried to do her part at home, for she tells me she has a grand Victory Garden.[89] Last year she put up several hundred jars of fruit and vegetables (actually has some left over! Imagine that?) and expects to do better this year! In her spring-like green frock and with her happy smile, she told me of her summer plans. So did Pearl Kelley who also put up many jars last year. It seems to me she said 600, but that seems an awful lot! Maybe I'm wrong! Henry Ryals has been five years in the Navy and is now serving in the Pacific. His brother, Percy Leroy, is at Charleston, South Carolina, while their father, with the help of his five remaining children, is busily starting his crop. Reuben Fiddle is at Ft. Huachuca, Arizona, where Richard Fourshea was also stationed prior to his departure for an unknown destination. Morton Clegg left two weeks ago for Camp Shelby. Sgt. Oscar Pickens (Aviation Squadron) is at Portland, Oregon. Henry Sanford, Jr., is at Ft. Benning, Georgia with the Medical Detachment. Also there are Willie D. Anderson, Booker T. Griggs, and Alex Harrell. Mound Bayou looked very soldiery with so many of her sons home on leave last Sunday. Besides Otis Glass, there was Joe Baker from North Carolina, Isaiah Dunlap from Missouri, Douglas Causey and Tommy Lee Conner from the Post Detachment at Ft. Benning, Georgia.

Of course, I couldn't go to Mound Bayou without going by to see

89. As part of the campaign to raise more food and fiber for the war effort, citizens were urged to plant Victory Gardens. Available arable space, ranging from window boxes in cities to newly broken farm lands, was utilized. The amount of food stuffs raised was prodigious. Canning and preserving efforts were also promoted in order to extend the useful period for the food. Extra sugar coupons could be obtained for those who were able to can and preserve food.

my old friend, Mary Bailey, who has made me so many beautiful quilts and sent me so much grand sausage through the years. I found her far from well and living in town since the death of her husband, Will. (I've always said he was one of the most perfect gentlemen I ever knew.) As Mary said, "There's nobody but them girls to make the crop now, out on the Lake place." But they (two girls) did it so successfully last year that they made six bales on seven acres, renting the rest of their land.

In his interesting book, *One American*, Frazier Hunt (noted foreign correspondent whose interesting broadcasts I'm sure you have heard) told of meeting far across the world in Siberia a woman from Brooklyn, married to a Russian, who said to him, "What a wonderful place America can be if she will only learn to dream again."[90] Well, in Mound Bayou, Mississippi, I found America dreaming again. Dreaming of the day her sons will come marching home; dreaming of better housing and hospitalization; dreaming of the day when education will really "educate" our farm boys to be made better farmers, proud and happy in their life work, in the dignity of plowing their acres and working with their hands, as the Lord intended eighty percent of us to do; dreaming too, of absolute fairness. And here in Bolivar County, there are many Southern white men and women, descendants of men and women who for eighty years have had their problems close to their hearts, who are dreaming with them that when our boys of all races, creeds, and color come home again to peaceful years, we may all work together to make our dreams come true. . . .

Yours for a better world.

Sincerely,
Keith Frazier Somerville

May 7, 1943

Dear Boys:

. . . .I had the luck one day last week to "hop a ride" to Duncan with Mrs. Ed Kossman, who was going up to teach a Red Cross Knitting

---

90. Frazier Hunt (1885–1967), *One American* (New York: Simon and Schuster, 1938). Less well known than some correspondents, Hunt was a prolific author and the first biographer of Douglas MacArthur.

class, so today I can report on some of your Duncan friends. There were about fifteen ladies who met at the lovely home of Mrs. Tom Boschert, and as their needles clicked I heard a lot of news. Mrs. Robert Smith not only has the loveliest iris I ever saw, but a son, Charles Weatherby, in Naval Reserves at State, who expects to be in uniform by June. Mrs. J.D. Haralson, as she knitted, told me of her son, Lt. R.T., a navigator in the Air Corps, now stationed at Greenville, South Carolina. He married a lovely girl, Vera Chapman, up there last August, so it goes without saying that he's happy in South Carolina. Dan Cupid has been busy shooting at those attractive Duncan boys lately! He hit Lt. Dick Mentrop of the Air Corps, too, away up in the Aleutian Islands, and he came home a couple of months ago and married Christine Taylor of Hushpuckena, who was teaching music here. She went as far as Seattle with him, when he returned to Alaska, and is now teaching in Duncan. Lt. Mentrop expects to be transferred to Florida in June. And by the way, Dame Rumor tells me that another of our Cleveland teachers is going to marry one of my pet "chillun" who is in the Navy one of these days!

And next week, Carl Reid Nelson of the Coast Guard, our mayor's son, is going to marry that sweet Martha Rushing who, since Delta State days, has been working for Elmer Nowell.[91] The Rushings live out at Dockery[92] and Keith is going to have the rehearsal party, so we're all excited over the wedding which is to be at the Methodist Church in Cleveland, with the maid of honor, Dorothy Rushing, and the bridesmaids, Eleanor Nelson and Alice Neff, all done up in pastel tints. I'm dead with envy, for they plan to live in a trailer, something I've always wanted to do![93]

Another of our Duncan friends hit by Cupid's dart is John Harris, who married on Washington's Birthday lovely Doris Reynolds, one of the South's beauties from Florida. Her mother lives in Washington now, but Doris has been modelling in New York and you know what

91. Elmer Nowell was a builder from Cleveland and owner of the Nowell Lumber Company.

92. Dockery is a small community just outside of Cleveland.

93. Trailer and mobile home living was a wartime expedient which helped to solve housing shortage difficulties near towns with military installations or war plants. At this time, virtually all such vehicles were truly mobile.

that means! Looks, glamour, and style! Well, John is a grand person and deserves the best, so all kinds of luck and happiness to them both down at Savannah, Georgia, where John is in the Air Corps. His brother, Dave, in the Naval Air Corps, is now at Martin, Tennessee.

As she cast on stitches, Mrs. John Miles talked of her son, E.W. Dumler, a machinists mate in the Navy, who volunteered the day war was declared. Since then he's been in Omaha, Miami, San Diego, on a "mosquito boat" in Panama, and is now on a subchaser in the Pacific.[94] I also learned that Z.A. Brooks is in India; that SSGT Vernon Parker is in Nashville; that Sgt. Otis Dunn, a Marine, is at San Diego, California; that Lamar Walton, Jr., is in the Navy, now at Millington, Tennessee; that Harvey Carpenter of the Air Corps is now at Ypsilanti, Michigan; and that George Bray and John Hastings are also "in" . . . present addresses unknown.

Then I went by to see Mrs. Wiley and learned that her son, Capt. Frank Bragg Wiley, Jr., had phoned her Saturday nite that he was out of the hospital at Camp Dix, where he had been confined with a severe cold. "You can't keep a good man down, mother," he told her. Frank, you know, had been at Camp Stewart, Georgia, and had only recently moved east. His wife, the former Edwina Smith and their cute babes (three years, one and one half years, and six months old) are in Clarksdale for the duration.

Had you heard that Bob and Frank, those identical Comfort twins, have been sworn into the Air Corps and are awaiting their call? That they'll be flying for Uncle Sam one of these days will bring small Comfort to the enemy. I'll guarantee! . . .

Yes, War has come to all the Main Streets of Mississippi, and I am more and more convinced each week that with all you grand boys in there enthusiastically pitching, and with all the people at home backing you, victory will eventually be ours. . . .

Sincerely,

Keith Frazier Somerville

---

94. Mosquito boats were high speed plywood patrol torpedo (P.T.) boats. Subchasers were fast pursuit craft equipped with torpedoes and depth charges. An early account of the exploits of P.T. boats is W. L. White, *They Were Expendable* (New York: Harcourt Brace, 1942).

May 21, 1943

Dear Boys:

I do wish you could have been with me last Sunday night when I went out to Pace to the dedication of their "Honor Roll," containing the names of Pace's sixty-nine boys who are serving their country. President Roosevelt, you know, had designated Sunday as "I am an American day," the especial day on which we people here at home were to stop and think and be humbly grateful that our flag still flies, o'er the land of the free and the home of the brave, and for the fact that you boys, since Boy Scout days, have been reared to honor and protect our flag and to love liberty and fair play. (All of those things will equip you to fight the tyranny and intolerance by which our enemies have smothered out precious liberty in so many lands.) Pace, that nite, honored not only her fighting sons but their parents, who in giving them have given their most priceless possessions. The exercises took place in the beautiful new Methodist church and it was truly a lovely setting for an inspiring occasion. The church was dedicated only last summer, . . . and against the background of its panelled walls and soft green carpets, the galaxy of flags and immense bunches of red lilies made an unforgettable picture. Add to that twelve of Pace's lovely young girls as a choir, all dressed in white and perched jauntily atop their soft shoulder length hair, bows of red, white, and blue ribbons. Honestly, I was so intrigued with those pretty girls that I couldn't keep my eyes off of them! We do have the prettiest girls in Mississippi, don't we? I wished for you boys to admire with me, but there was only one man in uniform present in that big audience, Pvt. John Boyd of the Supply Department at Jackson. His was the only mother who could proudly display her soldier son! The choir sang a number of patriotic songs, and Dinah Brown sang a lovely solo. Then Mr. Edward Tucker, the pastor, gave a beautiful message of hope and healing to anxious hearts in an anxious world. Many parents were present, thinking of their loved ones, for the front rows of the church, marked off by red, white, and blue ribbons like a wedding, were reserved for them.

Just behind me proudly sat Mr. and Mrs. R.C. Taylor, the only four star parents in the community. Sgt. Ralph is a Marine who has been "in" three years, and is now at Camp Lejune, North Carolina;

Candidate James R. is in Class 18 O.C.S. at Camp Barkeley, Texas;[95] Pvt. Curtis L. is with the Headquarters Battery, now on maneuvers near Shreveport, Louisiana; and their baby son, John Arnold, has just been sworn into the Air Corps!

Across the aisle sat lovely Mrs. Virginia Henry, who has long taught in the Pace school and whose three fine sons attest to her ability to train children. Her son, William Edward, is in the Navy and has taken part in many battles out in the Pacific; Sherwood, who left here with the National Guard two years ago, is now in England; and Richard, her youngest, got his call while at Delta State and is now at Camp Robinson, Arkansas. Next to her sat the Baptist preacher, Rev. E.E. Evans and his wife, whose son, Edward, is now stationed at Santa Ana, California.

Then there was Mrs. Frazier, whose daughter, Juanita, left here not long ago with Josephine Webb (Mrs. George) to train at Daytona, Florida, to be a W.A.C. (Josephine writes that the first week in a tent, with intensive drills, was a bit hard to take, but that now she's in barracks, twenty-five beds to a side. Tho her feet still ache, she reports the food good and that she's written a song for them to sing at a party they're giving soon, so you see she's fitting in beautifully as we all knew she would. Personally, I think with her voice and her piano playing and her capacity to make friends, she'll be a marvelous W.A.C.! Mrs. Stamps, out at the college, leaves about June 1st too, for a training camp, and she too with all her home science training will be a big addition to the Women's Army.)[96] Another of Mrs. Frazier's daughters, Ruby, sitting next to lovely Jacqueline Worrell, was one of the many beautiful girls in the choir who caught my roving eye. I wish I knew the names of all those pretty girls to give you, and I wish, too, that I had space today to give you news of all of Pace's sixty-nine sons who are in the service.

I owe this delightful evening at Pace to charming Mrs. H.C. Bizzell, who kindly wasted her precious gas to come in and take me out. Her son, Ens. William Hardy Bizzell, is with the Naval Air

95. OCS refers to Officer Candidate Schools, created during World War II to train officers for the war effort. More than 45,000 persons graduated from OCS during the war years.

96. Mrs. Stamps is Elizabeth Coburn Stamps, one of four faculty members from Delta State Teachers College who was on military leave of absence in 1943.

Corps, now at Pensacola. She, her husband, and her two attractive young daughters were among the proudest in that audience of proud families. And well they might be, for in addition to having a boy in the service, Mrs. B.'s brother, Kenneth Tucker, is a chaplain in the Army now at Camp McCoy, Wisconsin, but expecting to go overseas soon. Her nephew, too, Harold Mitchell, with Tommy Box, was one of those soldier-like young Scouts who stood at attention beside the flags on the chancel, and it made the tears gather in my eyes as I thought of the thousands of Boy Scouts of other days who are away now, fighting for us! . . .

After the service was over I had an opportunity to talk to many people and glean news of other of Pace's "serving sons." I learned that Buford Alexander is now a flying cadet at Coffeeville, Kansas, while his brother, Wilson, is at the Headquarters of the 9th Replacement Department in New Orleans. And Ellis Thompson Lott's sister told me about him being a prisoner of the Germans, taken in North Africa. Surprisingly, a letter from him, telling the news, came to his wife down at Monroe, Louisiana some days before the official announcement was received. The Red Cross is certainly on to their job. Floyd Thornhill is also in Africa, but hasn't been heard from since the Victory there.

Pace boasts two doctors in the service: Dr. Emmanuel Cohen, now at Camp Pickett, Virginia, and that good looking Dr. Howard Aylward, who is out in Hawaii. Dr. A's. brother, Francis, is at Camp Pickett, Virginia. Mrs. Williamson, in a gray dress matching her lovely gray hair, told me that her son, Carlisle, is now at Camp Davis, North Carolina. He was in training to be an officer, but because of foot trouble had to forego that when he found he was unable to take long hikes. He has my sympathy, for my feet won't take it either when I try to make them carry me in order to save gas! John B. Frazier is at Will Rogers Field, Oklahoma City. Harry E. Thornton, a Marine, is at Camp Elliot, California, while his uncle Lovis is down in Florida. Wayne Skelton is a radio instructor at Madison, Wisconsin. Robert Bell Smith was released (because of a bad arm) and sent home to farm, and John Hartman, Jr. (because of a bad knee) was also released from the Army and is now in a defense plant in Detroit. Leo Brown is up in the Aleutian Islands and Louis Thornton has gone overseas. John Pace, for whose family the town of Pace was named, is now in O.C.S. at Ft. Benning, Georgia. He's been living, you recall, in Little Rock, and it was there that he volunteered and got into the Army months ago. Since then he's been in California and it was from there that he was recommended and sent to O.C.S. He married a Little Rock girl, Sarah Reynolds, and she and his little red headed son, "Sandy" (so nicknamed by the soldiers), have been in California with him, but now they are in Little Rock with her family.

Mrs. Price Curd, Pace's efficient postmistress, was telling me that her daughter, Dorothy, is now working for the Fisher Aircraft Company in Memphis, while her husband, Howard Murphy, is at Camp Davis, North Carolina. Dorothy went to a defense school when her husband joined up, and he's been given two War Bonds for improved ideas for parts for the B25, being made by Fisher. The last bond was presented at a big public meeting at the auditorium! My, how proud we are of our girls, as well as our boys! Mrs. Curd is proud, too, of her niece, Katherine, who lived with her so long. (She was formerly Mrs. Weissinger, but has remarried and is now Mrs. Thomas.) She is now making parts for Flying Fortresses at Inglewood, California, while her husband and two sons are all away in the Navy! Guy Weissinger is on a submarine in the Pacific, and Roy, just thru at State, as a Naval Reserve is being sent to Notre Dame for training as an ensign. Another of Mrs. Curd's nieces, Helen Ellis of Rosedale, is married to Lt. Col. Allen Eldridge, who is associated with Col. Elliott Roosevelt in the Photographic Squadron in Africa.[97] Hats off to Mrs. Curd, working hard on the home front, and to her Patriotic family! English women say "the only way you can take war is to become a part of it," and our American women are finding it true, also. The English government, understanding this psychology, have realized the value of assigning each civilian a task. "In this way the immensity of the war can be reduced to manageable proportions," they say. The Russians, too, have found this to be true. A few months ago they decorated 3,654 women: some for service with the army, some for work as guerrillas, and others for work on the home front.[98]

97. Elliott Roosevelt (1910–1990), the second son of President and Mrs. Eleanor Roosevelt, was called to active duty from the Army Air Corps reserve in 1940.

98. Some 800,000 Soviet women participated in the Second World War on a par with men. An excellent work on this subject is S. Alexiyevich, *War's Unwomanly Face* (Moscow: Progress Publishers, 1988).

Mrs. Lois Hardee, who also has found her work in our local Ration Board a "boon," went out to Pace with me and proudly sat within the Patriotic ribbons, thinking of Lt. Norman, who has been flying in the Pacific for over a year, and is now in New Guinea, and of Ben, now attending a classification school at Washington and Jefferson College, Washington, Pennsylvania.

Cora Erwin, who teaches at Pace, told me that her brother, Frank, was home last week from Camp Maxie, Texas, and they had a regular family reunion to welcome him with both Myrtle and Martha here for the occasion. Charles, who is still building roads for Uncle Sam up in Alaska, of course, wasn't there. Martha (McCool) is now down at Keesler Field to say goodbye to her husband who is being sent to Michigan. . . .

Had you heard that P.F.C. Wade is one of the 38ers who is being sent home?[99] He's due here from Seattle about the 26th, and is Anne excited over the idea of having him back at his old post office job again!

Tech. Sgt. Kline Bedwell was home the other day, too, from Texas, but not to report back to the post office! He looks grand with that extra forty pounds he's put on! No, he hasn't found a girl yet, and yes, he likes Army life. "Might as well," he said, with a grin!

Robert Boyett, just turned eighteen, was home on furlough last week from Camp Bragg, North Carolina where he is with the glider-parachute troops. He enlisted with his mother's permission at seventeen, and since then he's been places! Now he's anxious for a chance at the enemy, preferably those treacherous Jap[anese]! And guess what? While he was home he got him a bride! She's lovely, blonde Jean Walls from Lynn, and she is only seventeen! They were married by Judge Watts and she is going to stay with his mother, here in Cleveland, while he's away. . . .

Because of a lot of information gotten from captured Jap[anese] diaries, all the Navy boys have had to burn theirs, and that was a real tragedy to Lt. LaValle House, who has kept his since Annapolis

99. After the spring of 1943, drafted personnel who were 38 years of age or older and not engaged in essential war work could apply for military discharge.

days.[100] If he could only have sent it home, how much his friends would have enjoyed reading of all the thrilling experiences he's had out in the Pacific! He did send home, tho', a grand picture of himself, taken aboard the battleship on which he is now serving. Did you know they censored pictures, too, as well as letters? This one had things cut off in the funniest shapes—right out of the background. Presumably they were guns of some especial kind.

Also in town this week is Tech. Sgt. William E. Spells, who got his wings at Las Vegas, Nevada, and is now stationed at Lincoln, Nebraska. Did you know that all four of these boys are now serving Uncle Sam? Another justly proud four star mother is Mrs. J.L. Spells! Albert, the only son who isn't flying, is in the Navy, now on one of our biggest battleships somewhere out from San Francisco. His half-brother, Hubert F. Brown, is an Air Machinist Mate, also somewhere west of the Golden Gate. And Lt. Ben Spells is a Bombardier with the 35th Bombing Squadron. He, too, is in a foreign land. The Spells live out west of town near the Bogue and I know you remember them from C.H.S. days.[101] When whole families walk out en masse to fight for us and liberty and to preserve our American way of life, how can we, here at home, sit back and do nothing! Come on out to the surgical dressing class, ladies, and make a few hundred dressings apiece for each of Mrs. Spell's patriotic sons! We hope they won't need them, but if they should, how ashamed we'd be if there weren't plenty of them.

I ran in the other morning to see Capt. John Wiley Erwin's lovely Canadian wife who is here this week for a visit, en route to London, Ontario, to see her parents. And listen boys, she is a honey! Really, I think she's one of the most beautiful girls I ever saw, and you know I have an eye for pretty girls, as well as for stalwart soldiers! Mrs. Erwin has been out at Tucson for a visit and brought Lenor home with her. They had quite a trip back, were side tracked for an entire day because of the Oklahoma flood, and then had to wait for dozens of troop trains to pass ahead of their train. John has gone up to study

100. Military personnel were under orders not to keep diaries, particularly if they were in a combat area. As a result, few such documents, especially from enlisted personnel, survived the war. One important exception is James J. Fahey, *Pacific War Diary* (Boston: Houghton Mifflin, 1963).

101. C.H.S. refers to Cleveland High School.

in an airplane factory where they are being made, the very biggest and newest of our fighting planes to which he is being assigned. They carry thirty men and will not be released to the Army before September.

We've all gotten a tremendous thrill out of the African victory, and are enjoying the rumors which the commentators tell us are coming out of a Europe, all jittery over the prospect of a near invasion.[102] "I don't believe in rumors," chants one of the new songs, but maybe there is a grain of truth in the rumor of a near-riot in Berlin over news of the defeat in Africa, and in some of the conflicting rumors coming out of scared Italy!

Well, once again our brave American boys are proving to the world that we here in the United States can and will fight, even to death if need be, for all we hold dear, and to help give back liberty to the enslaved peoples of the world! God bless you, boys! We honor you for all you're doing, whether it's driving Germans out of Tunesia, bombing Jap[anese] bases, fighting mosquitoes in the jungles, or peeling potatoes in "boot camp," for we know that it's in our united efforts, in the service and on the home front, that this war will be won.

With every good wish for each of you,

Sincerely,
Keith Frazier Somerville

102. On May 11, 1943, Axis resistance in North Africa came to an end.

2

Purple Hearts Are Getting too Plentiful Hereabouts

June 1943—December 1943

June 4, 1943

Dear Boys:

I went on a trip last week; in wartime, too! But I don't think Mr. Eastman would mind this one, even though I did take some soldier's seat.[1] For you see, it was a seat some of you used to use in years gone by, and not one of those precious train or bus seats you boys need now to bring you home on furlough! I went for a ride on a school bus! It's something I've longed to do for years, only before I never had a legitimate excuse! But I find you boys are on "open sesame," not only to people's hearts, but to all kinds of other things too! "Can you go on a school bus to gather news of the boys in the service? Why, certainly," responded my good friends, Mr. Parks and Mr. Harry Sanders, when I timidly broached the subject.

So on a perfect May morning, I started out on my adventure. The sun, after its pink advent into the world, was just turning into a big yellow ball, "flooding all the world with sunlight," in the words of

---

1. Joseph B. Eastman (1882–1944) was director of the Office of Defense Transportation during World War II.

the old poem. The dew was still on the rows of cotton, making them glisten and gleam like millions of diamonds as they stood up in straight rows like soldiers on parade. The cotton and the wonderful gardens along the route are truly our home soldiers, fighting with you for Victory. The English peas and the spreading tomato plants especially intrigued me, and I gloried too, in the flowers (pink and red poppies, orange lilies and blue larkspur) that flaunted their colors in the morning sunlight. Remember how fresh the air felt and how sweetly the birds sang on those past spring mornings as you waited for the school bus? Remember, too, how fresh the girls, big and little, looked in their starched ginghams and prints, as they embarked on their pilgrimage toward our educational mecca, the Cleveland Consolidated School? As fresh as the morning itself looked lovely Roxie Griffin as she gave me news of those fine brothers of hers. And by the way, did you know that their father, Mr. R.E. Griffin, is now on the School Board? With all his big family, I know he's a good one to be on, for there's nothing he doesn't know by now about schools— Clara Belle to give him the teacher's angle, and all the rest giving him, through the years, the other side of the picture! The Griffins are "four-starers" now, and the community is proud with them of their boys. Purvy, always one of my pet boys, having recently graduated at State, where he was in the Signal Corps Reserve, is now down at Camp Shelby, but expecting to go to New Jersey soon. Lt. (J.G.) Berlin is in the Naval Air Corps, you know, and now down in Panama. (Cecil Pleasants is down in that neighborhood, too, having been transferred from the Army to the Naval Air Corps. If you boys run into my old friend, Gen. Glenn Edgerton, Governor General of the Canal Zone, say hello to him for me![2] I loved the letter you wrote me, Cecil! And your mother told me of your buying bananas for five cents a bunch! Here we often hear, "yes, we have no bananas today," but we can easily do without them for the duration, while shipping is so needed for more important things. A broadcast from London last night said the commentator had seen no bananas, "nor a reasonable facsimile of one," since he'd been in the Isles, but

---

2. Glenn Edgerton (1876–1976) was Governor General of the Canal Zone from 1940–1944. Edgerton was a 1908 graduate of West Point, and Mrs. Somerville had met him while a student at the Castle.

he'd heard that there were thirty-six somewhere in England![3] Someone had raised them in a greenhouse and they were on display,
resting on cotton like precious jewels, and guarded by "bobbies!"
Well, they're not too plentiful here, but they're not extinct! You boys
enjoy them for us!) But back to the Griffins. (How I do wander!)
Corp. Delbert, in the Army Air Corps, is now at Santa Ana,
California. You knew, didn't you, that he married less than a year
ago? His wife, Ieola Lane, from Jackson, is with him in the west.
And Roy is in the Signal Corps down in Alabama.

Sarah Frances Hutchison, her brown eyes sparkling and her red
and white checked dress so becoming, talked of her brother, Raymond,
a radio man in the Army Air Corps, now at Hammer Field, Fresno,
California. She told me, too, of her uncle, Sgt. Marshall Faulkner,
now in England, and of J.L. Brown and Cecil Steen, who are in the
Navy, now at San Diego, California. Also that Hubert P. Waddell is in
the Army, somewhere in the South Pacific.

Charming too, in a fresh-as-a-daisy yellow frock which so well
suited her auburn locks, was La Verne Thresh, as she gave me news
that Branson Stewart of the Navy is now at Santa Ana, California.
C.D. Sims, still as irrepressible and delightful as he was in Grade
One, told me of his uncle, Melvin Sims, now at Camp Maxie, Texas,
and of another uncle, Ray Kendall, now out at San Diego. Told me,
too, of his cousins, Kelso and Hubert Sims, the former somewhere in
Alabama and the latter at Camp Shelby. When C.D. joins them to
fight for Uncle Sam, he'll make it hot for the enemy. "Red" Hood will
be a headache for the Axis, too! How full of life those boys are. And
what fun they had "whooping it up" and "ragging" the girls that
morning on the bus, just as you boys whose energy has now gone
into fighting used to do. Only the other day "Red" told me of his
brother-in-law, Leonard Leroy Hawkins, who is now at Camp Shelby.
Little Clara Sims, in a bright red dress, told me proudly that sister
Nettie's husband, James Raney, is also at Camp Shelby, and little
Jean Raney, precious in green gingham, her yellow curls bobbing,

---

3. Wartime shipping and transportation difficulties resulted in significant
shortages of tropical fruits of all kinds. Most available fruit was consumed by the
military forces. Special high Vitamin C fruits, such as tomatoes, were developed
to help counteract these shortages.

gave me news that her uncle, J.W. Jennings, with the Marines, is now in Chicago.

When the Olenes trooped onto the bus, their news concerned their cousins, Kildot, Clois, and "Red" Dart: Kildot, still "somewhere in the States," Clois, at Camp Shelby, and "Red," "across the water." Mrs. Dart, with the boys away, is now living with a daughter "in the hills."[4]

Humbert Shepherd tells me that brother Douglas is now at Camp Mackass, the new parachute camp in North Carolina. Harvey Lee Davis is an Air Corps pilot, and J.L. Dart is also in the Air Corps. B.S. Ray is a Marine at San Diego, while "Buddy" Matthews, another Marine, is "across." Guy McCool is in the Army. So is Corp. Woodrow McCool, now stationed at Kansas City, Missouri. Had you heard that he's married a Missouri girl since he's been out there? Congratulations to Woodrow.

Especially attractive was auburn-haired Lucille Harper, all dolled out in shades of brown and tan! Our girls DO know their color charts and all seem to remember the admonition of the great French dress-maker, Worth, . . . who urged women, "always dress to your eyes and hair."[5] Lucille told me of brother, Jonah, an air mechanic, now en route from Washington to some Kentucky camp, and of brother, Wester, in the Navy, now at San Francisco but looking to be shipped out any day.

Dorothy Frank told me of her cousins, the Blisset boys from down Lynn way, who have marched out four strong to fight for us. I know Mr. and Mrs. Will Blisset are proud of their four stars! They make ten families I've run into hereabouts with four sons serving us and Uncle Sam! (One hundred surgical dressings for each of those forty, four-star sons would be little enough for each of us women here at home to make to show our appreciation!) Basco Blisset is "across" —that seems to be the approved word—I heard it often on my bus trip. Expressive isn't it? What pictures it conjures up! Mighty billows, sea gulls, and salt spray across one's face; jungles and

---

4. "In the hills" is a reference to the area east of the Mississippi Delta, beginning around Grenada.

5. Charles Frederick Worth (1825–1895) was the founder of Parisian haute couture.

Jap[anese] and heat; Arctic ice, Northern lights, and dense fogs; Arabs and minarets and the blue Mediterranean; cathedrals and "trams" and bombed towns! Maj. Arthur Blisset is now in England and so is his brother, James (a radio man), and Spencer is back and forth "across" often, transporting planes. Dorothy Frank was in my room, years ago, when she was stricken with infantile paralysis, and I was happy to see her looking so well. She still uses one crutch, but apart from that, she is now a normal, happy girl. She's one example of what the President's Birthday Balls have done in our midst.[6]

Sgt. Obadiah McMinn, I learned, is now in the Air Corps, over in Greenwood, Mississippi and Sgt. William Gillespie is at Camp Maxie, Texas. The Blaylock boys, Otis and Howard, are in the Navy and Army respectively. Charles Kendricks (Seaman, 2nd Class) is at Camp Perry, Virginia. Edwin Clemons of the Navy, who was at Pearl Harbor, is now home on leave after three years in the service, and will enter an officer's training school soon, I was told, while his cousin, Fred Clemons, is now at Pearl Harbor, but with the Army, not the Navy. Corp. Willie Frederick is now in the Air Corps, (Camden, Arizona) and his brother, Jessie, also in the Air Corps, is now in New Mexico. The Greer brothers are in the service, too; Leon at Camp Beauregard, Louisiana, and Dorvell in the Navy (in Memphis, at present). John T. Chandler, of the Medical Corps, connected with a hospital up in Pennsylvania, is expected home soon on a furlough. They're getting ready for you, John! Willie Frank Howell is now a chaplain in Africa. . . .

Daughters, as well as sons of C.H.S., are getting out and doing things in this war world these days! Jean Jackson, having passed her exams to be a W.A.V.E., is just waiting to go to New Orleans to be sworn in after which Judge and Mrs. Jackson will have to remove the two star flag in their front window and substitute one with three! (Charles is still at Camp McClellan, Alabama, but Bobbie has been sent to the amphibian school at Norfolk. He'd sworn, so he wrote, that he wouldn't go to school anymore, but Uncle Sam had different ideas about that!)

---

6. The President's Birthday Balls were charity affairs begun in the early 1930s, to raise money for polio research, or as it was then known, infantile paralysis. Roosevelt was stricken with the disease in 1921. The Birthday Balls evolved into the March of Dimes and the Mother's March.

Dorothy Shands, in a Red Cross "overseas Mobile Unit," is still waiting in Alexandria, Virginia, to be sent "across."[7] Meanwhile she's helping with the U.S.O., enjoying going to camps near Washington, and practicing up on the kind of work she'll soon be doing "overthere."[8]

Joy Somerville's ninety-six pounds won't add much weight to the Chicago and Southern transport plane (Chicago to New Orleans) on which she'll soon be hostessing, but her joy in flying is so infectious that it will no doubt weigh heavily with any scared passengers. That she can serve a meal in the air without spilling a drop is the feat she's proudest of just now!

The afternoon after my bus trip, I had another nice sample of Hi School when a bunch brought a truck to the jungle that is my front yard for their annual load of honeysuckle to make the Class Day rope.[9] (Did they ever "rope" any of the boys into that job? I'd be terribly disappointed if they didn't come each May!) Again, I was impressed with the vitality and charm of our young people! While the boys cut and loaded the vines, a group of pretty girls sat in my swing and talked, and I noted beneath the gaiety that makes up commencement time, a tinge of sadness; the intruding thought that, even more than is usually the case, this class which has worked and played together for so long would truly be broken up soon because a lot of the boys in the graduating class expect to be in the service soon. Eight of them have already gotten their calls, deferred till after graduation, and will be inducted into the Army soon. Maxine Greer (still as lovely as she was as a little tot in first grade) told me that John Thomas Greer had "gotten his papers," as also have Hardy

7. An excellent contemporary account about the experiences of a Red Cross worker stationed in England, North Africa, and Italy during World War II is Eleanor "Bumpy" Stevenson and Pete Martin, *I Knew Your Soldier* (New York: Penguin Books, 1945). Also useful is George Korson, *At His Side: The Story of the American Red Cross Overseas in World War II* (New York: Coward-McCann, 1945).

8. USO is a reference to the United Service Organizations, founded in April 1941, to provide support services for military personnel and their families. For information about the work of the USO during World War II, see Julia M.H. Carson, *Home Away from Home: The Story of the U.S.O.* (New York: Harper & Brothers, 1946).

9. Honeysuckle ropes, or braided ropes of other flowers, were often part of graduation ceremonies at this time. The ropes symbolized the bonds which the graduates had forged during their high school years.

Britt, John Riley, Thomas Nelson, Jasper Jenkins, and Alvin Campbell. Charles Clarke, Nap Cassibry, and A.C. Lassiter have taken and passed their Naval exams and been classified V-12—which means they will be sent to some college where they will be in Naval Reserves.[10] Joe Farned and Lee Odom want to get in the service, too. Peppy "Billy" McCain told me of her two brothers who are already in; Lt. Paul McCain, now at Camp McCain..., and Sgt. Mitchell McCain, now at Camp Shelby.

Of course, I had to go to Class Day to see my honeysuckle and my "chillun" and, as always, it was lovely. Against the background of shrubbery on the campus, behind a white picket fence, draped with the rope of varicolored flowers which they had carried in, sat rows and rows of seniors: the boys in white suits, the girls in pastel shades. Truly it was a beautiful sight, lessened not a whit by the lowering clouds and faint drizzle which failed to dampen the enthusiasm either of the seniors or their admiring audience. On a pole at one side, the flag proudly floated (that flag which, from the top of the main building, has watched so many classes march in and out) and struck the keynote of the whole Patriotic program. The splendid quartet (Doris Evanson, Margie Crouch, Grapal McCain and Mary Sue Brown) sang "I Pledge Allegiance" and "America's Prayer." Also on the program, and doing their parts beautifully, were Mary Ann Brown, Mary Ann Catchings, and Harriet Causey, making seven as lovely girls as C.H.S. has ever turned loose on the world (now peopled by susceptible service men)! And the non-performers were equally attractive! I've seldom seen a class of prettier girls or finer looking boys.

Mingling in the crowd and shaking hands with old friends was Johnnie Merrill, "home from the War," looking in his Navy whites exactly like a Navy poster. My, he's one good looking lad! He's with the Amphibian forces, you know. Maybe he landed some of you in Africa. He was there all right!

10. V-6 and V-12 were the names given to the U.S. Navy programs created to produce young officers for the war. Two good memoirs which describe these programs are Douglas Leach, *Now Hear This: The Memoir of a Junior Naval Officer in the Great Pacific War* (Kent, Ohio: Kent State University Press, 1987) and Samuel Hynes, *Flights of Passage: Refections of a World War II Aviator* (New York: Frederic C. Beil, 1988).

Also present was Chaplain Evanson, home from Virginia, to see Doris graduate from Hi School, and Lester, from Delta State (Lester was in Army Reserves out there and reports to Camp Shelby on June 10th).

A lump came into my throat as A.C. Lassiter and Charles Clarke eloquently reminded us that "no matter what our ages, the times have made us men," and the thought came to me that this same scene was being enacted this month over the length and breadth of this great land of ours. From schools and colleges everywhere across our continent, our boys are marching out into the turmoil of war, with a laugh and a jest on their lips and deep enthusiasm for getting at the job of cleaning the world of dictators. Perhaps, I thought, we "builded better than we knew," for we have implanted somehow in our boys a love for liberty—'tis certain our enemies didn't expect this.

Mr. Parks has compiled a list of you old C.H.S. boys who are now in the service, and I just want you to know that a lot of us are remembering you boys who composed the happy classes of other years; remembering you with pride as well as with affection. As you faithfully perform your duties on the far flung battle lines of our country and in your training camps, always remember that your friends back home haven't forgotten to be grateful to you. And when many of the Class of '43 join you, as they soon will, they, too, will take with them our gratitude, our pride, and our abiding faith in you American boys. As I wore my poppy last Saturday for Memorial Day, proudly remembering that that first Memorial Day ever held in the United States was held at Columbus, honoring Mississippi soldiers of the Civil War,[11] and thinking, also with pride, of how the trees along our Cleveland to Boyle Memorial Drive have grown, since the day they were planted, into sturdy oaks, honoring Bolivar County's sturdy warriors of the last war, I knew in my heart that your deeds,

---

11. In 1866, Columbus, Mississippi, and Waterloo, New York, formally observed the honoring of the graves of those soldiers who had died during the Civil War. This custom eventually became a national holiday, known as Memorial Day or Decoration Day. Both Columbus and Waterloo claim to be the birthplace of Memorial Day. Following World War I, Memorial Day celebrations often included the purchase and wearing of symbolic poppies. The profits from the sale of the poppies were used to aid disabled veterans.

too, would ever be kept green in our memories.[12] Six of C.H.S. four hundred boys in the service have already given their lives: Charles Barbour, Charles Beeman, John Simmons, William H. Rice, Earl Beavers, and Otis Gannon. They, along with America's other brave soldiers from King's Mountain to Bizerte, have not died in vain.[13] "Greater love hath no man than this, that a man lay down his life for his friends." They died bravely in the fight to preserve liberty for us, their friends. We won't forget that.

God bless you, and may each of you come safely in "on a wing (or its equivalent in your branch of the service!) and a prayer."

Sincerely,

Keith Frazier Somerville

June 18, 1943

Dear Boys:

"America is on a matrimonial spree", says Kate Burr.[14] "The wedding cake may contain less sugar, the old shoes may have been safely put away for resoling, but marriage is a booming institution today! Every month 150,000 couples are married! Despite other shortages, there seems to be no priority on love!" Well, our Bolivar County youngsters are no exception to the general rule. They're at this marrying business, too, as I've told you before. Last Monday, out

12. In 1923, the local chapter of the Daughters of the American Revolution, at the suggestion of Mrs. Somerville's sister-in-law, Eleanor Somerville Shands, initiated a project to create a Memorial drive along the barren, three-mile stretch of road between Cleveland and Boyle to commemorate local men who lost their lives during World War I. The project provided for trees which could be purchased for a dollar each to be planted along the drive. Eventually, some four hundred pin oaks were planted along Memorial Drive to honor the twenty-five Bolivar County men who died in World War I.

13. The Battle of King's Mountain was an important battle of the Revolutionary War. It was fought near the boundary of North Carolina and South Carolina on October 7, 1780. Some 2,000 colonial frontiersmen surrounded the British troops on King's Mountain and killed or captured almost the entire force. The battle was noted as the first of a series of setbacks that led to the defeat of the British. Bizerte is a Tunisian port on the Mediterranean Sea. It was used by the Axis as a major supply center during the Tunisian campaign. Bizerte was taken by the U.S. II Corps and some French troops on May 7, 1943.

14. Kate Burr was a pseudonym for Lois Bryant Lane (186?–1943), a journalist and radio commentator from Buffalo, New York.

at San Diego, California, Billy Lowery and Myrtle Lindsey were quietly married. The bride's dad (Mr. Clyde Lindsey) accompanied her to the west coast to see the knot tied, and they had a Mississippian, Navy Chaplain Gatlin, to perform the ceremony. Billy is feeling super fine these days, but the Navy still has him doing "limited service". You know he was in all those early Pacific battles (Coral Seas, etc.) and was one of the first of our boys to be wounded in action.[15] Well, a pretty Delta bride should be all the tonic he needs! Jessie Ellis Lewis, who has been sojourning in a San Diego hospital following an accident, was the only home towner present at that wedding. By the way, he's about ready for a leave any day now.

On Friday, pretty Joyce Shular (fortunately entirely well now from a recent appendectomy which postponed her wedding) is to be married to Robert Hays, formerly of Port Gibson, but now working for the A.A.A in Washington.[16] The wedding will be at sister "Mary Margaret's" lovely home, with only the family and a few friends present. Too bad "Marine Melvin," still out in Australia, and Brother Bennett, up at Camp Pendleton, Virginia, couldn't be here for the occasion!

And as soon as he gets his wings (sometime this week) out at the Corpus Christi Naval Air Base, Nevin Sledge is coming home to wed that talented Brenda Wilson. The wedding will be sometime next week, at the Presbyterian church, and with no boys available, red headed Brenda has decided to use her red headed girl cousins for ushers!

That marrying bug has struck Pace, too. Had you heard that Robert Grantham, home on a twenty-day leave after a year in Hawaii, married attractive Edith Lott last week? He couldn't be letting brother Gray (a cook at the Port of Embarkation, New York) get ahead of him. (Remember what Pvt. Hargrove said about cooks? "That they had the best job in the Army.")[17] You know Gray married

15. For information on Bill Lowery's World War II experiences, see "Bill Lowery—Memories of War Remain Vivid," *Bolivar Commercial*, February 17, 1989.

16. AAA refers to the Agricultural Adjustment Administration, established in 1933 to oversee the various agricultural programs of the New Deal.

17. Marion Hargrove (1919–) wrote a best-selling, humorous account of his experiences as a young draftee titled *See Here, Private Hargrove!* (New York: Henry Holt, 1942). Hargrove also wrote for *Yank* magazine during the war years.

Ethel Quinton when he was home last December! And Rufus Aycock married recently too, a pretty Georgia girl. He's a paratrooper, up in North Carolina now; his brother, Clyde, is stationed at Camp Blanding, Florida and brother, Bobbie, is out on the west coast (Seattle) transferring Jap[anese] to inland camps. Hurrah for those "Fighting ay-cocks"!

But I'm not thru with Pace's weddings yet! Frank Thompson graduated from the Glider School at Lubbock, Texas, this spring and married Betsy Worrel the very same day! They've done some honeymoon tripping since then (by order of Uncle Sam), going first to Ft. Sill, Oklahoma, then to Louisville, and now Frank is an instructor in the Ground School at Sedalia, Missouri. George Kelly, Jim Hawkins, and Johnnie Jones (also of Pace) are down at Camp Shelby, wishing the old gent with the beard would send them out to see the world and meet the enemy! Leo Brown, up at Dutch Harbor, Alaska since last summer, says it was plenty cold up there last winter. Well, Leo, maybe you'll get over Kiska way ere long and find it a bit hotter! Our Chinese friends are all rejoicing that the Jap[anese] are being thrown back nowadays in China, and Lincoln Chann, a Pace radioman, now at Ft. Benning, longs to have the opportunity to broadcast total Victory for China, after their long valiant fight!

I hear that "Chunky" Clay is living a most satisfactory and happy life these days in his handsome Merchant Marine uniform down at the "Inn-by-the Sea," Pass Christian, where he's attending officer's training school.[18] He writes that the grandmother of one of his pals has been wonderful to him, and he speaks enthusiastically of pretty girls. But lest his mother think it's all play, he also mentions having fourteen classes and working from 6 a.m. till 10 p.m. . . .

Jeanette Kelso left this week to join Richard (who was himself at Keesler Field for quite a spell) at Wright Field, Dayton, Ohio. Fay McDearman is working at Wright Field, too, living in the house with a bunch of delightful flyers and their wives, and getting very airminded, too. Gosh, I wish I were a young girl these days! There are no closed doors for them! . . .

With all our boys and girls so air minded, after the war there'll

18. "Inn-by-the-Sea" was a famous luxury hotel on the Mississippi Gulf coast which was converted to military use during the war.

probably be a hanger in every vacant field, where one can drop in and have his tires changes, "fill'em up," and put water in the batteries, or whatever they do to service planes. I wouldn't be knowing myself, but I feel sure half the boys in Bolivar County will know. Maybe Wallace Conner and D.M. Fleming, Edward C. Peeples and Oscar Gillespie, and James Howard and Clyde Garrett will make their fortunes after the war with a chain of such service stations! Anyway, they'll be equipped to do so after their months of training on the Gulf coast!...

John Best is another of the thousands who will be "in the know" about plane service. He's studying radio at the Aviation Ground School at Scott Field, Illinois. His sister, Mary Stewart, with her precious seven months old daughter, is here with her mother, while her husband, Sgt. H.D. Putnam (formerly of Clarksdale) is attending the Engineering School at the University of North Carolina. Guess what the baby's name is! "Sonny Lou"! And you may be sure big "Sonny" is proud of his namesake!

Eckles and Ralph Jennings will probably have aviation jobs after the war, too. Eckles is down at Monroe, Louisiana studying to be one of those men on whom so much depends, a navigator of a big plane. Hard work, too, he says. Why, he had one exam that lasted seven hours! (Yes, he passed it!) And Ralph has finished his basic training at Miami Beach and is expecting to be moved somewhere soon (possibly Keesler), as the government is taking over a lot of the big hotels there for the use of wounded soldiers.

Jimmie Chiles is due to get his wings at the Victorville, California Air Base about July 10th and Mother Eva is hoping for a visit from him this summer. Meanwhile, he called her the other night and reported that he's still loving California, and that he's spent several weekends lately on a very foxy dude ranch! His "Aunt Emma Smith" is just back from having a fine time visiting with Capt. Milton Jr. and "Happy" down at Elgin Field, Florida. (Since we read that Gen. Doolittle's flyers made their preparations for the Tokyo raid there, Elgin Field has loomed large in our consciousness!)[19] Milton's lovely

19. In April 1942, General James H. "Jimmy" Doolittle (1896–) led a strike force of B-25 bombers in a raid on Tokyo. The raid had little decisive strategic effect on the war, but it greatly bolstered the morale of U.S. citizens.

bride won all Cleveland hearts on a recent visit here. Another Cleveland lad (with a lovely Frenchy-named New Orleans bride), also flying at Elgin, is Capt. Tom Blaylock, who made a flying trip home not long ago. Milton and Tom were both among those buying the 1,800,000 marriage licenses issued last year!

Have any of you boys had occasion to fly a "helicopter"? I see that the army has ordered a bunch of those flying machines, developed by the Russian, Sikorsky, who perfected the "Clippers."[20] That seems to be the plane I'll have to have, if I live long enough! (Lionel Barrymore, on his 65th birthday last week, said that's his ambition, too, "to fly a flivver plane"—Well, Mr. Kethley, out at Delta State had the nerve to tell me I was too old to take flying there, but believe me, Mr. K., actor Barrymore has a lot of years on me!)[21] Anyway, they say the helicopter is a nice little closed model with no wings, which can take off straight up in the air, land anywhere straight down, and carry enough gasoline for two people to trip far across country. And if its engine fails, it can land without power, unwinding leisurely earthward! So that's my baby!

Purple Hearts are getting too plentiful hereabouts. We're terribly proud when we see one, but it breaks our hearts to realize that our boys are being "wounded in action", and the fact that they showed bravery (which we knew they would), tho' satisfying, doesn't keep us from feeling bad over it!

Tech. Sgt. Raymond Malaby, who used to be assistant manager at Sterling's, has written his wife, Alma Blaylock, that his is being sent to her.[22] He was in North Africa for a long time, but has been back in England for many months and was stationed there on May 17th when he was wounded. He's a radio operator on a Flying Fortress, so he probably was wounded during one of those raids over the continent, maybe even Berlin itself. Just now he is able to be out of

20. Igor Sikorsky (1889–1972), a Russian-born, U.S. pioneer in aircraft design, is best known for the development of the helicopter. During the 1930s, Sikorsky helped to develop large "flying boats," known as "Clippers," which carried passengers and mail on transoceanic flights.

21. Lionel Barrymore (1878–1954), son of the stage actors Maurice and Georgiana Barrymore, was one of the most important character actors of the early twentieth century.

22. Sterling's was a department store in Cleveland.

the hospital and has gone to Scotland to recuperate. Even tho' he's been wounded, I can almost find it in my heart to envy him, for a trip to Scotland has been the unrealized dream of my life! Scotland, with its loch and glens and highlands, from whence all my ancestors came long ago: the land of Burns and Scott, of Wallace and Bruce, of the "Black Douglass" and "The Lady of the Lake"! . . . [23] "England", writes Sgt. Malaby, "is nice, but they just don't do things our way, and its hard to get used to their ways. I'm just beginning, after many months, to know my way around. One can't buy food and drinks like we used to, and it's a good thing I bought all the clothes I could need before I came over. Of course, there are no street lights anywhere, and without a flashlight it's hard to find your way anywhere at night." A recent article in *Vogue*, by one Toni Frisetti (in England with the Red Cross), told of hearing soldiers talking and singing on a London street one nite during a blackout, and the thrill she got when she suddenly realized they were American boys.[24] Berkeley and Grosvenor Squares, she said, looked like little America—so many American boys about! One of the commentators, speaking from London, told of groping his way around a blackened street one nite and suddenly running into someone playing Beethoven's "Moonlight Sonata." Stopping, the American found the musician to be a blind violinist who said, "Yes, he knew it was written by a German, but it was so lovely he thought it might cheer up some frightened person and remind them that moonlight had not always meant bombs, even to Germans, and would cease to do so again someday!"[25]

Lt. Winston Hale (with the 8th Air Corps Bombardier Command—recently promoted to first lieutenant) has been in England over a year. And perhaps he hasn't changed his job so much after all. For

23. These are references to Robert Burns (1759–1796); Sir Walter Scott (1771–1832); Sir William Wallace (1270–1305), one of Scotland's greatest national heroes; the Bruce family, to which two kings of Scotland belonged; Sir James Douglas (1286–1330), also known as Black Douglas, the champion of Robert de Bruce (King Robert I of Scotland); and, the 1810 novel, *Lady of the Lake*, written by Sir Walter Scott.

24. In order to diminish the accuracy of enemy bombs, blackouts were instituted during World War II. The popular 1942 song, "When the Lights Go On Again," referred to the blackouts of the Second World War.

25. By contrast, during the First World War, German and Austrian music was banned throughout much of the United States.

before he got into the Army, he was selling life insurance up in Memphis. Now he's working to insure "Life, Liberty, and the Pursuit of Happiness" for the world! His mother had a cable from him the other day (after not hearing for some time) reporting him O.K.

Up at Annapolis, Bill Berger is taking his "summer cruise" on a battleship close to his base. Those wonderful "summer cruises" in the past used to include the land of the midnight sun and other faraway glamorous ports, but no more! With Axis subs lurking, our future admirals are too valuable to take chances with. But at the rate they're rushing them thru the Naval Academy, those boys may yet be Norway bound, in time not only to see the Northern lights, but also to see the Quislings get what's coming to them![26] Charles House is at Annapolis, too, taking a Naval Reserve course, and Hugh Butler is at home now, with a ten day leave following his graduation from the Naval Academy on June 9th. (His mother and sister went up for June week and had a wonderful trip.) Ens. Butler is due to report at Jacksonville, Florida June 25th for some work this summer, prior to reporting to his ship. His brother, H.C., by the way, is now attending the Army Communications School at Scott Field, Illinois.

I wish you boys could all see the pink mimosa, blooming so beautifully on the college campus, and everywhere else in Cleveland, for that matter. Just the sight of them gives our spirits a lift and makes us inclined to see even war news through rose-colored glasses! Maybe that's partly the reflection of the rosy-hued view of life all our newly weds are taking!

So here's to a rosy future for all of you!

Sincerely,
Keith Frazier Somerville

July 2, 1943

Dear Boys:

David Cohn, himself a bachelor, has written a new book, *Love in*

---

26. Vidkun Quisling (1887–1945) was the leader of the Norwegian Fascist party in the 1930s. His collaboration with the Germans in their occupation of Norway during World War II established his name as a synonym for traitor. Following the liberation of Norway in May 1945, Quisling was arrested, found guilty of treason and other crimes, and executed.

America, an amusing analysis of marriage, in which he arrives at the conclusion that American men do not like women![27] Well, maybe he's right, but the preponderance of weddings nowadays seem to prove him wrong. You boys may prove him wrong. You boys may not like 'em but you "shore does" love 'em! He says everyone expects too much of marriage (himself excepted!). Well, he's right there, but personally, though I roared mightily over some of his witticisms, and think some of his premises well taken, I don't think he's quite fair to women, or to men either, for that matter. "It's a very strange thing," he remarks, "that American literature contains no work of any note on love as a psychological phenomenon," so forthwith he sits down to write us one, pointing out exactly, in the Dorothy Dix manner, what's wrong with American marriages![28] (How scornful he would be of a stupid woman reacting like that to his treatise, for he makes all manner of fun of Dorothy Dix who, he points out, now receives $70,000 a year, has world-wide readers, competitors, and imitators, all for giving advice to the lovelorn, thoroughly miserable, married folk!) Well, boys, don't let his pessimism stop your wedding! With all its ups and downs, marriage is still a pretty good institution, preferable with all its imperfections to unmarried bliss! I gather from the fact that everyday I hear of another of you "stepping off" that most of you haven't seen this book. If you had, you wouldn't dare chance a lifetime of living with some pretty, dumb, neurotic girl, interested only in movie stars, beauty parlors, and happy-ending stories in women's magazines! Lt. A.L. Mellott writes me, "Judging by your last write-up, I must be the only single soldier left in existence, and I'm afraid that I'll end up in the Smithsonian Museum as the last of the species!" Gracious, A.L., have you read the book and taken the vow of celibacy? Just for that I'm going to send you the address of one of the prettiest girls I know, who lives in Charleston, South Carolina! Maybe she'll go swimming with you out at Ft. Moultrie, and help you "haul in the bad little boys" you chase from their

27. David Lewis Cohn, *Love in America* (New York: Simon and Schuster, 1943).

28. Dorothy Dix was the pseudonym for Elizabeth Meriwether Gilmer (1870–1951), the writer of a widely circulated advice column for the lovelorn. The name was apparently chosen as a deliberate effort to recall Dorothea Dix, a nineteenth-century social reformer who was a crusader for the mentally ill.

"hilarious nightlife" in that lovely old city. But watch your step, son, or you'll be buying a license, too! Remember, "pride goeth before a fall"!

Lt. George Boozer's June bride is appropriately named June! She was June Lange, of El Paso, and they were married on June 5th in the Chapel at Ft. Bliss, with Army Chaplin Barney performing the ceremony. I went down to see your mother, George, and thrilled with her over the El Paso papers with "the brilliant details of the wedding." It must have been lovely, with those girls in "misty marquisette" (canary yellow, green, and pink) carrying pink amaryllis. And your June bride! Words fail me! Her picture is so lovely in her filmy wedding gown, her short veil, those adorable lace gauntlets straight from pre-war "Paree," carrying her white orchids, that I don't blame you a bit for falling for her! I loved the picture, too, of her cutting the huge tiered, flag-topped cake, and you beside her wearing such a broad grin! Much happiness to you both out at Marana Field, Tucson, Arizona. I saw brother Bobbie's picture, too, and learned that you and June had been down to see him. It must have been a happy meeting after two years of separation. I understand he's finished his "basic" at Ft. Stockson, Gibbs Field, Texas. And I practically had a fit over a marvelous picture of brother James (Lt.—flight commander) in his plane with his mascot "Lady," a white, wire-haired terrier (the picture which appeared in the *Spokane Daily*). Honestly, that's the best picture that's come out of this war! Please send me one, James! Just a glance at it would set my spirits soaring! Also, I think you should paint in a cigarette and then send it to the tobacco companies! I'm sure they'd pay you countless thousands to ornament their billboards announcing, "I smoke Lucky-Strike-Philip-Chesterfields!" Does "Lady" really eat carrots like you flyers, "to help her night sight," and always meet your incoming plane out at Ephrata, Washington?

The town is all agog over another wedding to be solemnized July 10th in the Chapel of Davidson College (North Carolina): Jane Gaines (Boyle) and Fernie Wood. Fernie is an Air Cadet up there. The wedding plans are still nebulous, for those good old days when wedding plans were perfected to the last candle, months in advance, are a thing of the past. But I hear that Jane is hoping to take along several of her Mississippi friends to stand up with Fernie's soldier pals.

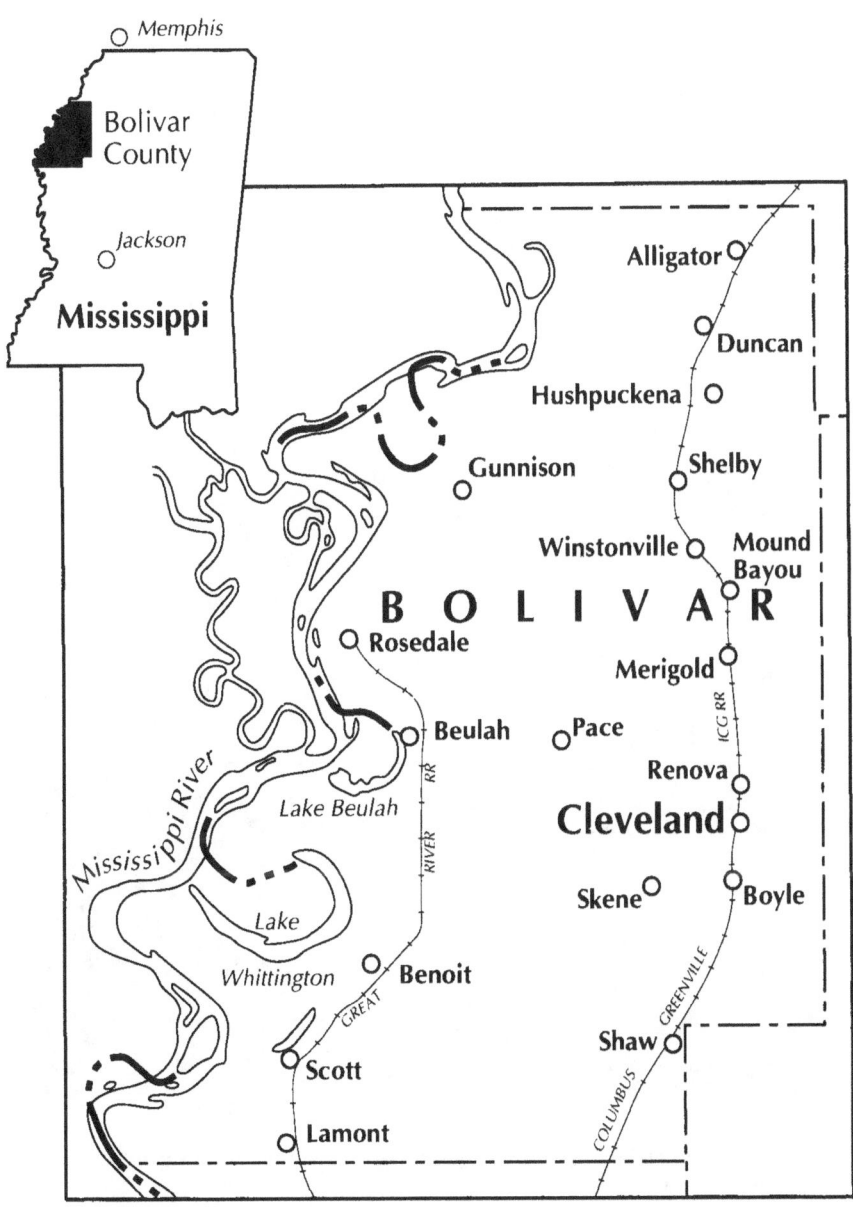

Bolivar County
Cartography: Bill Pitts

Graduation portrait of Keith Frazier, Ward's Seminary, Nashville,
Tennessee, 1904

Above: Governor James B. Frazier and Keith Frazier at the launching of the U.S.S. *Tennessee,* Philadelphia, Pennsylvania, November 1904; *Right:* Keith Frazier, Somerville, Ca. 1945

The "Dear Boys" column as it appeared on the front page of the
Bolivar Commercial

This Christmas 1942 V-Mail from Rowan Thomas, one of Keith Frazier Somerville's "Dear Boys," is an example of the many cards and letters which Somerville received from Bolivar Countians in the service.

This page and opposite: Examples of advertisements from local businesses in support of the war effort published in the *Bolivar Commercial*

SOLDIER SOY
IS A FIGHTING BOY!

Increased Production of Soybeans Is Essential to Meet Greatest Demands for Oils and Fats In History of Nation

American farmers are asked to make another tremendous increase in acreage planted to soybeans. They are asked to grow more soybeans because this crop produces many important products urgently needed on the Home Front and on the Battle front.

American farmers are asked to grow twelve million acres of soybeans for beans in 1943.

The demand for oils and fats is the highest in history. Production of more soybeans is a necessary to keep oilseed needs in supply of vegetable oils from the Far East and South America. Normal stocks of fats and oils in the United States have been drastically reduced. The current rate of consumption of fats and oils is the highest on record and enormous quantities are being purchased for Lease-Lend shipments.

The Secretary of Agriculture has announced that prices of soybean or green soybeans will be supported at not less than $1.66 to $1.79 per bushel, depending on its location.

How Soybeans Are Helping Win the War

The highly versatile plywood made from soybeans is being used in the manufacture of army tanks, mine sweepers, cargo vessels, army landing boats, defense housing, ship equipment, food, and shipping containers.

Soybeans, soybean oil, and soybean meal, are used for many other purposes, some of which are as follows:

— Soybean flour	— Other food products	— Soap	— Paints
— Lecithin	— Cardboard	— Printers ink	— Linoleum
— Margarine	— Plastics	— Glycerol	

Mississippi farmers are asked to grow 725,000 acres in 1943. This is 54 per cent above the 1942 acreage of soybeans harvested for beans in the state.

Bolivar County's 1943 Goal Is 37,200 Acres

Every farmer is asked to grow as many beans for beans as he can. If additional seed is needed, see your county agent.

WATTIE BISHOP   T. T. WILLIFORD

This message furthering an essential Agricultural crop is published in the interest of Food for Freedom.

PLANT SOY BEANS FOR VICTORY — PUT YOUR FARM IN THE FIGHT

World War II poster on the importance of letter writing
Credit: National Archives

A bunch of our boys have been home lately on leaves (or is it furlough? I never know which is correct to use when!)[29] Corp. "Bunny" Carpenter was here for a week but has now returned to Nashville, where he's connected with headquarters of the 2nd Army. (Three of our colored soldiers, too, reported back to the Quartermaster's Department at Nashville this week after a visit home: Oscar Bridges, Earl Dean, and Willie Williams. It probably makes Bunny feel at home to have them help him!) Wife Dot's brother, Jimmie T. Robinson, is now taking his preflight training at Grove City College, Grove City, Pennsylvania, near Pittsburgh, and loving it. He reports that it's one lovely spot and that the bunch of Southern boys who were sent up from Keesler Field are having a big time up in Yankeeland.

Capt. Rowan and beautiful blonde, Barbara Thomas, were here for a flying visit last week, too, after three delightful weeks on Broadway as the guest of Winston and Company, the publishers who are to bring out Rowan's book, The name of the book is still undecided, the publishers favoring *Born in Battle*, the name of the air squadron to which Rowan was attached so long.[30] Now the Thomases have gone to Dalhart, Texas, where Rowan will get further orders. Nathan House, Cleveland's own artist, did the cover design for the book, by the way.[31] We are all on tiptoe for the advent of the book, which is due off the press in September. Artist Nathan has a big part in this war of ours, too, for he's making pictures which are being used in camp classrooms all over the land. He lives in New York, but just now is down in Florida, studying photographing and drawing an especial new type of big gun, whose operation a new set of boys will soon be studying... Hay fever sufferers can all envy George Turner, for he's stationed up at the "Soo" (Saulte St. Marie), the only place in the United States where that is an unknown disease. George, too, was home last week to tell us of the beauty of the rapids, the bigness

29. Leave is the navy term for authorized absence from duty. Furlough is the equivalent army term. Enlisted personnel were allowed thirty days leave or furlough each year.

30. *Born in Battle*, by Rowan Thomas, was published in 1944 by the John C. Winston Company.

31. Nathan House (1908–1947) was a graduate of Delta State Teachers College and a well-known artist of the 1930s and 1940s.

of Lake Superior, and about his job of helping guard those important locks there. Before the war, it was said that more tonnage passed through the "Soo" than through the Panama and Suez canals combined, and now, as it's doubly important that all that iron ore, coal, and wheat reaches its destination, George has a vital job. He gets his mail at Ft. Brady, Michigan, but is often working on the Canadian side, just a stone's throw away, and wears a ribbon for Canadian service. On steaming hot days like these, I recall with longing how cold I was atop those lochs a few summers ago, and tho' George probably didn't admit it at home, I'm betting he was pretty glad to get back to his pleasant summer resort! . . .

They seem to be cutting down somewhat on the number of boys they're taking into the Army nowadays and sending them home for any little old thing. Looks like the powers that be have decided we don't need eleven million men in uniform. Anyway, only ten of the thirty-seven who went down to Camp Shelby last week were kept. "Sonny" Mann (Skene) was among those accepted, but much to their sorrow, Jerome Hyman, James Garratt, and Erwin Mizze were sent home. Erwin and wife, Alma, have now gone over to Savannah, Georgia. You know Erwin worked there, shipbuilding, for quite a while. His twin, Corp. Erlin, has been in England a year this August and likes it a lot. He says the English people have been wonderfully nice about inviting him for weekends in their homes. Just lately he's been on a leave, and he and a bunch of his friends took an apartment in the south of England and had a delightful time. Erlin's wife, Violet (a Bogalusa, Louisiana girl), is out at our hospital, patriotically nursing in his absence. Brother R.B. (with his wife, Sue Roberts, and baby, Linda) is now stationed at Mission, Texas.

Milton Weinstein (staff officer and senior purser on a brand new Liberty ship) was in England, too, when "Miss Fannie" heard from him the other day.[32] He wrote, "War has played hell with this

32. Liberty ships were specially designed vessels which could carry 10,000 tons of cargo about 8,000 miles at a speed of eleven knots. A later version, called the Victory ship, could carry the same cargo about 12,000 miles at speeds slightly in excess of fifteen knots. The standard designs allowed rapid construction at a wide variety of locations. In total, 2,708 Liberty ships and 414 Victory ships were built. For additional information, see Frederic C. Lane, et. al., *Ships for Victory: A History of Shipbuilding Under the U.S. Maritime Commission in World War II* (Baltimore: Johns Hopkins University Press, 1951).

country and these people have gone thru, and still are going thru, plenty. They talk about a little sugar and coffee rationing at home, but there everything to eat and wear is rationed, a damn little ration, too, but you never hear any complaints. I have met people, wealthy before the war, now living in small places, their homes bombed and their business gone, but they're doing the best they can. They can't do enough for us here. Between different service organizations we could run until our tongues hung out if we wanted to. They even send ladies down to the ship to give us programs. I've seen a lot of things I never expected to see: among them the 'land of the midnight sun' on the way here. We stopped at a place where it is daylight twenty-four hours a day. It got us all mixed up and we'd sit around and talk all night, as none of us were used to going to bed in the daytime." To prove that rationing isn't bothering Uncle Sam's boys, he enclosed a menu of a luncheon at sea on June 13th, a regular Thanksgiving dinner with soup, turkey, and all the regular fixings including cauliflower, asparagus, yams, mashed potatoes, pumpkin pie, and coffee! And this letter ended by saying, "The voyage was a bit rough in weather and other ways too, but I never felt better. Buy some bonds every month, whatever you can afford. It's our duty." . . .

Corp. Lauress Early writes from North Africa that the food is better and the band is playing more, but that they're not sleeping as much, leaving his mother to guess why! He's been moved lately, he reports, tho' from where or to whence he, of course, doesn't say. However, he did mention gorgeous scenery en route, which reminded him of his loved "Blue Ridge Mountains of Virginia" and swimming in the blue Mediterranean, tho' for his part, he avers, he'd swap it for a dip in the Sunflower River. Lauress, you know, went into service with the Millsaps band (he played with them while there in college) and a number of those boys are still together, playing in the 175th Engineers Band "over there." . . . [33]

Owen Roberts is now at Ellington Field, Texas and studying to be a navigator. Military life has agreed with him so much that he's gained thirty-five pounds. Which reminds me to tell you of such an

33. The Sunflower River runs through an eastern section of Bolivar County. Millsaps College is in Jackson, Mississippi.

interesting article I've just read on the "Post-war World" by Owen
Roberts (same name, but this one a justice of the United States
Supreme Court)![34] Said Justice Roberts, "The present war is witness
to the fact that in world crises, begotten by race prejudice, by lust
for national aggrandizement and by selfishness, international law is
powerless and the sentiment of the majority of civilized men insufficent
to deter some nations from flaunting covenants to which they were
party. We have learned that treaties, agreements, and voluntary
submissions of disputes to a world court fall short of reaching the
goal. What other recourse is there? Our own national experience as a
federation of states seems to point to at least one avenue to be
explored. How about a world government, with a representative
assembly, and executive to administer laws, police to see to their
enforcement, and a judiciary to which disputes must be submitted.
When the war ceases, great populations will be without governments, in utter confusion. If, when peace comes, a strong union of
democracies speaks with a united voice, and holds out, even to the
conquered people, opportunity for ultimate entrance into this
Suprastate, a very different picture would be presented! But our
nation will not take her stand for international cooperation unless her
leaders are convinced that it is the will of the people. The man in the
streets is capable of saying whether he wishes his government to
embark upon a daring, but hopeful experiment, in world organization. It would be as unfair as it would be fatal to leave our
representatives in the equivocal position in which President Wilson
stood, after the proposal by him, and acceptance by our Allies, of the
League of Nations. Unless the United States responds promptly, and
vigorously urges such a project, none such will reach treaties, and
we may as well throw up our hands and let the world roll on again
into chaos." This is the sixty-four dollar question: "What do you boys
think about it?"[35] It would be a big undertaking all right, and many
think it wouldn't ever work. But many people also thought, in the

34. Owen Roberts (1875–1955) was associate justice of the United States
Supreme Court from 1930–1945.
35. Sixty-four dollars was the highest amount of money that could be won by
a contestant on a popular quiz radio program, "Double or Nothing." The
program began in 1940 and the phrase "the sixty-four dollar question," became a
catchword for a difficult question.

beginning, that our Articles of Confederation and our Constitution wouldn't stand up, and they have for 150 years. I know you boys all want to preserve this Peace you're working now to attain for the world, so take a bit of time out and think about how you think it can be done!

Here's wishing a peaceful future for this war torn world to each of you.

Sincerely,
Keith Frazier Somerville

July 16, 1943

Dear Boys:

I certainly showed my ignorance, when I asked in a recent letter if any of you had run into a helicopter, didn't I? But honestly, I didn't know, 'till *Life* informed me, that one of Bolivar County's own sons, Col. Frank Gregory (of Shelby and the Engineering Division of the Air Forces Material Command) was one of the two most expert helicopter pilots in the Army, and "the man more responsible than any other military man for its development!"[36] Your mother tells me, Col. Frank, that you are hoping to fly home in one before long, and she's promised me, on the word of honor of a very charming lady, that she'll let me know when you land that amazing invention in your hometown so I can rush up and see it (and you) in action! I am thrilled over the prospect as a child awaiting Santa Claus, and much more excited than I was many, many years ago when I made several treks out to see if that much touted flying machine of the Wright brothers would stay up in the air over the Potomac! Because I know this one will fly, and I was a bit skeptical about that one! (My father at that time was a member of the United States Senate Military Committee which had agreed to buy the machine if it worked. Frankly, they and the House and Army men, too, were all a bit doubtful about it!) So after many days when I went and it didn't fly because of weather conditions, I got disgusted and went to a party

36. Colonel Gregory was featured in "Helicopter: Sikorsky's Flying Windmill Helps Celebrate Air Mail's Anniversary," *Life*, May 31, 1943, p. 28.

the day it finally did make its successful test.[37] Now, I can't even remember who had the party I thought more important than flying in my early youth! Which only goes to prove—well, among other things, that patience is a virtue and that frivolity doesn't pay, for missing that flight has been one of the "regrets" of my life! But I promise you I won't miss seeing you fly a helicopter, even if I have to camp in Shelby for a week! I elected it "my baby," the plane I'd fly in my old age because of an article which said it was "foolproof," but *Life* rather disabused my mind about that when they said that even Igor Sikorsky himself doesn't fly it with any appearance of ease. Nobody does, it appears, except our own Col. Gregory and a Maj. Cooper! And it's very discouraging for me to read that it's far from easy to fly, with its wobbly stick and over-sensitive controls, and that it will take years to perfect it to absolute safety and mass production. But Mother Gregory tells me that our flying colonel is quite sure, as is Sikorsky, that it's the "flivver of the future," so I refuse to give up yet the idea of eventually owning and piloting one! Meanwhile, I got a vacarious thrill out of *Life's* interesting pictures of him at the controls and rescuing sailors at sea. The Gregory brothers entered the regular Army twelve or fifteen years ago and have both been tremendously interested in aviation. Now Col. Frank divides his busy time between Wright Field and Connecticut. (He's a bachelor, too, tho' when I gazed on his "Great Profile," I wondered how he'd escaped some girl laying claim to him!) His brother, Lt. Col. Louis is now stationed at Deming, New Mexico as head of the Bombing school there. (Yes, married to an Oklahoma girl seven or eight years ago!)

My, aren't we proud of our Bolivar County boys! Had you heard that Norman Hardee had gotten the Distinguished Service Cross out in the Pacific? And that Raymond Malaby had received the Oak Leaf Cluster in England?[38] Sgt. Malaby sent wife, Alma, a clipping telling

37. The Wright Brothers, following their successful flight at Kitty Hawk, North Carolina in 1903, demonstrated the capabilities of their aircraft before large audiences of members of Congress and other dignitaries. The young Keith Frazier was a witness to some of the flight exhibitions which occurred along the Potomac River.

38. The Distinguished Service Cross is awarded to any person serving in combat with the Army who has distinguished himself by extraordinary heroism in military operations against the enemy. The Oak Leaf Cluster is awarded by the Army for an act meriting an award identical with one already received.

about him shooting down a German fighter plane, and he's a radio man! Burch Williams, out in India, has added the Oak Leaf Cluster, too, to his string of honors.

I went to Shelby the other day and as I visited around with Joe Shelby (Mrs. George) on lovely shady porches, and in cool, darkened living rooms, I quite forgot, in my interest in hearing news of the boys in the service from there, that the thermometer had climbed to near the 100 degree mark! First, let me tell you that Fred Shelby has come home to join the Crop Corps. After going up the hard way, private, corporal, sergeant, nine months in England where he taught in O.C.S., he was himself sent home to attend O.C..S. at Ft. Benning, Georgia.[39] Then recently, just before getting his commission, he came face to face with an "agricultural emergency" when his father, already in bad health, fell and broke his knee cap.[40] So with Gwin in service and his mother unable to manage the place, there was nothing for him to do but come home and try to save the crop. No, naturally he didn't want to get out, and hopes to return later, but his commanding officer told him it was the only thing for him to do, so "he seen his duty and done it," like the good soldier he is! Fred loved his months in England and made many friends there whose memory he will cherish always; the beautifully mannered young son of a Royal Engineer who called him "Uncle Freddy;" the cultured vicar, his "horsy" daughter and her friend the little Russian princess; the spinster organist of the village church who practically adopted him. Yes, Fred loved England and the English people and really didn't want to leave when Gen. Lee sent him home for O.C.S. He zigzagged across the Atlantic on an unescorted transport, surprised his family by a call from New York some five months ago, arriving home looking hale and hearty. Since then, he's been at Benning, till

39. Among the many Officer Candidate Schools which were established by the Army during World War II, the most well-known and highly respected was the Infantry Training Center at Fort Benning, Georgia. A January 1943 article in *Life* magazine described the thirteen-week training program at Fort Benning as "the largest, most efficient, and most ruthless educational institution in the world" ("Officer Candidate School," *Life*, January 7, 1943, 73-89).

40. Occasionally, military personnel were granted leaves to help with agricultural emergencies at home, or, in some instances, they were discharged for this purpose. In addition, selective service boards sometimes gave agricultural deferments to persons engaged in essential agricultural work.

recently called home. I see where the Memphis *Commercial Appeal* is offering an A flag, similar to the Army and Navy E flag which will be unfurled over many farms next fall, signifying those which have rendered meritorious service in agriculture to the nation in war time, and I'm betting (if he didn't get home too late) that Fred will get one, for he's as good a farmer as he was a soldier![41] These flags are being offered as an extra incentive to farmers to meet the pressing need for more food, feed, and cotton. With their higher quota, mid South farmer-soldiers are faced with many difficulties, but most agree that by combined hard work, the allotments can be reached.

The other Shelby son, Gwinn, after serving at Algiers, Key West, and Seaman's Institute (New York) is now in charge of supplies at the United States Coast Guard Depot in Miami. . . . I got a kick, Gwinn, over your reading one of my letters when you went to have a day with Brooksie Eckles! She was home last week and so enthused over her work, having lately been transferred from Nautilus Hospital (Miami) to be Red Cross Recreational Director at the Pan Coast Hospital. She's met lots of interesting personalities who have come to amuse the wounded men, among them charming, white haired, Mrs. Eddie Rickenbacker.[42]

Four stars hang in the doorway of Mrs. W.W. Denton's Shelby home, and she talked proudly of her four fine sons. Maj. Billy is at Wright Field in Ohio (experimental equipment laboratory) and Laura Alice and the boys are with him, but he doesn't "stay put" for long, as he's always tripping about collecting airplane parts to be tested at Wright Field. Maj. Joe is still out in Texas (Camp Howze) and Marian and their babies are living in nearby Gainesville, on Denton St., by the way! The twins, Davis and Jack, in the Tank Corps, are both at Camp Campbell, Kentucky. Jack got married not long ago to lovely Lola Louise Walton over at Benoit. Florence Ogden, writing in the Rosedale paper said, "The Delta really looks good when it

---

41. The Army/Navy "E," or "excellence," flags were awarded during World War II to businesses and industries which had matched or exceeded their wartime contract specifications. They were sought by firms to indicate their strong support for the war effort.

42. Mrs. Eddie Rickenbacker was the wife of World War I air ace, Captain Eddie Rickenbacker.

goes on dress parade! When Lady Halifax came to Memphis she said she'd never seen so many beautiful women.[43] Well, I just wish she would come down when the Delta pulls off a big wedding! She ain't seen nothing yet!" Judging from the lovely pictures, Jack's must have been something extra-special, even in Delta weddings!

Mercy, here I am back on weddings again! Well, I can't help it if "that old black magic called love" just keeps hoo-doo-ing you boys into doing it, can I?[44] You know I warned you how awful David Cohn said it was, but you go right on doing it!

Now there's Sgt. Pat Philen who up and did it, too, last Thursday up a Camp McCoy, Wisconsin. He married Virginia Streakland, a Wisconsin girl, and Mrs. Philen went up for the big doings, which included a wedding reception and a dance. Pat brought Virginia down on his last leave and Shelby loved her so that he went straight back and married the gal! His brother, Robert Philen, is 1st Class Petty Officer in the Navy, now at Pensacola. He bought one of those licenses last year and married Connie Robinson on one of his trips home! Those Philens are all in there pitching, for Lloyd is now at Camp Carson, Colorado, doing office work in the hospital and is no longer a patient. He was wounded ("a slug in the wrist") in Alaska.

When I first came to Bolivar County ("blows and centuries ago"), there was what they called "the German settlement" out west of Shelby.[45] About fifteen families had sold their Illinois black land and bought equally black Delta land at a much cheaper price. Thru the years some of them moved back and some died, but I thought it interesting to find that the German settlement had provided at least three soldiers to fight with Uncle Sam against Nazi Germany. They are Louis Agner, Jr. and Stanley and Milton Campany, grandsons of the original Agner settlers. Stanley is in the Navy (Millington, Tennessee) and Milton expects to be called up shortly. . . .

Mrs. Katie Harris, herself serving Uncle Sam, is trying to keep the busy telephone lines clear, tells me that her twins are busy, too,

43. Lady Halifax was the wife of Edward Frederick Lindley Wood (1881-1959), 1st earl of Halifax and the British ambassador to the United States from 1941-1946.

44. Mrs. Somerville is quoting the words of a popular World War II song, "That Old Black Magic."

45. Mrs. Somerville came to Bolivar County as a young bride in 1912.

these days. Sgt. Roy is now with the ground Air Force at Dyersburg, Tennessee and sister, Floy, has a state job in Jackson.

Taylor Stone finishes his pre-flight training this month at the Teachers' College, Kutztown, Pennsylvania. His bride (Jean Harris of Duncan) is there with him. James Dixon (Navy) is up at Millington, and his brother, Milton, is now studying mechanical engineering at Westover Field, Massachusetts. "These two sons," says Mrs. Dixon, "are all the children I have, and I'm very proud to be the mother of sons giving their services to their country." That's the spirit I find everywhere, boys. Your mothers, and all the rest of us, are proud of you!

J.T. McDonald is now in Africa with the Quartermaster's Corps, and his wife is in Columbus while he's away. Corp. Alec Belenchia is also in Africa and writes, "I am very glad the Tunisian campaign is over.[46] I had several very close calls, but, with the protection of God, came thru it without a scratch. I know I have lots to be thankful for, after all I've seen." His brother, Paul, is with the 6th Armored Division at Camp Chaffee, Arkansas, and his cousin, Sgt. Jimmie Belenchia is in the Air Corps, Keesler Field. John Orizette is also in Africa, while his brother, Jim, is somewhere out in the Pacific. Lt. Jerry Lillo is also overseas, and Lt. Vincent Rogers, who was in Australia for many months, is now back in this country and, after a visit home, is now at Ft. Sheridan, Illinois. Sgt. Johnnie Rogers is still out in the Pacific. Paul Camponova is down at Camp Shelby and Charles Curcio is at Camp Crowder, Missouri.

Mrs. Cowan, with two sons and sons-in-law in the service, is a busy lady these days. "Boy and Bill" (Mrs. William Russell and thirteen-month old William, Jr.) have just left to join Lt. Russell of the Signal Corps at Asbury Park, New Jersey. Going to a popular resort for the summer sounds like pre-war stuff, doesn't it? But Mary Allen and baby, Julia, are still with her, as "their man," Dr. Hubert Baird, left Norfolk recently for overseas duty. Mrs. Cowan's son, George, was home last week on leave from Camp Campbell, Kentucky, just about the time that "Doc" (James Chilton) left for Emory University, Georgia, for Naval training.

46. The fall of Tunis to the Allies on May 7, 1943 marked the end of the Tunisian campaign.

I found Mrs. Edwin Wilkerson making peach preserves and looking amazingly cool and unruffled! How she did it, and where she located peaches to put up are, I suppose, her own "Military secrets," but she made no secret of her feelings about those grand boys of hers! Tommy, who took advanced military training at Ole Mississippi, is now at Camp Croft, South Carolina. Horace Edwin is now at Camp Livingston, Alexandria, Louisiana, surprisingly in the Ordnance Department when he's just finished a course in the School of Finance at Indianapolis! And Kenneth, having completed primary and secondary ferry command training (Millington) is now awaiting his next orders. Those other Wilkersons, Van and J.K., are still together at the Link Instruction Training School, Furman University, Greenville, South Carolina. They have previously trained together at Moorhead and Georgia Tech. . . .

Well, the name Shelby has been synonymous with patriotism since the days of Col. Issac Shelby of Revolutionary fame, and not only are the sons who bear that historic name, but every son of the beautiful little town of Shelby, living up to the name.[47] Practically all of them are off fighting for America's future. In this one letter I've only scratched the surface of Shelby's sons in the service, but I'll give you more news of others another day. Meanwhile, "may the Lord bless and keep you" is the prayer of your friend,

Sincerely,
Keith Frazier Somerville

July 30, 1943

Dear Boys:

With what excited interest have we heard that thousands of our American boys, with their English and Canadian cousins, are on the island of Sicily, and how proudly, yet fearfully, have we listened hourly for news from there and from Italy.[48] Few spots upon the surface of the globe are more beautiful than Sicily . . .

I doubt if many of our boys there have had time these past days to

47. Colonel Issac Shelby (1750-1826) was the Revolutionary War hero of the Battle of Kings Mountain of 1780.

48. The invasion of the island of Sicily began on July 10, 1943. The island was completely in Allied hands by August 25, 1943.

rhapsodize over the beauty of the isle, or to mull over the archaeo-
logical treasures like the mighty columns of the temple of Juno, and I
doubt, too, if the great amphitheater of Syracuse (cut out of solid
rock) witnessed, even in the days of contests of the gladiators
centuries ago, anything to even compare with what they saw the day
Syracuse fell! And the bombings go on, in Sicily and on the continent, preceded by warnings to the civilian population. One of our
own flyers, Joe Saia of Shaw, brought home one of those warning
leaflets (in Italian) which he himself had dropped in great numbers
over Italy. It read like this: "Harbor Workers and all Workers—In
1940 Mussolini declared war on us. In 1940 Mussolini insisted on
participating in the bombardment of England. In doing so he has
sown the wind, and condemned you to reap the whirlwind. A
tempest of bombs will fall on the harbor, factories, and Italian U-boat
bases. This is a warning of the R.A.F. Evacuate immediately. You are
attacking us over and under the sea. We are going to fight back. In
October, 1942, before we bombed the factories of northern Italy, we
warned you. Today we warn you again that the sea and undersea war
from now on will be fought also in your harbors, your factories, your
U-boat bases, with English and American bombs! Evacuate your
families! Evacuate yourselves! Anyone who remains near a military
objective is in danger of death." And ominously, the warning carried
on both sides a black skull and cross bones. So they can't claim they
didn't know what was coming to them!... Sgt. Joe Saia, a gunner
with 348 official hours of combat flying to his credit, won the Silver
Star, the Distinguished Flying Cross, and the Distinguished Service
Cross for outstanding bravery in North Africa. He was recently back
in Shaw and his stirring adventure would fill a book. In one engagement, his wrist watch was shot off, in another, he literally came in on
a wing and a prayer, for "with two motors gone," part of a wing and
fuselage shot off, "they still carried on" and landed safely![49] Joe went
to Utah City, Utah after his rest in Shaw and thence to Salina,
Kansas, where he is now an instructor.

Shaw has an amazing number of boys already serving overseas. I

---

49. Mrs. Somerville is quoting from a popular song of the period, "Comin' In
On A Wing and A Prayer," supposedly based on the reply of the pilot of a
crippled aircraft in response to the question of how he would land.

was down there the other day and heard of them on every side. Those last heard from in North Africa are probably in Sicily now! Capt. Joe G. Peeler has been in Africa since last December, doing a grand job in a hospital there, dressing wounds and boosting morale. He himself was in the hospital for awhile, but is out now, so his wife told me. She is a sister of Mrs. Bill Kennedy in Cleveland, and, with her two youngsters, is living alone in their attractive Shaw home, not liking it any more than do the other millions of service wives, but like all of them, carrying on bravely. Vera Fields' husband (Dr. Lt. Ivar Ward Gessler) is also in Africa, and Vera is with Dr. and Mrs. Fields in their lovely new home. Her brother, Lt. Mike, was home last week, and having finished his internship at Charity Hospital in New Orleans, left Sunday for duty at Carlisle Barracks, Pennsylvania. James Harvey is in Africa, too, and so, at last report, was V.D. Powell. V.D. is in a "crane division" and my guess is that he'll soon be unloading tanks onto the toe of Italy's boot! Mr. S.P. Powell is justified in being proud of his five boys! Elmer B. has been in the Navy three years, while Robert and Aubrey are both in the Navy now, too. Robert's wife is in Shaw, but Aubrey's wife is doing war work in a factory up at Martin, Tennessee. And brother Charles is working in a shipyard in New Orleans to make sure his four brothers have boats aplenty to go sailing on! In Africa, too, are the two Lamensdorfs, Teddy and his cousin, Rollins. Teddy (Navy) writes the most delightful letters home and his sister, Jeanette Moss, let me read one in which he said he'd just received, all in one day, ten letters from home! In one, Jeanette had enclosed some sticks of chewing gum, for which he thanked her, adding, "now if you could only send me a couple of cold cokes, for we're having our share of hot weather, too"! Teddy's mother, by the way, was Bingred Borodofsky, and came to America at the age of nineteen from Warsaw, which was then a part of Russia. Rather gives point to Russia's claim to Poland after the war, doesn't it? She can still speak Russian, and has been tremendously interested in the great fight the Russians have been putting up. Up to the time the Nazis entered Warsaw, she still heard from her uncles, who were surgeons with a large private hospital there. Teddy's father came from Austria at the age of five! (This wonderful America, "the melting pot" of the world!) "Now," said his sister, "we are proud and happy that our beloved boys can go back and fight to give freedom to the oppressed peoples of the countries from which our parents came!" Lt. Rollins Lamensdorf, with Army Intelligence, wrote of swimming in the Mediterranean, leaving his clothes on the shore, and having them stolen, wallet and all! "I don't mind so much about the money," he reported, "but I had a chocolate bar and they took that too!"

Another Shaw boy of Russian ancestry is Irving B. Rubenstein, whose father came to this country at the age of seven. He is now stationed at the proving grounds, Aberdeen, Maryland, in the Army Ordnance Department. His adorable twin brothers, Louis and Leonard (age five) aren't ready yet to help their Uncle Sam win the war, but give them time and they'll be a big help to him in the years of peace to come!

Not only are "Shavians" (how about that word for inhabitants of Shaw, Mississippi? It's what the admirers of George Bernard Shaw, the erratic, brilliant, English author, call themselves!).[50] Now I'll have to start all over again, for a paragraph beginning like that would never pass censor of the English language! What I started to say was that "Shavians" of Chinese, as well as of Russian descent, are watching with interest the progress of the war in their native land, so Joe Ying Kee tells me, and he is proud indeed of his nephew, Edwin Howe, who is now a sergeant out at Camp Crowder, Missouri. Also at Crowder is Billy Bursed, attending "school there" after finishing his radio course at Mississippi State.

Out in the Pacific fighting area Shaw is well represented, and I'm betting they're all grateful to Felix Sweat, working in an A.P.O. in Seattle, hurrying their home mail to them.[51] Fred Rogers (Navy) is out there somewhere, while his wife, "Boots" Turner, is in Shaw for the duration. Vernon Hammett, a real Marine veteran after many months there, is now in New Zealand, where after escaping showers of Jap[anese] bullets, he has been laid low by his appendix! But he's recovering nicely from his operation and will soon be back in the scrap. Claude Hines Alford, also a Marine, is out there, too, and so is his brother, John Wiggins (Navy). The third Alford brother, Elbert

50. George Bernard Shaw (1856-1950) won the Nobel Prize for Literature in 1925.

51. APO was the abbreviation for Army Post Office and FPO for Fleet Post Office.

R., is soon to be commissioned a 2nd Lieutenant at the Air Base, Miami, Florida. Three of a kind, those Alford boys,—the patriotic kind! In the Pacific, too, for eons, has been Charles Eason Williams (Nettie Helen Litton's husband), a Navy radio man. Gracious, how many of the Litton family are in there fighting for us! Bill is at Barton Field, Florida, Ramon at Ellington Field, Texas, Larry, expecting soon to be stationed near home, over at Camp Campbell, Kentucky, Robert at Pine Camp, New York, and John at Virginia Beach, Virginia! Bolivar County salutes the six fighting Littons!

Now I know you're wondering what's become of those fine Ferris boys. Well, Will D. is a sergeant major at the Herbert Smart Airport, Macon, Georgia, while "Boo" (David) is now giving physical training instruction at Randolph Field, Texas. "Boo", you recall, is Bolivar County's number one baseball player, former Mississippi State star, and "property" of the Boston Red Sox.[52] He's still playing baseball, tho' with the Army now, and his airbase team is leading the league in ballgames won. The Jap[anese] you know, play baseball too, and I read an interesting article the other day in which an American, who was for years the captain of the Shanghai baseball team, which played an annual series with the Japanese team, said, "The Jap[anese] are the greatest baseball fans in the world, so long as their team is winning. But if they have a losing team it's a different story. They always walk out in the seventh inning if they realize defeat is inevitable. So I think they'll crack under pressure. I never knew it to fail." Here's hoping he's right! As the Jap[anese] play baseball and the government frowns on weather talk, the commentators this summer will have to be extra careful about mentioning stands full of palm leaf fans and cold drink vendors, else Japan might deduce that it was ninety-nine in the shade! Remember how easy it was for us sit-by-the-radio-football fans last fall to deduce rain and mud and slippery fields when the ball was fumbled often, even tho' Ted

52. David "Boo" Ferriss was a pitcher for the Boston Red Sox for six years. He joined the Red Sox in 1942, but his baseball career was interrupted when he was drafted. After his military discharge in the spring of 1945, he resumed his baseball career. During the 1946 season, Ferris won twenty-five games and lost only six. He pitched a shutout over the St. Louis Cardinals in the 1946 World Series. In 1960, he returned to Cleveland to become head baseball coach at Delta State University, a position he held for twenty-six years.

Husing and his ilk studiously stayed away from the weather?...[53]

Do you know Victoria Mutzi, out at Shaw's White Palace?[54] Well, you've missed something if you don't, for she's a "raring, tearing beauty" of the pure Castillian type that the famous old Italian masters used for their angels and madonnas. (Cleveland's own David Joseph married her pretty sister, by the way.) Well, Victoria was telling me about some of the thirty-five boys of Italian descent, members of the Christopher Columbus Club, who are serving Uncle Sam. The president of the club, A. Angeli, and Mrs. Costa Spadina, president of the St. Francis Circle of the Catholic church of Shaw, have done a grand job keeping in touch with those boys, and also in helping the Red Cross. The dance they sponsored last winter netted $560 for the Red Cross. Which reminds me to tell you that Geraldine Farrar, the famous Metropolitan singer, herself of Italian descent, has a Red Cross unit in Ridgefield, Connecticut, composed exclusively of women of Italian ancestry.[55] Our good Americans with Italian ancestors are many in Bolivar County and their patriotism is unquestioned. Most of them are several generations removed from the Italy of Mussolini and it is America which is their land and the Delta the home for which they are fighting! Take the Ferretti boys, for instance, another three of a kind! Gay "Gee" is in the southwest Pacific, Tullio in Hawaii, and Lars with the ground Air Force in Texas. Dominic Danna (Air Corps) is at De Ridder, Louisiana, and Nello Gasparini is an M.P. at Ontario, California, while his brother, Bruno, is still at Camp Shelby. Victor Blardnell is in Australia, Romero Bagoli and Louis Durastanti, of the Air Corps, are in Oklahoma City. They're marrying too, in Shaw, same as elsewhere. Darile Cabucci did it on his furlough. His bride is Christine Smith, formerly of Philadelphia, Mississippi, who has been working in Shaw. Pete Kittle and his bride, Helen Fox, are now pleasantly located in Orlando, Florida. Helen went to Delta State, you remember....

53. Ted Husing (1901-1962) was one of the best-known play-by-play sports broadcasters of the prewar period. Husing and other broadcasters were not allowed to describe the weather because knowledge of the weather was thought to be useful to the enemy.

54. Shaw's White Palace was a small cafe located on Highway 61 in Shaw.

55. Geraldine Farrar (1882-1967) was a leading soprano with the Metropolitan Opera in New York City during the early twentieth century.

"From how many different countries and creeds have sprung the people of Shaw," I mused as I wound my way homeward up the highway with its blooming border of cotton. And then I bethought me of an article entitled, "Back Home," ... which had so impressed me that I'd torn it out and saved it. The author had returned to the house of his childhood, and this is what he wrote. "As I walked slowly and let the memories flood back, it seemed to me that my neighborhood was a miracle. Here people came from every corner of Europe, Asia, Africa, the near East, and China, and lived side by side and didn't cut each others' throat. They lived side by side and rubbed shoulders in the streets and wonder of wonders, managed to get along with each other. That is my neighborhood's contribution to history. That is why my country is the greatest country in the world. For there, somehow people of different races and creeds develop a good natured tolerance toward each other instead of a narrow, galling hatred. There was something in the air we breathed that made us feel that maybe the other fellow's beliefs and background were all right, too. Here, boiled down to its essence is what we are fighting for (a way of life the whole world could adopt and profit by), tolerance and faith in the dignity of all people."

Goodbye, dear boys, and may we all live to see the day when the peoples of the countries of the world may live, side by side, in harmony and peace, as do the fortunate people of Shaw, Mississippi!

Sincerely,

Keith Frazier Somerville

August 20, 1943

Dear Boys:

You all have something to live for besides, of course, the day when you'll hear that Hitler and Tojo have faded from the picture, as Mussolini already has done![56] After this war, you'll be veterans, and as such, for the rest of your lives, will have the right to go to the wonderful Army and Navy Hospital at Hot Springs, Arkansas![57] I

56. Hideki Tojo (1884-1948) was the premier of Japan during World War II. Mussolini (1883-1945) was deposed and jailed on July 25, 1943.

57. Hot Springs, Arkansas, is a resort area. Its forty-seven thermal springs were set aside as a public reserve in 1832 and became Hot Springs National Park.

wonder how many of you who are now "seeing America first," prior
to taking a grand tour of foreign lands, have ever seen Arkansas' Spa,
just across the "muddy Mississippi" from home? Or are you, perchance, like the old man in the poem, who lived all his life just
eighteen miles from the French castle of Carcassonne, was always
planning to see it, yet ended his days with the wail, "And I have
ne'er seen Carcasonne!"[58] So many of you are like that about things
close to home. Well, the government hospital at Hot Springs, with
its huge square towers, its massive buildings on a hilltop dominating
the entire valley, looks not unlike a medieval castle. As old age in the
form of neuritis is pursuing me, my family sent me over recently to
take the baths, but I wouldn't advise you (or anyone else) to go
unless you need it badly, for in the wildest stretches of my imagination, I can't imagine anyone going there for fun! To me, the hot baths
(100 to 120 degrees), the steaming vapor, and the room where they
put glazing towels on you and wrap you up in a sheet like a mummy
(ditto, in two supposedly cooler rooms) were all one long torture!
However, if it helps, I'll probably forget my suffering. But, of
course, you are men and strangely enough, most men seem to
like it!

I th't often of you boys as I ran into servicemen everywhere, but I
looked in vain for a familiar face in the uniforms. However, on the
day I left, when I went up to the hospital to leave some magazines
and books, I heard there were some Mississippi men there, home
from the Pacific to have the fever boiled out of them. But none from
Bolivar County. . . .

Since early childhood I've read everything that came my way, and
feeling as I did like a limp and dizzy dishrag, reading was the only
bright spot in my stay at Hot Springs. But I did enjoy two new books
by two of my pet radio friends, Clifton Fadiman and Franklin P.
Adams, those experts on "Information Please" that I've dreamed of
one day being able to "stump"! Both were anthologies, liberally
sprinkled with their compilers' opinions. Fadiman's is called *Reading
I've Liked* and contains 900 pages from books he's reviewed in the

---

58. Carcassonne is a well-preserved medieval city in south central France. It
was the subject of the poem, "Carcassone," by Gustave Nadaud (1820-1893).

past ten years. . . .[59] For years I've tried to hide from the world the fact that the average things that make people laugh (like most jokes, the funnies, and Bob Hope) leave me cold.[60] And I'd definitely decided that I have no sense of humor! Why, last winter when *Life* published a page of pictures of men like Jesse Jones and the English King, laughing uproariously, and gave the jokes which so amused them, I didn't crack a smile, and was I worried![61] Jesse practically "busted a button" over this one—"Man having a manicure, asked manicurist for a date. "You'd better ask my husband," she said. "He's shaving you." Very, very funny? Well, not to me! Then along comes Mr. Fadiman, a man who admits out loud in print that that type of humor leaves him cold, too, and publishes *My Life and Hard Times* by James Thurber, with the preface that he'd howled over it five times and once even tried, unsuccessfully, to read it without a chuckle.[62] I tackled it with misgiving, doubting if I'd laugh. But I did! I howled gleefully through it, and you can't imagine the relief I feel to know that everything in life isn't "real and earnest" to me! Do read it if you run upon it, and try reading it with a straight face!

Fadiman reviewed and printed excerpts from another, which he calls a "disturbing book," *The Managerial Revolution*, by a professor of philosophy named James Burnham.[63] "One should never underestimate professors of philosophy," he warns, "Socrates was one." Briefly, that book announces that the world is now in the grip of an irreversible revolutionary process; that the world of our immediate future will be a world of superstates, three in number (Europe, Asia,

59. Clifton Fadiman (1904-), author of *Reading I've Liked* (New York: Simon and Schuster, 1941), was a popular editor and radio personality. Franklin P. Adams (1881-1960) wrote a column, "The Conning Tower," for the New York *Herald Tribune*, and he also appeared on the radio. Fadiman and Adams, along with Oscar Levant and John Kieran, were regular members on "Information Please," a radio quiz show from 1938-1948. Questions were sent to a panel of experts, and, if they failed to answer them, a set of the *Encyclopedia Britannica* was awarded to the questioner.

60. Bob Hope (1903-) toured all over the world entertaining service personnel during World War II.

61. Jesse Jones (1874-1956) headed the Reconstruction Finance Corporation during the war. The RFC was responsible for lending funds to construct many of the war plants which were built. His memoirs are entitled, *Fifty Million Dollars: My Thirteen Years with the R.F.C.* (New York: Macmillan, 1951).

62. James Thurber (1894-1961) was a main-stay writer for *The New Yorker*. His book, *My Life and Hard Times* (New York: Harper, 1933), was a best seller.

63. *The Managerial Revolution* (New York: John Day, 1941) by James Burnham (1905-1987) was one of the most widely discussed books of its time.

and America) in which the master class will be "managers," with bureaucratic, technical, and military assistants, the final objective of each, world mastery, obtainable by war. We are now, so says the professor, in the first phase of the first managerial war, which will be won by those states which most efficiently substitute managerial techniques for the outmoded democratic capitalist ones. All this Fadiman thinks means the death of the individual, for all will be slaves to the state, and so arts and literature will perish. "I do not admit no alternative," he says, "but I am not so naive as not to see that the system of superstate obtains already overlarge portions of our planet, and is growing. The new Dark Age has begun." From which gloomy outlook we turn with relief to Franklin P. Adams, *Innocent Merriment*, wherein we find one answer anyway, to the oft repeated question, "When will the war end?"

> Actual evidence I have none,
> But my aunt's charwoman's sister's son,
> Heard a policeman, on his beat,
> Say to a housemaid in Downing Street,
> That he had a brother, who had a friend,
> Who knew when the war was going to end![64]

Well, we all agree that the end is indefinite, so Uncle Sam goes strenuously on with his training program up at the Great Lakes Training Station, where on August 20th it will be Ens. Nason Brock. Nason's brother, E.V., is now with the Ferry Command down in Brazil. He finds it an interesting country, but a bit lonesome. "What wouldn't I give," he writes "to be able to walk down the streets of Cleveland to see friends!" Home last week was another of our newly commissioned ensigns, C.P. Brocato, who has been assigned to sea duty and just came home a few days to see the folks and show off that brand new uniform after finishing at Columbia in New York. His brother, Anthony, down at Keesler Field, has recently been assigned to take specialized craftsmanship training in the Air Corps, following a recent perfect score in mathematics.

Also home last week wearing the new wings he acquired at Victorville, California, was Lt. Jimmie Chiles. After a visit home, he has now gone back there to be an instructor.

---

64. Franklin P. Adams, *Innocent Merriment* (New York: McGraw-Hill, 1942).

The Ruscoes are having a regular homecoming for Willis, home from the new Eagle Lake Air Base near Ft. Worth, Texas, which the Navy has recently taken over from the Marines. Willis is a parachute rigger there. Sister Frances is home, also, from Texas. Her husband, W.L. Glenn, is one of the engineers working on the big new Denison Dam, the largest "mud dam" in the world, so I have been told.[65]

Alice Margaret Clark Root gets daily letters from her engineer husband, now working down in Brazil. Capt. Root used to talk of someday settling in South America, but after his long months there, he's decided he prefers life in the U.S.A....

W.A.C. Webb, our own Josephine, having finished her Florida training, is now stationed at the Air Base in Greenwood. She was home last Sunday and looks simply marvelous in her size 16 uniform!

W.A.C. Stamps, now in training at Oglethorpe, Georgia has the unique distinction of being the only D.A.R. regent, so far I can find out, serving Uncle Sam actively. People in past years have made much fun of the Daughters of the American Revolution for talking so long and so often of preparedness, but time has proved us right. Is it not so? Mrs. Stamps, who has taught for many years at Delta State, writes amusingly of the varying degrees of culture she's encountered, but seems very happy and interested in new work.[66] Yet she likes the food too—quite a tribute to Army cookery from a domestic science teacher. Her daughter, Elizabeth, a student at the University of Tennessee this summer, joined her this weekend for a sightseeing trip around my old home town, Chattanooga. Dorothy Shands has arrived in Africa with a Red Cross Club Mobile unit, and is now handing out "Java and Sinkers," (coffee and doughnuts) to the Yanks there. Her sister, Eleanette, with her three sons (the youngest, James, two weeks old) expects to join the "Home-for-the-Duration Club" soon, as her husband, Lt. Hunter Leake (Navy) leaves Friday

65. Huge dams made of earth were constructed throughout the semi-arid west to husband water for irrigation purposes. Denison Dam, located along the Red River on the boundary of Texas and Oklahoma, forms the 225 square-mile reservoir, Lake Texoma. Denison Dam was completed in 1944.

66. DAR is the abbreviation for the Daughters of the American Revolution. Mrs. Somerville was a founding member of the local chapter of the DAR. Elizabeth Coburn Stamps, who served with the WACSs during World War II, taught home economics at Delta State Teachers College for many years. She was a former State Regent of the Mississippi DAR.

for overseas duty. My Keith and Eleanette are changing locales, for Keith and her two little girls left this week to join Joe Rice (Lt. Dockery, Coast Guard) who is at present located in New Orleans.[67]

Lt. Leon Young, recently commissioned at the Army Tech Air Force School at Yale and following a week's leave at home, is stationed at Clovis, New Mexico and is now at Alamogordo, New Mexico. He's full of enthusiasm for his engineering maintenance battalion work. Even the thermometer, which reaches 120 degrees some days, doesn't bother him much, he writes, for because of the altitude and lack of humidity it doesn't seem as hot as Mississippi. . . .

Well, time to sign thirty and say goodbye![68]

Sincerely,

Keith Frazier Somerville

September 3, 1943

Dear Boys:

The cotton is opening in every field; the pickers are dragging their bags; the gins are humming; and the Saturday crowds on our streets are getting bigger and bigger. All of which means to us, and to you, that fall is here. But it's still hot and the "lightening bugs" are out nightly in full force, making the world fairy-like after dusk. Remember how you used to catch 'em and put 'em in bottles so you could watch 'em, when you were a little tyke? Remember, too, how we always qualify our remark, "gosh, it's for the cotton?" I saw some figures the other day, which pointed out that for each man in the service, one cotton worker toils to equip him, so all your Delta friends left behind are working hard these sultry days to see that you are properly fixed up. Last year over seventy percent of the total cotton production went to equip servicemen. Did you know that cotton is used in self-sealing gas tanks of all United States planes, tanks, jeeps, and cars?

Speaking of heat, I saw where up in Memphis (at Millington) last

67. Keith and Joe Dockery's two children were Keith Douglas and Hughla McKay.

68. Thirty or -30- was the telegraphers's code for "the end." As much news was sent back to newspapers by wire, thirty was widely used to indicate the end of a news or feature story.

month, a Naval officer in command decreed that this is the tropics, and ordered his men into shorts for the duration of the heat spell. (I hear you boys don't like shorts—feel undressed without your long pants. How about it?) The *National Geographic* magazine in an article entitled, "Fit to Fight Anywhere," telling of precautions taken to build up soldiers, spoke of the maneuvers in the "deep South," as being held there because conditions are so similar to those in the South Pacific.[69] So maybe we do live in the tropics! I've thought so often this summer when the thermometer was soaring! A Frenchman, asked what he did in the French Revolution, once replied, "I survived."[70] Well, that's what we want you boys to do—survive! So you're being "acclimatized," as you probably well know! The experts were asked how long a soldier retains "acclimatization." Will men retain it long enough to cross the ocean? And their answer is—yes, it lasts three or four weeks. "1943," they say, "sees a vastly different Army from the Rough Riders who died by the thousands in heavy clothes in Florida in the Spanish-American War, or the soldiers in World War I, for everything that science and experience can produce is being used to train, condition, and equip our Army. Out in the Mohave Desert and down in Louisiana the boys are being conditioned to heat, and up in the northwest to cold. Did you know, talking of climates, that the average temperature of Boston, Massachusetts, is lower than it is on Iceland? My, what a lot we're learning about the world during this war!

I understand the proposal to use some of you soldiers to help harvest the crops this fall, owing to labor shortage, is not greeted with rapture in the camps. "Ha," snorted one soldier on the radio, "No, I don't like the idea at all of having to dig the potatoes before I peel them!'..."[71]

---

69. Frederick Simpich, "Fit to Fight Anywhere," *National Geographic,* August 1943, p. 233-256.

70. This remark is generally attributed to the French statesman and diplomat, Charles-Maurice de Talleyrand (1754-1838).

71. Shortages of farm workers in the United States, especially at harvest time, led to the use of some military personnel in agricultural work. In addition, agricultural workers were imported from the Caribbean, Mexico, Canada, and Newfoundland, and, east of the Mississippi River, prisoner of war laborers were assigned to agricultural work. Teenage children also became part of the harvest forces.

I noticed in the Memphis *Commercial Appeal* where a Memphis boy, home from the South Pacific, said all he wanted was to sleep. That seems to go for all you boys, for Robert isn't the first returning hero I've found enjoying the luxury of sleep! The bugler who gets you up in the morning isn't very popular, I imagine, (not even the southern bugler who has jazzed his calls up so successfully that he's being sent on a tour of the camps to teach his technique to others.) Speaking of sleep, did you hear about the mighty snorer out at Fresno, California who was recently discharged from the army because they finally despaired of finding him a sleeping place within bounds and out of earshot? Dames with snoring husbands will just have to make up their minds to put up with them, for Uncle Sam doesn't want them!...

Donald Lewis, who left home twenty years ago at the age of seventeen to join the Navy, is now an ensign and down Panama way. He went up the long, hard way, but I'll wager he knows all there is to know about the Navy now, and is probably quite amused at you new ensigns who get commissioned at training schools in a few months.[72] Maybe he even thinks you're all "wool-gathering" like the Naval-trainee who, 'tis said, was asked on an exam, "Where is the Suwannee River?" and dreamily answered, "Far, far away!" Ens. Lewis has a son of fourteen, who with his mother is now living in Jacksonville, Florida. (Donald married a Pensacola girl when he was stationed there years ago).

Another of "Prior-to-Pearl Harbor" Navy men, Lt. Lorance (good looking Snooks) was home for a few days recently, en route back to the Pacific after helping to man and deliver an aircraft carrier from Pearl Harbor to New York. Soon he'll be sailing on another carrier, his fifth! His four major battle stars attest to the fact that those big boats are right in the thick of it, wherever fighting is. One of the four he's served on has been lost, but the others are still going strong. His brother, Harold, is now with the Amphibian force up in the Aleutians, and brother, Cecil, now at Ft. Sill, is soon to start training as an Air Corps cadet flyer.

Charles Rodgers, too, was serving Uncle Sam before that fateful

72. Young officers who received this concentrated training were often called "ninety-day wonders."

December 7th that made soldiers and sailors of all you boys. As a matter of fact, he was home on furlough when the news came, and his father recalls the intense excitement that prevailed at their house as he phoned his base and was ordered to report back immediately. Now he's stationed up at Little Falls, Minnesota (Camp Ripley) with the ground Air Corps. His nephew, Arthur Glen Rodgers, is now stationed at Ft. Benning, Georgia, with the mechanized cavalry. (He married a Columbus girl, Catherine Clemons.) Mrs. Rodgers' son, J.P. Mason, is serving with a replacement division at Camp Shenango, Greenville, Pennsylvania. And don't you dare, ever again, call him "Baby Mason," for he's a soldier now! . . .

Herman Mullins is an Air Cadet up at Nashville and his wife (Fay Green of Wilson, Arkansas) is with him at present. By the way, his white-haired mother looks exactly like the "mother waiting at the mailbox for a letter from her boy" that Rockwell Kent painted for the back of a not-so-long ago *Post*.[73] To Nashville soon, also, will come Fernie Woods to continue his air pilot training. His bride, Jane Gaines, is expected home for a visit when he leaves North Carolina. . . .

A big blue bus rolled away from our local draft board not long ago, bound for Camp Shelby, and loaded with grinning faces. When I waved and called "goodbye and good luck," one of my "little boys" called back, "I'll send you a card from Tokyo, Mrs. Somerville!" Well, son, I'll be waiting for it, and hoping and praying it will come soon! Someone wrote, "Don't know what Tojo and his war lords are doing to the nerves of the current Emperor, but Hirohito's father was daffy in the last years of his life and had to be removed from the throne."[74] Well, when you boys get to Tokyo, the present ruler will probably go "nutty" too! Wouldn't be surprised if he's getting jittery already! . . .

Sgt. Braskel Naron is now overseas, somewhere east of New York. His last letter from Washington Barracks, Missouri, reported him anxiously awaiting the arrival of the W.A.C.S. to take over his job so he could go to fighting. He wrote, . . . "It makes me feel pretty insignificant to be sitting up here in an office where nothing but

73. Mrs. Somerville is referring to the May 8, 1943, cover of the *Saturday Evening Post*.

74. Hirohito (1901–1989) was the Emperor of Japan during World War II.

Army paperwork is going on and someone else is out there doing the fighting! I guess my time will come though, and when they're ready for me to fight, I'm ready to go. I've enjoyed all the privileges that these United States stand for, and now I am ready to fight for them. The foremost thought in my mind when I say this is the fact that I have as fine a mother and daddy as anybody in the whole world and I hope that in some small way I may be able to measure up to the high standard you have set me." Braskel may not like having his tho'ts and feelings broadcast like this, but it's such a wonderful letter that, with his mother's permission, I just had to publish it! You just can't beat an Army composed of our boys who feel like that! The other Naron son, Lt. Lamar, is assistant engineering officer (Air Corps) at Bear Field, Ft. Wayne, Indiana.

From Africa, Lt. Fred Evans of Boyle wrote his mother, "Say, I bet you can't guess who I saw yesterday! Dorothy Shands! She's been across ten days and is with the Red Cross. We had a drink, a long talk, danced a little, and had a good time. She told me about everybody at home." Lt. Evans is with the Ferry Command (Troop Carrier Division) and his group of fifty-three planes landed the first paratroopers on Sicily. A later letter says he was "in the water four hours when his plane was shot down on a later trip"—but made no mention of being hurt. Yet the War Department notified his family last week that he had been "wounded in action"—so he's probably been a busy lad, seeing lots of flying. We're all hoping we'll hear soon that his wound is not serious.

What do you know about this? Donna McClellan (yes, Snag's little sister) wants to be a Ferry Command woman pilot. . . . Isn't it amazing and wonderful what girls do these days![75] Louise Woodward is leaving soon for Alexandria, Virginia to be a "decoder". All women love secrets and I'm sure Louise can keep Uncle Sam's well!

Lt. Jerry Adams (Dr. "Junior"), who has been stationed at Atlantic City, was home not long ago en route to his new station, Scott Field,

---

75. In 1942, Nancy Harkness Love (1914-   ) organized the Women's Auxiliary Ferrying Squadron (WAFS). When the Women's Airforce Service Pilots (WASPS) was organized by Jacqueline Cochran (1910-1980) later in 1942, the W.A.F.S. was incorporated into it. More than 1,000 women served as ferry command pilots, delivering aircraft and performing other flying duties, during World War II.

Belleville, Illinois. His wife, Corinna Harris of Memphis, accompanied him. They were married several years ago when he was interning up at the John Gaston Hospital.

Remarque, author of a best-seller about World War I, *All Quiet on the Western Front*, says, "I've been a student of history for many years and I've studied military campaigns—Caesar's, Hannibal's, Napoleon's and Hitler's. In each case, humanity was saved by a man's one mistake."[76] Well, they say Tojo's mistake was in not going into India last year, and Hitler's was in going into Russia at all—so maybe it will be true again![77]

So here's to our enemy's mistakes! May we make none of our own!

Sincerely,
Keith Frazier Somerville

September 24, 1943

Dear Boys:

Remember the poem, "My Soul Today/is Far Away,/Sailing the Vesuvian Bay;/ My Winged Boat,/ A Bird Afloat,/ Swings Around the Purple Peaks Remote"?[78] Well, today our "winged-boats" (Flying Fortresses and Liberators) are sailing about the peak of Vesuvius, and certainly all our thoughts, if not our souls, are sailing the Bay of Naples, landing with our reinforcements, and our thought waves of hope, cheer, and pride are with our brave American boys who have been fighting so valiantly in sight of the volcano—Etna first, now Vesuvius, perhaps tomorrow, Fujiyama![79] And just the other day in geography classes those volcanos seemed as far away as Byrd's

---

76. Erich M. Remarque (1898-1970), *All Quiet on the Western Front* (Boston: Little, Brown, and Co., 1929).

77. The German invasion of the Soviet Union began on June 22, 1941.

78. This is the first verse of the poem, "Drifting," by Thomas Buchanen Read (1822-1872).

79. The Allied invasion of Italy began south of the Bay of Naples, at Salerno, on September 9, 1943. Allied troops entered Naples on October 1, 1943, after fighting off very heavy Axis counterattacks. Allied troops also landed behind Axis lines at Anzio, a small port on the west coast of Italy about twenty miles from Rome, on January 22, 1944. The Allies did not break out of the Anzio beachhead until May 23, 1944. Rome fell on June 5, 1944. This secured southern Italy to the Allies.

expeditions to the South Pole.[80] Now, two of them at least, are American history! Pictures of the 5th American Army, with tents pitched among the ruins of Salerno, bring the ancient history of your school days up to date, too! Salerno eons ago was a Greek settlement, regarded as the greatest medieval educational center in Italy. Greek and Roman nobles walked under the twenty-eight mammoth columns of the great Cathedral of St. Matthew, where today American soldiers are encamped and where only last week German troops streamed past. Disdainfully, that great pile must have looked upon the avenging Nazi, as filled with anger against the Italians for deserting them, they attempted to destroy the town before leaving. They were able to ruin food, medical supplies, water, and transportation systems, but in their hurried retreat before General Clark's army, they hadn't time to demolish the Cathedral.[81] Surprisingly, the Nazis were even in too big a hurry to take the money out of the banks! Terrible oversight! . . .

I saw a picture the other day of an American soldier hugging an old grandmother he'd never seen before in Sicily, and I expect there'll be many a family reunion in Italy.

From much-bombed and beautiful Naples came the father of one of our Bolivar County boys, Sgt. Frank Lillo of Shaw. Frank, when last heard from, was at the Replacement Center, Ft. Bragg, North Carolina. Perhaps by now he's on his way to visit his grandparents' home and incidentally to take a few shots at the Germans, as he's reputed to be a fine marksman. Doubtless many of you boys will thrill to the idea of fighting for the homes of your ancestors, as well as to preserve the sanctity of your own homes in Mississippi.

Recently, I spent a wonderful day in "Sunny Italy" right here in Bolivar County. Visiting about among the people of Italian descent who live around here, I was offered the Italian hospitality, unrivalled anywhere. I gazed into sparkling black and deep brown eyes; was shown a marvelous accordion, inlaid with mother-of-pearl, and reminiscent of the street singers of Naples; given flowers and food and

80. Admiral Richard E. Byrd (1888-1957), the Polar explorer, was famous for his intrepid efforts to study the climate of Antarctica and glacial movements.
81. General Mark Wayne Clark (1896-1984) commanded the Allied forces during the hard-fought, but ultimately successful, Italian campaign against the Axis powers in 1943-1944.

receipts; and, above all, provided with much news about some of you boys now serving Uncle Sam. The ancestors of many of you boys of Italian descent, I find, came from Ancona, in the province of the Marches, halfway up the boot of Italy on the Adriatic Sea. I've wondered if their nearness to the tiny, free republic of San Marino inspired them to seek their fortunes in our "land of the free.". . . "The parents of Corp. Lee J. Mei (85th Air Squadron) came from Ancona, and Lee is probably in Italy right now as he has already served both in Africa and Sicily. He married a cute little Russian girl from Detroit, who is living and working there in his absence. Such delightful letters he has sent home from his foreign service and how they are prized! (I was privileged to read some of them.) From Africa, many moons ago, he wrote, "I've been to Alexandria on leave. Got a fine room in a hotel, but I rolled and tossed all night, trying to get to sleep in a soft bed! Which only goes to prove, you can get used to anything! It's not bad out here; good food, but one gets fed up with the same old life. I like change. (Well, Lee, you've probably had plenty of change by now!). . . There's nothing like having lots of kinfolks and knowing they are thinking about you. We can all be thankful that 1943 looks better for us than for the Axis. This is our year to dish back some of their own medicine to them, 'cause only through Victory can lasting peace come, and we can come home and actually sit back and enjoy life like we used to." A later letter from Sicily reports, "Our squadron insignia is 'Flying Skull,' a gruesome emblem, but we're rather proud of it. If Jerry sinks the boat with my American cigarettes on it, he'll never hear the last of it, but better my package than some of our boys."[82] Lee spent last Christmas in the desert and wrote interestingly of midnight Mass in the desert, the altar the back of a G.I. truck, and confession heard in the cab. "It was a beautiful night," he wrote, "with a full moon. Only one candle was burning, because of the black out. It opened with all of us boys singing 'Silent Night,' and it was hard to fight back a lump in our throats 'cause each of us was thinking of our folks back home. If ever a time when memories come back, it's on an occasion like that. They're really fresh in our minds then." (Here's hoping, Lee, that you may hear Christmas mass this year in the Vatican!) Lee

---

82. German troops were often referred to as "Jerry."

and five other Mississippi boys have been together since leaving Chanute Field, and he says they spend their spare time debating the price of cotton in the Delta and talking about how nice the girls in Buffalo were to them, adding, "after this is all over, the places we've visited and the wonderful things we've seen will be worth all this trouble." Which is a marvelous way to look at war, isn't it? Lee has a cousin, same age, whose people also come from Ancona, who is also "over there." . . .

The Sunday afternoon after my visit to our own "Sunny Italy," I had a visit from another Italian friend, Renato Casselli, from Nitta Yuma, Mississippi who was best man when my Keith married Joe Dockery (now Lt. in Coast Guard.). . . Just before Italy and the United States got into war, General Casselli, who had served in the Italian army all his life, was retired. Whether he was called back into service, as so many in our country were, his son does not know, for he has heard nothing from any of his family since war began. The husband of one of his sisters is also a colonel in the Italian army, and Renato, himself, served his compulsory year and a half in the Army before coming to Mississippi. Needless to say, he, like all Americans of Italian descent, is watching with breathless interest, developments in Italy today. We're all confident that you American boys who are there today are competent, with the help of your English allies, to take care of the situation. Our prayers are with you.

One more thing before I say goodbye. Don't worry about your families at home. They're all fine and terribly proud of you. And all hoping that in the happy days to come when war is no more, that Italy and the United States may ever afterwards live in peace and friendship.

God bless and keep you all.

Sincerely,
Keith Frazier Somerville

October 22, 1943

Dear Boys:

Has anyone written you about Cleveland's latest excitement? It's that we have a U.S.O. at the Legion Hut for the soldiers watching guard over the thousand Italian prisoners who are picking cotton hereabouts. What the status of those prisoners is, now that Italy, ... after her unconditional surrender, has gotten into the war on our side, nobody seems to know exactly.[83] I was told that the day after Italy declared war against Germany, a request appeared on the bulletin board at the camp here that the letters "W.P." (war prisoner) that they wear on their backs be changed to "N.A." (new ally). "N. A. or nothing," asserted the Italians! Father Rotundo, who has been holding mass for them in Italian, tells me that a number of the men here are college graduates from the Universities of Florence and Milan, and that they feel badly to think Americans consider them cowards who surrendered too easily. Also he gathered from conversations with some of the men that the majority did not like Mussolini, hated Hitler and the Germans, and, if given a say, would vote to go back and fight with us against the Nazis.

Anyway, the boys guarding these men are living in tents out east of town. There are several hundred of them under Maj. Bill Schmitt, former Clarksdale lawyer, and they all seem enthusiastic over the "hut." I've been up several nights hostessing and it seems odd to see soldiers swarming all over the place, playing Ping-Pong, reading, writing letters, and listening to the radio.... Most of them seem to be from Pennsylvania, Connecticut, Massachusetts, and New York, and some tell me they've been in as many as four southern camps, and this is the first place they've really met and talked to any Southerners. We admit ours can't equal the Stage Door Canteen in New York, which served over 500,000 men in uniform last year and boasts Grace Moore, Tallulah Bankhead, Marlene Dietrich, and Helen Hayes as hostesses, but we think General Chairman Helen

---

83. On December 31, 1943, the *Bolivar Commercial* headlined an article, "War Prisoners Do Good Job in Picking Cotton." The article reported that there were approximately 5,000 prisoners of war in five Delta counties. For further information, see the "Heritage" section of the centennial edition of the *Bolivar Commercial*, June 27, 1986. Also useful is Merrill R. Pritchett and William L. Shea, "The Enemy in Mississippi (1943-1946)," *Journal of Mississippi History*, 41 (November 1979): 351-371. As the Allied forces were approaching Salerno in the late summer of 1943, the news was broadcast that, as of September 1, 1943, the Italian government had agreed to surrender, effective September 8, 1943. The premature news of the surrender meant that the Allied landings, which began September 9, were known beforehand. Stiff German resistance resulted in heavy Allied casualties. The remnant Italian forces joined the Allies as cobelligerents.

Levingston and Lola Bell Eustis (assisted by the whole town) have
done a bang-up job.[84] Mrs. Bolling at the piano, playing old favorites
last Sunday night while a bunch of boys sang, made a home-like
picture. After all, there are times when a mother is just as welcome
as a glamor gal! (Brother Bolling says since Dick's in the service,
Mrs. B. mothers every soldier-boy she sees, and they certainly
seemed to like it.) I, myself, especially enjoyed two very attractive
young soldiers, just over eighteen, both of whom had graduated from
high schools only last June: John Beavers from Washington, D.C.
High and Anthony Pikulsky from one in New Salem, Pennsylvania.
Anthony's parents both came to America from Warsaw, so of course
he was excited when we heard over the radio how close the Russians
were to the Polish border, and that the fall of Kiev seems imminent.[85]
Kiev, you remember, is the capitol of the Soviet Ukraine. Hitler, in
1930 said: "If the unending cornfields of the Ukraine lay within
Germany, under National Socialist leadership, our country would
swim in plenty." It looked for awhile last year as though he would get
it, but inch by inch the brave Russians have pushed him back, 'till
now they are said to be about to retake Kiev. Maurice Hindus
(author of *Mother Russia* and *Russia by Japan*—both fascinating and
enlightening books) described the Kiev he knew as a city of hills,
gardens, trees, flowers, historic museums, and old churches, "one of
the world's most beautiful cities, representing the height of Russian
culture, abounding in charm and gaiety."[86] They could have declared
it an open city, like Paris, and saved it, yet the Russians "forgot
history, sentiment, beauty, art, investments, and remembered only
to hate the enemy and so destroyed all their age-old treasures with
their own hands." It must take an especial kind of courage to destroy

84. The Stage Door Canteen was a famous, celebrity-run USO facility in New
York City. Its hostesses included singers and movies stars such as Grace Moore
(1901-1947), Tallulah Bankhead (1903-1968), Marlene Dietrich (1901-), and Helen
Hayes (1900-). Another celebrity-run USO was the Hollywood Canteen. A somewhat similar facility in Piccadilly Circus in England was called Rainbow Corner.
   85. Advancing Russian armies retook Kiev on November 6, 1943.
   86. Maurice Hindus (1891-1969) was a Russian-born authority on Soviet affairs
who immigrated to the United States in 1905. He wrote numerous books on
Russia including *Mother Russia* (Garden City, New York: Doubleday, Doran and
Co., 1943) and *Russia and America* (Garden City, New York: Doubleday, Doran
and Co., 1942).

one's treasure and the work of one's hands as the Russians have done everywhere. I'm just back from a visit with my daughter, Ashton, who lives up at Norris Dam (Dneiper Dam was built, with the aid of American engineers, much like Norris), and as I looked on that huge structure, representing so many years of work, so much money, and such great industrial activity, I could not help but shudder as I thought how the T.V.A. would hate to have to destroy their work if an enemy threatened it.[87] Would we do it as thoroughly as Russia did, I wondered?

A lot of our boys have been home lately on leaves. Lt. E.V. Brock (Army Air Transport Command), after many months in South America where his work was supervising airfields and seeing that transport planes to Africa got thru with speed, was recently sent to New York for an intensive three week course in "special service study." After a visit home, he returned to South America to travel about disseminating the knowledge he acquired in New York. E.V. tells me he's picked up a lot of Portuguese, that they have classes in it there for the soldiers, and that he's a strong advocate of language study for all soldiers who are to serve in foreign lands. He has gained in weight, looks wonderful, and tells interesting stories of life in Latin America and about noted personages he met when they stopped over en route to the Mediterranean battle areas. Lt. Bob James (Shelby) of the Air Corps is also home this week from Wright Field, Dayton, Ohio, looking smiling and fit. . . .

Our young people keep on with this marrying business. Bobbie Wall, of the F.B.I., made a hurried trip to Memphis not long ago and married Joyce Hoffman, who graduated in his class at "Ole Miss" where the romance began years ago. They are in Washington for the present. And Burch Williams, back in the states after almost two years in India and China, holder of a string of air decorations, has

87. Norris Dam, completed in 1936, was the first major dam to be built by the Tennessee Valley Authority (TVA), on the Clinch River in eastern Tennessee, near Knoxville. It provides power, flood control, and recreation for the area. The dam is named for Senator George W. Norris (1861-1944) of Nebraska, who cosponsored the act that established TVA. The giant Dnieper Dam, thirty-seven miles south of the very large industrial complex of Dnieperpretrovsk, was heavily damaged by the Russians in their "scorched earth" policy practiced during the retreat before the Germans. The area was reconquered in November 1943.

also taken unto himself a wife, Margery Maxim of Scarsdale, New York, a friend of sister, Betty. The town was charmed with her when they came by, en route to Lt. Burch's new station as instructor at Orlando, Florida.

And the new babes are still holding the spotlight. The arrival of Pamela Ann Smith (daughter of Capt. and Mrs. Milton Smith, Elgin Field, Florida) makes a grandmother of Mrs. Emma Smith. Delia Liddell Hallam, daughter of Lt. and Mrs. Louis Hallam, has two grandmothers here to ooh and ah over her and try to console mother, Delia, for the fact that Louis, out on the West Coast, hasn't yet laid eyes on the beautiful babe. But at the hospital, Mrs. G.N. Chanaca (she was one of the Strawbridge girls from Skene) is mighty glad that her husband is no farther away than the Greenville Air Base and can get up to see his very young son. . . .

Guess what? Lt. Bobbie Jackson and Dorothy Shands went swimming together recently at Palermo, Sicily! That's a long way off for two Bolivar County friends to get together, isn't it? The New York *Times* carried a picture recently of an erst-while swanky winter resort club, just outside Palermo, which has been taken over by the Red Cross, so their two mothers deduce that it was there that Bobbie and Dorothy were in the swim together.

Bill Lowry and his wife, Myrtle Lindsey, are back in Cleveland and nicely settled in an apartment on Victoria Street. Billy, you recall, was in the Navy for years and was one of the first of our boys to be wounded in action. He looks fine, but Uncle Sam has decided that his bad arm makes him unfit for further service, so he is being welcomed home by his many friends.

I hear that G. Feretti (Shaw) is home, too, having also been discharged for physical disability. Curtis Poe is now in a hospital at Miami Beach. He's only been in service a short time and its tough luck he got laid up so soon. B. Gordon, from out west of Shaw, is in a New York Hospital, having been wounded in Sicily. And the War Department reports young Ed Hill has been wounded in action. From someplace in Sicily, Lt. Fred Evans (Air Corps, Boyle) casually wrote his mother, "I got decorated yesterday—got the Air Medal and the Purple Heart. The colonel presented them to me and about forty other boys—some enlisted and some officers. Had a good time at the rest camp and wish I could have stayed a bit longer but we gotta win this war and can't be staying in Mountain Camps."[88] It distresses us all terribly to hear that any of you need hospitalization, but we do know that Uncle Sam is providing the best America can produce in the way of medical attention for his nephews. I have but lately seen the mammoth new Woodrow Wilson Hospital at Staunton, Virginia, which literally covers miles and is said to be the most up-to-date in the land. And I talked at length to Dr. Elkins, head surgeon of the wonderful hospital now housed in the big hotel, the Greenbrier, at White Sulphur Springs, West Virginia. Before the war, the Greenbrier was considered the most beautiful resort hotel in America (most expensive, too). Now it holds 3000 wounded, and a beautiful place it is to get well in, let me tell you. The huge lobby, with its sinky-in couches, easy chairs, rugs, and lovely hanging is unchanged, and I understand that the rooms are unchanged, too, not even the draperies taken down, except in operating rooms. The doctor personnel there, as elsewhere, is the finest the United States can offer, and we'll match our doctors, like our soldiers, against the best the world can offer!

Have you noticed the wondrous Hunter's Moon lately? Its been simply beautiful here..... Not so many hunters this year, the papers tell us too many of you boys are out hunting big game this fall! But wherever it is shining down on you, I know you're remembering other moons in other places. "Moonlight and Roses", Moonlight and Romance—maybe even the nursery rhyme assertion that the moon is made of green cheese (why green, do you suppose?).[89] And the way Delta dance bands used to beat out "Harvest Moon, For Me and My Gal."[90] Across the world or here at home it's the same old moon. Which makes the world seem a smaller place, doesn't it?

Goodbye and good luck to each of you.

Sincerely,

Keith Frazier Somerville

88. The United States established several rest and rehabilitation "Mountain Camps" in northern Italy and Switzerland. They were frequently used by aircrew personnel who had completed their quota of missions.

89. "Moonlight and Roses" was a popular pre-World War II love song sung by Betty Grable (1916-1973) in the 1940 film, *Tin Pan Alley*.

90. "Shine On Harvest Moon" was a famous vaudeville song introduced by Nora Bayes (1880-1928) in the "Follies of 1908."

November 12, 1943

Dear Boys:

For the first time in forty-eight years there is not a football team at "Ole Miss," so this year there'll be no Ole Miss-State game for us to get all "het-up" over at Thanksgiving![91] But there's a war on, and someone (I forget who) once said that "war is an age old game whose rules never change but whose implements get better." It takes perfect timing for our sky warfare teams, and only perfect teamwork between all the service branches landed our troops safely on the beachheads of Africa, Sicily, Italy, and the Pacific islands. So those past days of playing and watching football were useful, for they taught vividly those lessons of teamwork and timing. Practically all of the famous [Mississippi] State-Ole Miss football stars of recent years are now, like you, in the service. For instance, to name but a few, Merle Hapes of Ole Miss, who used to thrill us with his running, is now flying for Uncle Sam, and the Poole brothers are Marines, out in the Pacific, . . . [and] are in there running interference, blocking and tackling the enemy![92]

From the way things look now, the score this year, with Ole Miss and State and all the other colleges pitted against our enemies, will not be a tie.

91. Following the entry of the United States into the war, many colleges curtailed sporting activities, especially as the male population dwindled. The wartime ban on nonessential travel made it difficult for persons to attend sporting events. However, President Roosevelt noted that sporting events were good for the morale of the country. Professional sports continued on a somewhat limited basis, and substantial funds for the war were raised at games. Many athletes played on military teams. For an interview with Hank Soar, a tailback and safety for the New York Football Giants, which includes important commentary on the status of professional sports during World War II, see Bill Parrillo, "'A kind of chill came over everything,'" Providence *Journal*, January 17, 1991. It should be remembered, however, that sporting events were less important in the lives of Americans during the 1940s than they are today.

92. Merle Hapes played football for the New York Giants in 1942, and, following his wartime service, in 1946. The four Poole brothers were excellent football players. Barney played for the New York Yanks from 1949 until 1951; the Dallas Texans in 1952; the Baltimore Colts in 1953; and, the New York Giants in 1954. James played for the Giants from 1937 until 1941. Following his wartime service, he played for the Chicago Cardinals in 1945, ending his career with the Giants in 1946. Oliver played for the New York Yanks in 1947, the Baltimore Colts in 1948, and the Detroit Lions in 1948. Ray played for the Giants from 1947 until 1952.

I was all pepped up one day last week to have a call from Lt. D.M. Fleming, home for a few days en route to Purdue University, Lafayette, Indiana where is is to study engineering. "Seems funny to be going back to school again," said D.M. "but one doesn't question Army orders." His wife, Margaret, and baby daughter were here with him for several days.

I glimpsed Lt. Lee Catchings and Joy Somerville dating one night last week; he, en route for four months training at Ft. Benning, following his long months in the west, and she, leaving next day to "catch a flight" in Jackson and back to her airline hostessing (Chicago and Southern) which she finds fascinating. Her dad (Maj. A.D.) was here, too, from Camp Robinson, Arkansas. "Son Doug," said Abe, "now outranks me, for he's a Captain in the Merchant Marines."[93]

Speaking of that service branch, Milton Weinstein, all brown and hardened, has been home, delighting "Miss Fannie" and all his friends with interesting stories of his many voyages. He left Sunday to join his ship in New York. Chunky Clay, a Merchant Marine cadet, is now doing his sea duty but expects to be back in New York at his studies again by February. He'll probably be sent to the "Annapolis of the Merchant Marines" at Kings Point, Long Island which was recently dedicated. It was built and equipped in record breaking time (begun in 1942); cost almost seven million dollars and now houses 2,607 cadet-midshipmen. Commander Hugh Andrews reports that the spirit of his corps is marvelous! Little things like submarine attacks don't effect the morale of those youngsters! Tom Kimbrough, who previously trained there, expects to return to Kings Point, too, when his months of sea duty are finished. Not long ago he had a bone shattered by a piece of flying shrapnel in North Africa and was in a hospital for awhile, but is back with his ship now, tho' he admits his knee still troubles him at times. Sister "Doll" is still with the Navy Department in Washington and La Frances is in Seattle with her husband, Capt. Charles L. Abernathy (Coast Guard). He was formerly a resident of Dumas, Arkansas, and his mother hasn't seen him for three years, so she is rejoicing with Mrs. Kimbrough over the prospect of a visit from them around December 1st. How

93. Merchant Marine personnel were not part of the regular military service. A captain in the Merchant Marine was the commanding officer of his vessel.

those two grandmothers will enjoy little six month old Elizabeth Ann on her first trip to the South!...

The first of our drafted fathers are back in town for twenty-one days before reporting for duty back to Camp Shelby. Fred Roberts is enjoying Eunice and his three "chillun," hating the thought of leaving them, yet happy, too, to get in. "I'd hate to think I wasn't physically able to pass," he told me the day he left for Camp Shelby. I'll tell you of others who are now in, another time.

Lt. Paul R. Magee, former head of the music department at D.S.T.C., is now personnel adjunct in a war prison camp in Italy.[94] Here in Cleveland we're all hoping you're out of the hospital by the time this reaches you, Lt. Paul, but here's some musical notes to mull over during your convalescence, if you're not yet fit. According to a poll, the five best selling (hence most popular) songs in America today are "The White Cliffs of Dover," "Praise the Lord and Pass the Ammunition," "There's a Star Spangled Banner Waving Somewhere," "When the Lights Go On Again,"and the "Army Air Corps." From the number of times I hear them, I'd add the "Marine Corps Song" and "Coming In On a Wing and a Prayer." Also Japan, discovering an American fifth column in their midst, has banned American music, fearing that Jap[anese] boys and girls dancing to "Mr. Five by Five," might become contaminated, perhaps! Isn't that silly! We, ourselves, banned German operas in World War I, but we seem to have more sense in this war, and neither we nor England have done it this time, realizing sensibly that music, a universal language, is in no way responsible for the chaotic state of the world. We certainly know that their authors, long since dead, had nothing to do with the Nazi regime. Maybe that's the way Japan figures, too, for I understand that two songs escaped the "no United States music ban"—"The Last Rose of Summer" and "Home Sweet Home." Noel Coward's latest song, "Let's Not Be Beastly to the Germans", they say, has Britons seething with wrath and writing indignant letters to the London

---

94. DSTC is the abbreviation for Delta State Teachers College, now Delta State University, in Cleveland, Mississippi.

Times.[95] I can well imagine that after all they've endured, it might well strike a discordant note with them! And did you hear the command performance (broadcast to overseas troops) which Bob Hope closed by saying that if the boys wanted Ginnie Sims to purr another number, "just tear off the top of a Zero and send it in"?[96] Well, Air Corps boys out in the Pacific took it literally and sent her a hunk of a wing with the Rising Sun on it! Which I should class as A1 applause!...

Douglas Levingston visited home a bit, ... last week but has now returned to Ft. Benning. His new title is Lt. Levingston, for he received his commission at Benning last month. And by the way, I have a new title, too (I and all the other non-military housewives here about who neither rivet nor weld but remain behind to keep the home fires burning! We are to be called W.I.N.K.S.—"Winks" Echols Eustes no longer has the only claim to the name Women In Numerous Kitchens! tho' I admit her priority claim!

Lt. J.D. Stephens (M.P.) is now somewhere in England and no doubt still collecting beautiful girls with his contagious grin! Wonder if he greets them, "Hi, yah, babe?" I see where the booklet gotten out so the English people may better understand you Yanks tells them that that greeting is equivalent to saying "Lovely day!" Well, maybe the boys from Brooklyn may greet the gals that way, but I'll wager J.D. will have a more subtle approach! Anyway, I don't think our Southern boys use that expression. Or do you? (It's been so painfully long since I was whistled at, that I wouldn't be knowing!)

Speaking of England, did you see the model form (written by men of the 8th United States Air Force over there) for Dr. Goebbels to use?[97] "Just copy and use this daily, Dr. G., and it will relieve you of the burden of writing a daily communique—'large formations of huge American bombers attempted to penetrate Western Germany today, but were driven off by hordes of our brave fighter pilots. One of our fighters was lost. One of our cities is missing!'"...

95. The English songwriter, Noel Coward (1899-1973), wrote "Let's Not Be Beastly to the Germans," in an effort to lighten spirits in England. However, in some instances, the song brought forth the negative response mentioned by Mrs. Somerville.

96. Zero was the nickname given to the Japanese fighter airplane. Radio shows for children often gave small prizes to those persons who sent in a box top from the product that sponsored the program.

97. Joseph Goebbels (1897-1945) was the minister of propaganda for the German Third Reich under Adolf Hitler.

Quenton Reynolds, author of *Only the Stars are Neutral* (which I consider the best of the war correspondent's books) and the latest correspondent to join the ranks of radio commentators, tells of returning lately from Moscow by way of Sicily and enjoying a reunion with Gen. Montgomery.[98] "Tell me," said the General, "is it true that girls in New York are wearing berets like mine?" We can assure the General that not only in New York, but also in Mississippi, his berets are stylish, tho' we must admit that our girls go bareheaded oftenest. I did see that lovely Re Thweatt with a hat on the day of the D.A.R. Blood Plasma Drive, but it wasn't a beret. She was radiantly beautiful, but whether because she'd just sold almost enough tags to buy a whole pint of blood or because of the lovely corsage and sparkling diamond she was wearing, I'd hesitate to say! The ring, which presages the loss to Cleveland of another of our pet girls, came from Capt. Roger Lambright (Air Corps), formerly of Brookhaven, Mississippi, lately of the Greenville Air Base, and now stationed at Smyrna, Tennessee. . . . In passing, did you know we have no blood banks in Mississippi? Uncle Sam and the Red Cross have decided we all have malaria, dormant or otherwise, so they will have nary a drop of our blood! But our drive to contribute to the work in other states went over in a big way, thanks to the untiring efforts of Mrs. Parker West, chairman.[99]

Goodnight and best of luck.

Sincerely,
Keith Frazier Somerville

98. Quentin Reynolds (1902-1965) was one of the most famous journalists of the Second World War. He had a knack for turning his war correspondent activities into entertaining books. Many of his pieces also appeared in *Collier's Magazine*. *Only the Stars Are Neutral* (New York: Random House, 1942) was just one of his best sellers. His memoir, *By Quentin Reynolds* (New York: McGraw Hill, 1963) contains a significant examination of how the Allied peoples perceived World War II. Field Marshal Bernard L. Montgomery (1887-1976) led the British 8th Army in North Africa. Under the command of General Dwight D. Eisenhower (1890-1969), he also conducted the Normandy invasion of June 6, 1944.

99. Malaria is caused by a parasite carried by mosquitoes to a human host. The disease attacks red blood cells and frequently remains dormant in the host's blood cells. For this reason, human blood with the potential of causing malaria could not be used in blood transfusions during World War II. There were no blood drives in Mississippi during the war because of fears of a malarial outbreak. However, Mississippians often held tag days to raise funds to sustain blood drives in other areas of the nation.

Dear Boys:

Someone has written that Americans, more than any other people, love success stories and are hero worshippers; that we "thrill to brilliant deeds of boys from small towns and small jobs which remind us that heroes are made of the same stuff we are." Perhaps he's right, for the evergrowing list of Bolivar County boys who have been found courageous, outstanding heroes, certainly does give each of us a thrill. Just lately there's been Eph McLean (Commander in the Navy) who received the Navy Cross with a presidential citation;[100] Bill Litton (Maj. in the Air Corps) who is credited with shooting down three Nazi planes in a raid over Yugoslavia; and Ed Hill (Paratrooper) who was given the Silver Star in Sicily.

Lauress Early has sent home from Sicily a wonderful collection of coins and paper money, including some of the allied occupation money now issued to our overseas troops. I hope the occupied countries realize that that money is not like the worthless "Occupation Marks" the Nazis have strewn over Europe, but is backed by most of the world's gold, safely packed away in Fort Knox.

Out near Skene last week the Harrison family had a reunion, the occasion being the desires of them all to see Gordon (Medical Corps) home on leave. So from up in Indiana came brothers, J.M. and E.W., with their wives and children, and over from Drew came Cledith (Mrs. J.W. Abels), and they had a wonderful time, and so that they'll always remember it, they had a marvelous family group picture made.

There was a happy family group gathered at the Beavers, too. Truman (Navy Fireman 3rd Class) was home from the Great Lakes Training Camp, having finished his basic and been chosen one of the two in his class to attend Service School. Tech. Sgt. Clarence, too, was home from Moody Field in Valdosta, Georgia, to tell the family all about beauteous Bernice Jacobs of Valdosta, Georgia, who has consented to marry him in the near future. Elaine was home from Camp McCain, Mississippi and Sybil and baby Larry arrived to be here for the duration, for her husband, L.E. Tyer, Jr., reported to

---

100. The Navy Cross is awarded to navy personnel who have shown extraordinary heroism in combat operations against an armed enemy.

Shelby last week for induction. Needless to say, their happiness in being together was tinged with sadness, for their thoughts were often of Tech. Sgt. Dennis, now serving with the Signal Corps in Italy, and of Brother Earl who gave his life for his country in Africa many months ago.

Happiness was evident in the Camise home, too, when J.A. was home from Ames, Iowa (Navy V-12, State College) and Charles, with a medical discharge, is now home for good. Dominic Danna (Shaw) also has recently been given a medical discharge, after spending six months in La Garde Hospital, New Orleans. Milton Weinstein (Merchant Marine) is now at the Marien Hospital in Chicago. No, he isn't sick,—just stationed there for the month. Merchant Marine reminds me to tell you that Joe Dockery's boat, "Azara" (which he offered to the Navy the day after Pearl Harbor), has just recently been taken over by the Merchant Marines for a training ship. So perhaps some of you "Sea Scouts" who have enjoyed peacetime outings on it may find yourselves training on it in earnest one of these days.

And speaking of hospitals, Henry F. Watts is in one in Oran, Algeria, with a broken jaw bone, acquired when his truck went over a cliff somewhere in Italy. He is lucky, at that, for the two men who were with him were killed. Knowing nothing of his accident, his mother recently had sent him a whole box of chewing gum. Opening it in a ward where fourteen other patients were all being treated for broken jaws, he solemnly passed it around! Well, it served its purpose, for the boys all laughed (to the best of their ability) at the irony of fate!

From a hospital in Sicily, Dorothy Shands (Red Cross) writes cheerfully of a fractured kneecap which has her laid low. She was disgusted that it didn't merit a "Purple Heart." She only got it by falling down stairs. Poor "Dah-dah" and her brittle bones! She got the first one broken when she fell out of her baby bed at three months old!... [101]

---

101. Dorothy Shands described her hospital experiences in a letter to Mrs. Mose Hyman, chairman of the Bolivar County Red Cross, which was published on the front page of the February 18, 1944 issue of the *Bolivar Commercial*. Dorothy Shands concluded her letter with the comment: "I trust that you are having larger crowds at the [Surgical Dressings] Club. The dressings serve two purposes: more and more of the materials are needed here and when the soldier knows that the people at home are devoting their time and energy, he is reassured that America is worth fighting for."

Two more of our loveliest Cleveland girls are displaying beautiful engagement rings. Nan Bond's is from Lt. Lawrence Murphy (Greenville Air Base, formerly at Natchez and Mississippi State) and Le Point Cassibry's is the gift of Lt. Warwick Smith (Jackson Air Base and Ohio). That so many of our fairest daughters are flying away with the Air Force is, I'm sure, sad news to a lot of you boys! However, when this war is over you boys will be bringing home the lovely lassies you've acquired elsewhere! That's life! Lt. Cecil Pleasants (Naval Air Force) makes no secret of the fact that he's lost his heart to a Spanish beauty in South America (he was here on a flying visit recently and looks wonderful), and I heard the other day that one of my pet boys, now in England, is really in earnest about the daughter of an old friend of mine up in Tennessee! "Latest Lohengrin statistics indicate that December's end will produce at least two million new brides in 1943, or about fourteen marriages per 1000 population."[102] During World War I, we had eleven marriages per thousand, so you boys are doing better than your dads did! . . .

All of us are almost afraid to open telegrams these days, so we don't blame Mrs. Long for hesitating a long time over one she received the other day, for Ralph has been on the *Card*, that famous ship which has the record of sinking more subs than any unit in the Navy.[103] But the wire contained the good news that her son was on his way home! Lt. Long (Navy-Skene) is another of our heroes, for he is credited with sinking a sub himself! He has been in active combat since last April. . . .

Goodbye and God bless you all. There wasn't a home in Bolivar County where you weren't remembered last week on Thanksgiving Day, and many were the prayers, in churches and in homes, that went up for your safety.

Sincerely,
Keith Frazier Somerville

102. *Lohengrin*, the romantic opera by Richard Wagner (1813-1883), was first performed in 1850. Act III opens with the celebrated "Wedding March."

103. Telegrams were often the harbingers of bad news as notification of wounds, deaths, or prisoner status were often conveyed by this method. Planes from the U.S.S. *Card*, an escort carrier, sank three German submarines from August 7-27, 1943 and a fourth on October 4, 1943.

December 17, 1943

Dear Boys:

A Merry Christmas and a Happy New Year to each of you and how we wish everyone of you could be in Bolivar County for these holidays! But we know, as the song says, "Christmas Eve will find you where the love light gleams. You'll be home for Christmas, if only in your dreams!"[104] Isn't that a grand song? "A White Christmas," which swept the airways last year, didn't mean much to us, did it?[105] For I doubt if many of you had ever seen White Christmases before the war. I've lived here thirty years and we've never had one in all those years. No, Christmas doesn't mean snow to us. Some years it means warm sunshine, when one can be outdoors without a coat, and maybe a lonesome red rose is blooming on one of mother's bushes and the company stands about in the front yard, talking crops and politics, while mother and the girls finish the last touches of that big dinner. Other years it means fog and rain and mud; crowds in the damp clothes crowding Main Street, doing last minute shopping on Christmas Eve, not a parking space available; the Christmas lights gleaming palely through the fog-encrusted windows of the stores; the little trees beside the door at Denton's glimmering in the rain; and all across the top of the streets, the strings of colored lights shining merrily and the little trees along the sides of Court Street and in all the house windows giving out a warm glow thru the mist. It means little boys selling fireworks along the sidewalks (maybe you were once one of them) and surreptitiously setting off some "crackers" now and then to startle the passers by and add to the grand hilarity, where everybody is gay and talkative, greeting friends and dropping packages.

Or maybe Christmas means Carol singing on the Court House lawn the nite after school closed for the holidays. Remember the strings of lights down the front of the Court House, the big trees alight on the porch, the crowds, the high school band, the Delta Singers, the kindergarten children in their black and yellow lined capes (maybe you were one of them), all pealing forth "Silent

104. This is a paraphrase of Bing Crosby's (1904-1977) 1943 hit song, "I'll Be Home For Christmas."

105. "White Christmas," by Irving Berlin (1888-1989), was sung by Bing Crosby.

Night?" Remember how our tall white Confederate soldier looked down on those peaceful, happy scenes, doubtless hoping that another war would never disturb the serenity of his Mississippi, for even a man of stone must have rejoiced in those nites![106]

But maybe you'll remember best the dances during the holidays at all our little towns in those bygone days of plenty of gas, when the family car was yours and you and your girlfriend rushed madly from one to another. Even if your car stuck in the mud coming home from Rosedale, or somewhere else, on Christmas night, that was part of it too!

Well, that kind of gay, merry, carefree Christmas is gone for the moment, but they're part of what you're fighting for. They'll return one day, and meanwhile we all remember them, and to you, wherever you are, we're saying that time honored phrase, "Merry Christmas, and sending up a prayer that "the lights come on again, all over the world" soon.[107]

I ran into John Thomas Greer, home from Ft. Bragg, North Carolina, at Denton's the other day. He looked grand in his uniform and was being made much over by a group of cute "sweater girls."[108] (Going to Denton's, "Cleveland's Country Club," for a coke or a sundae is probably another of your Christmas thoughts of home! So, to all of you who remember happy hours there—Merry Christmas!)

And a very special "Season's Greetings" to all you boys whose address is "Care of Postmaster, San Francisco."[109] Luck to you and may your island hops bring you daily closer to Tokyo and home! I do wish I could send each one of you a copy of that delightful book, *C/O Postmaster*, by Corp. Thomas R. St. George, which tells in amusing

106. An Italian and Georgia marble statue, honoring fallen Confederate soldiers, was dedicated on the lawn of the Bolivar County Courthouse in Cleveland on May 14, 1908.

107. This is a reference to the 1942 song, "When the Lights Go On Again (All Over the World)", made popular by Vaughn Monroe and his Orchestra.

108. The original "sweater girl" was Lana Turner.

109. Mail to military personnel who were stationed overseas was routed through military post offices established in large coastal cities. The mail was then sorted by the Army or Fleet Post Office number which had been assigned to each military unit. This system was devised to ease the task of sorting the immense amount of mail that was dispatched overseas during the war years as well as to insure that the specific geographical locations of units would not be available to the enemy.

detail all his experiences from the time there appeared on the bulletin board in place of "Tomorrow's K.P." (gleefully crossed out) his new address "C/O Post Master, San Francisco," to the moment he boarded, in a hurry, a windowless transport and was off for active duty[110]. . . . Merry Christmas to all of you out in the Pacific; to our Navy boys; to Capt. Eph McLean (and I didn't need any medals or presidential citations to tell me you were extra special Eph!); to Lts. LaValle House, Lawrence Wiggins, "Snooks" Lorance, Hampton Ballard (former Shaw star athlete); to Ens. "Bubber" Ely (Shaw) on a P.T. boat; and to Doyle Lusk (Merigold) on a "sub"; to E.W. Dumler (Duncan) on one of those "fish-boats" the Jap[anese] would like so much to catch; to the Robertson boys (Merigold); Owen on an aircraft carrier and Paul, a radio operator, at Pearl Harbor; and to hundreds more of you I haven't space to name, Merry Christmas!

To all our Marines, our pride along with the Seasons Greetings, for to be a Marine is to be forever enshrined in the hearts of America! To name but a few among the many, Merry Christmas to Harra Mullins (Merigold); to A.T. Janis, Sidney Mayo and Dick Alexander (Boyle); and to our boys who were at Guadalacanal; Melvin Shuler, Charles Collins and Charles Cuffman (Merigold).

And to all our boys who have flown so far and so high and are showing the might of our air power—Merry Christmas (and we think you are wonderful!) to Lts. Norman Hardee and James Owen Thomas (Merigold) and to Sgt. John Parks (Merigold). And a "Merry Christmas" to you, Charles Renfro, "down below the equator where it's so hot." I suppose Ruby has written you all about Mary Alice (Waldron) Rice's wedding. Another of our girls who has succumbed to the fatal charm of those Greenville Air Base lads! The groom was Sgt. Donald Hatcher. Ruby was maid of honor, Sgt. Boyd Shields (also from the Greenville Air Base) was best man, and Brother Bolling performed the ceremony in the beautifully decorated, ivy hung, candlelit Renfro home. The weddings keep occurring! Sgt. Jamie Cuming (Pace) now at Collegeboro, Georgia, married recently Mary Ferguson of Great Falls, South Carolina.

A Merry Christmas to Van Hallman (Merigold), Charles and

---

110. Corporal Thomas R. St. George, *C/O Postmaster* (New York: Thomas Y. Crowell, 1943) provides a good account of the life of a draftee.

Kimball Glassco out in Hawaii; to Kirk Park (Army radio—spending his second Christmas in the Pacific—your mother loved the Bible the English minister you visited brought her, Kirk!); to Bill Ashley and Lt. Lewis Callaway (two Shaw friends who recently got together out in Australia); and to Corp. Pete Kettle (Shaw) who is operating anti-aircraft searchlights; to Carl Gordon and John Alford; and to James Jacks (who is one of those busy Seabees—who land with the combat troops and begin building roads and air fields even before the enemy is cleared out! Your brother Roy is now at Camp Crowder, Missouri, Jimmie.)

And Merry Christmas to Capt. Louis Hallam (that new daughter of yours is a little beauty! She bids fair to rival her lovely mother); to John Ward and David Joseph and two of the Fondren boys (Lt. George and Lt. Ernest) and to Lt. Berlie Griffin.

I do wish, while I'm sending greetings across the Pacific, that I could include one to Charles B. Carranay (Duncan) who is a prisoner of the Jap[anese]. He talked recently on the radio from Japan and said he was O.K. A record of the broadcast was made and sent to his mother. C.B. built and installed a radio station in three hours just before he was taken prisoner!

And an especially "Merry Christmas" to all of you whose address is "Care of Postmaster, New York." You're doing a grand job over there! Many of you who are in the Mediterranean are spending your first Christmas in the southern countries, where early Christianity still reigns, have doubtless been surprised to find that except for the creche in churches, all else that means Christmas to us is lacking. For the "barbarians of the north," forest-born, introduced tree worship (Christmas trees and the Yule log), and mistletoe came from the Druids, while we English speaking people have made of it the children's festival, set to the tune of carols. The ancients, too, held December 25th sacred and as someone has written, "we still flout old winter with a green tree and mortality with child worship." December 25th is certainly THE day of the year for us, so to you boys, pounding at the south of Hitler's "fortress Europa", may it be a gladsome day.[111] "Merry Christmas" to Capt. Frank Wylie (Duncan),

111. Hitler called the defense against invasion by the Allies, "Festung Europa."

to Lt. Bobbie Jackson; to James Harvey and the Lamensdorf boys (Shaw); to Riley Naron, Frank Moore and James Howard; to Maj. Bill Litton (Shaw), shooting down Nazi planes over Yugoslavia; and Wade Purvis (with a bombardier squadron); to Corp. Joe Lewis (Shaw) with the 5th Army on the road to Rome, Merry Christmas (and has your brother N. E. written you that he and his wife have moved into a new house, just back of me, and that he now has the Memphis *Commercial Appeal* route to Belzoni, Mississippi? Your brother, Webster B. Lewis, is still at Camp Gordon, Johnston, Florida). And Merry Christmas to Shaw's Lt. James Williams and Sgt. James Bishop.

And not only "Merry Christmas," but congratulations, too, to Billy Witt Cochran (Merigold) who has been awarded a medal for distinguished services in the Atlantic patrol! And the best of wishes to Sgts. Gilliland, William Cockrell, and Norman Gordon; to Maj. Billy Fondren (at Headquarters of the 7th Army!); to John T. Erwin (Merigold) with a tank destroyer battalion, and Sgts. Braskel Naron and Dennis Beavers.

And may all you boys in England have a real Dickens-y Christmas! As Tiny Tim would say "God bless you everyone." (Did your grandmothers say "God bless you" every time you sneezed? Well, I hope this isn't applicable and that none of you have the flu that we hear is raging in England, even to Buckingham Palace, but if you are sneezing, say "God bless you" again!)

And Merry Christmas to Lts. Cullen Bedwell, J.D. Stevens and Malcolm Hale; to "Son" Schmitt of the Signal Corps and to those other Shaw boys, Larkin Turpin and Hugh Smith, who enjoyed a get together when Hugh came down from Ireland; to Sherwood Henry (Pace) and to thoughtful Curtis Seawright (Merigold) who cabled home on his daughter's first birthday; to Merigold's Chinese Dan Gong, who has been making raids over Nazi Germany of late as a tail gunner on a Flying Fortress, probably wishing that he could gun for Jap[anese] and help drive them from China's rice bowl! And Merry Christmas to Corp. Tom Gunn, one of my colored friends who used to work at Jordan's (Your "season's greetings from Great Britain" is one of my nicest Christmas presents, Tom! Thanks for thinking of us!)...

I'd like to send very WARM greetings to each of you whose address is "Care of Postmaster, Seattle," where Felix L. Sweatt (Shaw) is doing a wonderful job in the Army Postal Service these days, rushing your Christmas mail to you. Dr. Jim Westerfield (Merigold) writes that he's not looking forward to his third white Christmas in Alaska: "I wouldn't swap one acre of Mississippi soil for the whole of Alaska," he writes, "but I'd spend the rest of my life here before I'd let the Jap[anese] have a foot of it!" . . .

A "Merry Christmas" to you, too, Virgil Williams, up in cold Alaska! You never dreamed when you were a little boy listening to me tell about Admiral Byrd's first Polar Christmas that you'd be spending two Christmases there, did you? . . .

Up in "Alaska's frozen waste" also is Billy Denton, at the Winterization Testing Station, after his long stay at Wright Field, Ohio. I'm sure, Maj. Denton, that your wife and young sons will have a happy Christmas with your mother in Shelby, but you'll be often in their thoughts. I hope you won't need to be rescued by an Esquimau, but I do hope you'll find helping hands in Alaska so that you, like Admiral Byrd, can tell the youngsters in your family that you saw Santa at the North Pole![112] Your brothers are still scattered: Maj. Joe and Marian are at Camp Claiborne, Louisiana; Lt. Jack (Air Force) is now at Maxwell Field, Alabama; and David is still at Camp Campbell, Kentucky.

Up at Merigold, recuperating from wounds he received in the battle for Attu (Alaska), is Dole Prewitt, who has been honorably discharged and is home for Christmas this year.[113] And warm greetings, too, to Lt. A.B. Leverett (Merigold).

"Care of Postmaster, New Orleans," takes our greeting to those of you to the South of us; to Capt. Kenneth Thigpen (Shaw—Coast Artillery) and to Eleanor Shand's husband, Lt. Hunter Leake, both in Panama; to Lt. Cecil Pleasants (Naval Air Corps); to Lt. E.V. Brock (Ferry Command).

"Care of Postmaster, Miami," says hello to Merigold flyers, Lt. Alfred Pink in Cairo and Capt. Monroe Wynne, who flies a transport

112. "Esquimau" is one of a number of spellings given to the name of the native population of the Polar north during this period. The preferred term is "Inuit."

113. Attu is a small island at the western extremity of the American Aleutian chain. It was seized by the Japanese on June 7, 1942. In late May 1943, American forces regained control of Attu.

on the India-Chungking route and had written his family that he would leave Tibet in November for a visit home. Then he cabled he couldn't make it, so immediately Merigolders started wondering if perchance he might have flown some of the Chinese officials to Cairo—maybe even the Madonna herself.[114] Well, it's fun to speculate, and she couldn't have gotten a better pilot, for he is a veteran flyer with more than a million miles with American Air Lines to his credit.

And to all of you still in the U.S.A., Merry Christmas! If paper wasn't so scarce I'd beg Mr. Langford to print twenty-five pages this week so I could send a personal greeting to every boy in the service from our side of Bolivar County![115] As that can't be, remember, all of you not mentioned by name, that you have many friends here in Mississippi whose thoughts are with you! Especially are we remembering our boys in hospitals all over the world and sending our best wishes for a speedy recovery. . . .

This letter was written in time to reach you for the holiday season, but in case it doesn't, it at least will bring you the belated message that you were all remembered during Christmas week in the land of cotton.

Well, I began with a song, so here's one to end with. "All I want for Christmas is to keep what I've got!" Thanks to you boys who are away from home this Christmas helping to make that best-of-all-presents possible for all of us.

Sincerely,
Keith Frazier Somerville

114. The Madonna is a reference to Mei-ling Soong (1898-   ), the wife of Chiang Kai-shek (1887-1975), the president of China and Allied Supreme Commander of the China Theatre of Operations. Mei-ling Soong was educated at Wellesley College and knew how to manipulate the American press very well.

115. Paper became very scarce during World War II because wood pulp, from which it was made, was a major source of gun powder. The paper scarcity was alleviated by recycling campaigns, newspaper collection drives, and the use of prisoner of war labor to cut pulp wood. Russian pulp wood arrived in the U.S. in reverse lend-lease as well. See David C. Smith, *A History of Papermaking in the United States, 1690-1969* (New York: Lockwoods, 1970). Chapter 14 gives this story in detail.

3

How You Bolivar County Boys
Are Scattered
all over the World

January 1944—May 1944

Dear Boys:

Gosh, how you Bolivar County boys are scattered over the world in this year of 1944! It makes me dizzy trying to keep up with you! Not to even mention the many thousands already overseas, just a partial list of you in camps here at home, reads like a railroad timetable list of United States cities (and flagstops! Stars and Stripes flag of course!) Chaplain K.I. Tucker (Pace) is at Fort Custer, Michigan; Corp. E.I. Sims (Shaw) at the Station Hospital (Ward 3), Bradley Field, Connecticut; Lt. Thomas Yates (Bombardier Squadron) at Ephrata, Washington; while up in Virginia there's "Snag" McLellan, now a Seabee, at Williamsburg; Lt. Otis Dunn (Duncan) at the Marine Corps School at Quantico, Virginia; Sgt. M.D. Strawbridge (Merigold), Anti-Tank Battalion, at Camp Lee, where also is stationed Thomas Nelson (Quartermaster)...

The colleges, too, are filled with you boys getting trained. Joseph V. Brocato (Merigold) at Notre Dame; James Burrus (Merigold) back from Africa for Officer's Training Candidate school at Dartmouth; Elgie Burrus (Merigold) at Tulane; James Davis at the University of

Missouri; Anthony Brocato (Cleveland) and E.C. Meek (Merigold) at the Citadel (South Carolina), while John P. McLaurin is at "Ole Miss" and Ray Beckham (Shaw) is at State.

Down in Florida there's Henry Varner (Pace) at Jacksonville; Lt. (J.G.) W.H. Bizzell (Pace) at Pensacola; Carolyn McLean and her husband, Lt. Webb DeLoach, are there too, tho' Carolyn is home just now on a visit; Will D. Ferris (Shaw) is in the beautiful lake country at Orlando; Richard Weileman (Shaw—Air Corps) is at Miami Beach and Gwinn Shelby (Shelby—Coast Guard) is also there; Bernard Maurice Adelson (Merigold—Quartermaster Department) is at Venice, Florida; Thomas W. Bernard (Merigold) —Navy) is at Key West and Lt. Curtis Hutchinson (Merigold—Air Corps) is at Tyndall Field, Panama City; Lt. Charles Jackson is at Camp Blanding and Lt. Richard Haralson (Duncan) at McDill Field, Tampa.

Out in California, William Henry (Pace) is at Treasure Island; Louie Grantham (Pace) at Camp Haan; Harry Cook (Duncan) at Port Hueneme and Kenneth Walton (also Duncan) with the amphibian tractors at Oceanside; Bernard Holt (another Duncan boy in the Medical Corps) at the Navy Hospital in San Diego; Lamar Wells at Camp Roberts; Tech. Sgt. A..E. Davis (Merigold) at Van Nuys; E.C. Ouzts (Merigold—Navy) at San Diego and Jack Patty (Shaw) at Pittsburgh, California.

In Texas there's Charlie Capps at Camp Fannin; E.G. Evans (Pace) at Houston, and countless numbers of you at San Antonio, including David "Boo" Ferris (Shaw); John A. Taylor (Pace); Lt. James Moody (Shaw); Lt. Robert Brooks (Duncan).

Up in Tennessee, there's Corp. "Bunny" Carpenter (Quartermaster 2nd Army Headquarters); Capt. R.T. Litton (Shaw, with the Student Training Detachment at Smyrna); Bob Comfort (Duncan— one of the twins; the other, Frank, is at Selma Field, Monroe, Louisiana—both in the Air Corps). At Memphis there are a bunch of our Navy boys: Guy Tidwell; "Buddy" Bernard Garfinkle (Boyle); M.J. Coward and Charles D. Cochran (Merigold); and John Walton, Jr.

Still in Mississippi are Lt. R.H. Jones (Merigold) with the Troop Carrier Command at Grenada; Harry Malone (Pace) and Louis Agner

(Merigold) at Gulfport; Oscar Sizmore (first father called from Pace) and David Dean (Shaw) at Camp Shelby.

Our "gals" too are scattered far and wide! Lt. Anna Danna (Shaw—a nurse) is at Camp Rucker, Alabama, and Francis West (Red Cross Recreational Director, also of Shaw) is at Maxwell Field, Alabama. Have you run into Lt. Joel Barrard, Fran? He's there, too. Phyllis Drott (that pretty D.S.T.C, W.A.V.E!) is at Corpus Christi, Texas, while our own lovely W.A.V.E., Jean Jackson, is at "United States Naval Barracks" (alias the Robert Clay Hotel!) in Miami; Brooksie Eckles (Red Cross Recreational Director) is also in Miami; W.A.C. Juanita Frazier (Pace) is in San Antonio, while SSGT. Marie Frith (W.A.C.—Shaw) is now at Ft. Dix, New Jersey expecting to "go over" before long. . . .

Nan Bond and Le Point Cassibry married their flyers (Lts. Murphy and Smith), the latter in a big wedding on New Year's day and flew away. And now all the town is excited over Bitsy Pleasants' approaching marriage to Newman Briggs, formerly of Burlington, Vermont, where he was a state auditor. There's one Yankee anyway who likes the South! Guess where she met him? Why right here at home! He was one of the boys who was guarding the cotton picking Italian soldiers! Now he's stationed down in Florida, but he was back for a weekend just the other day!

The latest babe is the young daughter born to Lt. and Mrs. Bill Boyd (Camille McLean) down at Ft. Benning, Georgia. Another late arrival is Patricia Crutchfield, the daughter of Lt. Oscar and Mary Elizabeth House. She's another of the V-Mail babies![1] You knew, didn't you, that if a baby is born after the father goes overseas, Uncle Sam will send its picture by V-mail to the dad! What priceless treasures those pictures are now, and will be in the future years! . . .

1. V-Mail was a special form of correspondence developed by the U.S. government during World War II to help save space in scarce wartime transport. Letters, written on specially designed 8½ by 11 inch stationery, were photographed and the film shipped in canisters overseas. The developed film was then distributed to the troops as a letter in the form of a 4 by 5½ inch photograph. V-Mail made it possible to transform letters with a bulk weight of 2,500 pound into film weighing only 45 pounds.

Yours with hope for a "Federation of the World," and with every good wish for each of you for 1944.[2]

Sincerely,

Keith Frazier Somerville

January 21, 1944

Dear Boys:

I got a big kick the other day when a friend in Washington, D.C. sent me a clipping, with the inquiry, "Is this a friend of yours"? It was all about Capt. Jack Firestone, whose wife is the former Jean Jones of Cleveland, Mississippi. Of course he is, for we claim all our girls' husbands and are proud with them of their hero husbands! Of course, you remember Jean. Her mother, Mrs. H.O. Jones, is one of the "Seelbinder girls" and is staying at the Seelbinder's this winter. Capt. Jack, so the clipping reported, was the leading navigator of a combat wing which participated in the big American raid on the German port of Kiel recently.[3] At a United States bomber base in Britain, Capt. Firestone is quoted as saying: "It was Schweinfurt all over again. The Germans threw all the fighters they had against us—Messerschmitts 210s, 110s, and 109; Dorniers 217s and Focke-Wulfs 190; applied all the well known fighter tactics and employed one new one (towing anti-aircraft bombs on wires)."[4] Though born in Baltimore, Capt. Firestone has lived in Washington since he was nineteen months old. After graduating from high school, he worked for a short while in an ice plant before joining the Air Corps and receiving his wings at Hondo, Texas (November, 1942). Jean lives with his parents in Washington during his absence and is working in

2. Prior to the founding of the United Nations in 1945, persons who supported world government often called for a "Federation of the World."

3. The German port of Kiel, on the Baltic Sea, was the site of a state-owned shipyard which built diesel engines and submarines. The shipyard underwent thirty-six attacks by American and British bombers.

4. The Schweinfurt-Regensburg raid of August 17, 1943, was designed to attack and destroy the ball bearing manufacturing capacity of Schweinfurt as well as the Messerschmitt factory at nearby Regensburg. Of the 376 bombers which participated in this daylight attack, sixty were shot down. Martin Middlebrook, *The Schweinfurt-Regensburg Mission* (London: Alan Lane, 1983) is the standard account.

the British Embassy. Jean is a cousin of those fighting Smiths (Clarence, Marine Corps, Jackson, Mississippi; Lt. Robert, Tank Corps, Shreveport, Louisiana; Capt. Milton, Air Corps, Elgin Field, Florida. They were all together recently on leave); of Lt. Jimmie Chiles, Air Corps, Victorville, California; of Roy Barner, Ruleville, Air Corps now stationed at Columbia, South Carolina; of Ben Moore Seelbinder, V-12, Tulane University; and of the Boschert girls. Louise's husband, L. D. Murphy, has for many years been attached to the Engineering Board (War Department), Fort Belvoir, Virginia; Catherine's husband, J.J. Helm, is "commuting property man" (inspects government warehouses as far away as California and the Mexican border), also attached at Ft. Belvoir; and Helen has recently joined them in Washington where she has a very "hush hush" war job with the Signal Corps. My, how much that one patriotic family is contributing to our war effort! And grandfather and grandmother Seelbinder were both born in Germany, coming to this country at the age of sixteen. They, strangely enough, came on the same ship, though they did not know each other. Each came to visit relatives in Mississippi, met, and were married at Durant, moving to Greenwood where they were soon naturalized and became American citizens.

Down in San Antonio (Randolph Field), Aviation Cadets Jimmie T. Robinson and Rufus Walt are living "just across the street"—company street—from one another. Jimmie T. has been there some time, but Rufus has only recently joined him, after finishing up at the University of Oklahoma (where he made such a high grade that he was one of five, out of one hundred twenty, allowed to skip part of the college work and go on to the business of flying). Rufus loved that, for he loves flying. Gleefully, he recalls the day he flew home from Moorhead and flew right above our street, all the way home, and then dipped and dived for the benefit of mother and grandmother just over the house, scaring the wits out of them. "No stunt flying here," he regretfully states. There are a "powerful lot" of you boys who are being trained to take off for Berlin and Tokyo! There are the McCarty boys (Merigold); SSGT Eldon is at Boca Raton Field, Florida; and Elmo at Brayton Flying Service, Cuero, Texas. Flight officer R. F. Thompson (Pace) is at the Glider Training Center, Bowman Field, Kentucky; F.W. Bishop (Air Corps) is already in England and finding it interesting. Lt. James M. (Preacher) Goudelock is also in England where he was recently promoted to First Lieutenant. He's with the Army Postal Unit. I see from a London dispatch, boys, where the B.B.C. can't joke about American soldiers now, and they even have put a "ban on the Southern accent."[5] (Can't even say "honey chile, shet yo' mouth.") Well, personally I'd rejoice over a like ban in America! They never get us right, do they? I hear, too, that there are so many American soldiers in London that Piccadilly looks like Times Square![6]

Dorothy Shands writes me (from somewhere in Italy? Sicily? A.P.O. 550, C/O Postmaster, New York) that she "saw a boy from Boyle today and he was saying how much he always enjoyed your newsy letters." And why didn't you tell us the boy's name, Dorothy? Well, thanks anyway, and we're all glad to know you Bolivar Countians are getting together overseas and happy to know that your leg is about well and you're able to be back on your job. Glad too, to know that Christmas there "was busy and exciting, much decoration, music, and food (at the Red Cross), with soldiers wandering around swinging the socks Santa had filled for them, the girls going about singing carols, and a big turkey dinner for every one." Dorothy also writes, "Looking out my window I see hugh palms swaying in the wind against the background of snow capped mountains, a very unusual scene." A letter from Ens. C.P. Brocato (written January 6) says that he and Ens. Harry Buckley went together recently into a Red Cross officer's club and saw on the bulletin board the names of five from Cleveland, Mississippi, among them Dorothy Shands and Billy Fondren. They didn't see them that day, but were going to make another visit and try to get in touch with them. Those Fondrens, tho' far from home, seem to manage to keep in touch. Louis Hallam and Ernest got together out in Australia! Don't know whether Lt. George (Marine) ran into any Cleveland friends while he was confined to bed with malaria recently or not! Hope so! He was on Guadalacanal.

Over in Egypt is Pvt. Willie Romandi (Shelby) who writes there are several Mississippi boys in his unit. Speaking of Shelby, I don't

5. BBC is the abbreviation for British Broadcasting Corporation.
6. Piccadilly Circus is a traffic hub in the West End of London.

believe I told you about "Jiggs" Neblet being killed in a plane wreck, en route back to his Virginia camp after a Christmas visit home. The whole community was sad with his wife (Mary LeMoyne Wilkerson). Jiggs' term as District Attorney was not out (a Clarksdale lawyer had been running it in his absence). Now the governor has called a special election for February 1st to fill the vacancy. Our own "Bill" Simmons (former mayor of Cleveland, who was once District Attorney) is a candidate and if our people will only come out to vote that day, we can elect another Bolivar County man to succeed Lt. Jiggs. (Two Clarksdale men, Luckett and Chrisler, are running against him, which should split the Coahoma County vote and give us a good Bolivar County man, but only if we can get out a good vote to offset the other counties in the district.) But you're not interested in politics. Or are you? Since they've been making such a to-do in Congress over the "soldier vote," I've wondered, "Will you boys vote if it's arranged for you to do so?"[7] So many of us here at home are careless about it! It shouldn't be so, but it unfortunately is! I have such faith in the American people that I think we'd have better men in office if all of us would remember to exercise the privilege of voting!

SSGT Joe Pursell (who used to work for the Virden Lumber Co. and another of our "heroes" who received the Air Medal and the Oakleaf Cluster for distinguished service in submarine warfare in the Caribbean) was last heard from "neath the palm trees in Cuba." Your parents and two small brothers down at Belzoni, as well as all your local friends, are mighty proud of you, Joe!

7. The "soldier vote" was an important issue in 1944. In January 1944, the U.S. Congress began debate on a federal ballot bill to allow persons on active duty to vote in the fall elections. Debate on the bill was rancorous and centered on the racial issue as well as the "states rights" issue of whether state governments or the federal government should determine voting qualifications. Franklin Roosevelt voiced strong support for the federal ballot bill, but many "states rigbts" congressmen from the south were opposed to it. A "states rights" ballot bill, designed to prohibit black servicemen from voting by preserving local voting qualifications, was sponsored by Congressman John E. Rankin (1882-1960) and Senator James O. Eastland (1904-1986), both from Mississippi. This "states rigbts" ballot bill was passed on March 31, 1944. President Roosevelt said that the "states rights" bill was inadequate and allowed it to become law without his signature. Although the "soldier vote" was not significant in any major contest during the fall elections of 1944, tbe length and severity of the debate was an indication that voting rights would become a major postwar issue.

Speaking of sergeants reminds me to tell you something interesting. Did you ever hear of any of those (proverbially!) "tough" fellows getting together and giving anyone a Christmas present? I thought not! Well, down at Camp Shelby, the mess sergeants did just that! They presented a beautiful fitted case of cosmetics to W.A.C. Elizabeth Stamps as a token of their regards!...

Have you boys up at Camp Pickett, Virginia, contacted each other? There are two from Merigold, Henry Allday and Hoyt C. Daves, and Elgin Lester (Duncan)—all with the 155 Infantry. Sgt. Bernice Steede (Boyle) is there, too, in the hospital, Ward A-9. Get together, boys, and laugh over the homefolks, suffering (?) over sleet, snow, and "busted" water pipes. Corp. James B. Reid (Louise Sanders' husband) would say "that is to laugh," for he's been up in Iceland where it was forty below months ago. Heaven knows what it is now! He's an aviation engineer....

Thanks for your nice letter, Jesse White, and we're all proud to hear you are now "Pharmacist's Mate, 1st Class, in the greatest Navy in the world," Norfolk Naval Hospital, Portsmouth, Virginia. I run into the store often to see your family. You certainly gave your mother an unforgettable trip!...

Our wedding for this letter is Tommy Griffin's. She married a "Yankee," from Detroit, Pvt. Clarence Houghton, up at her sister's (Mrs. Virgil Miner) in Clarksdale. The groom is stationed at Como where the couple will reside for a while!

Babies? Of course! Had you heard about Sallie Crawford Magruder? She's the daughter of Lt. Lawson and Mary Ann (who is now in Houston with her parents while Lawson is overseas, somewhere across the Atlantic).

After a year in Africa and a vacation in Shaw, Dr. (Capt.) Joe Peeler is now at the Government Hospital, Butler, Pennsylvania. Another of Shaw's doctors, Capt. Charles Watkins, has recently been transferred to Columbia, South Carolina. Mike Field (Dr. Richard to the Army) is now at Kearns, Utah, and Nino Bologna is down in New Orleans and probably doing as fine a job of doctoring for Uncle Sam as he did for Mississippi State when he was president of the student body there. Another "soon will be Shaw doctor" in the service is Guy Dean, now a medical senior at the University of Virginia. (His brother, L.G., by the way, is a Naval Aviation Cadet at Ohio

Wesleyan, Delaware, Ohio. That's where Milton Dunn, (Duncan) is, too, while Charles Smith, (Duncan) is a V-12 at Lafayette, Louisiana).

Well, its time for me to "Lay that Pistol (Pen) down, Babe"! It's a comforting thought to reflect that I have lived through "Yes, We Have No Bananas, Today", "The Hut-Sut Song," and "The Merry-go-round broke down", so in all probability I'll survive the "Pistol Packin' Mama"! But I don't claim to like it![8]

Yours for better music in a better world.

Sincerely,

Keith Frazier Somerville

February 4, 1944

Dear Boys:

The whole world is interested in the Mars, "the giant flying galleon," world's largest aircraft, now in the United States Navy service, and we here in Cleveland have a special interest in it because one of our boys, Clovis Norwood, is one of her crew.[9] (The first pilot is a Mississippian, too, by the way. Lt. J.T. Baker of Pocahontas.) One morning last week the Memphis *Commercial Appeal* carried a picture headed—"No Substation: Just the Mars," —picturing the huge control board indicating every phase of activity and operation aboard. Below the picture were the words, "In charge here are Clovis Allen Norwood of Cleveland, Mississippi, Chief Aviation Machinistmate, and Ens. Geck of California, Flight Engineer. Well, half the town rushed over to the Norwoods to be sure they saw that picture of handsome Clovis! Why, of course I went too, and what an interesting time I had looking at pictures of Clovis and the Mars!... It is positively enormous! Mrs. Norwood told me, "I called my daughter last nite and told her that Clovis had just landed in Hawaii. She asked how I knew. 'Just heard it on the radio,' I replied. That's one advantage of having a boy aboard such a famous ship." On this trip to Hawaii, the Mars carried only 13,860 lbs. of

---

8. Mrs. Somerville is quoting from a version of a popular and occasionally risque song of the period, "Pistol Packin' Mama" (1943). Her other songs are well-known nonsense songs: "Yes, We Have No Bananas," (1922), "The Hut-Sut Song" (1941), and "The Music Goes 'Round and Around" (1935).

9. The Mars, developed by Martin Aircraft, was a large transport airplane.

mail, twenty passengers, and some high priority war materials, but on a recent trip down Bermuda way, she carried 35,000 lbs., and can carry 175 persons with room to spare. It is as big as a fifteen room house and weighs seventy-five tons when loaded. And it's fast, too, for it made the trip from San Francisco to Pearl Harbor in exactly the time the "Clipper" (not half its size) takes—thirteen hours and eighteen minutes! No wonder! It has four 2200 horse power engines! Clovis is one of the nine members of the crew who has been with the Mars from its initial run. In fact, his address is still, Care of Postmaster, Glen Martin Company, Baltimore, Maryland. How intensely interested Mrs. Norwood is in those boys of hers and their interests, and who wouldn't be! You know she has two more in the service. Forest (Marshall F. to the Army—so many of you boys we hardly recognize by those first names they insist on calling you by in the service!) brought in a picture of one of those giant balloons, with himself and his crew (also appearing small) grouped in front of it. He's with a "balloon barrage battery" at Camp Tysen, Tennessee.[10] And Bryson is a radio man (Air Corps) now at Hensley Field, Texas. Her oldest son, Le Roy Taylor, was called up recently, too, but was deferred for the present.

Another Bolivar Countian who made headlines all over America recently was Col. Frank Gregory (Shelby), who was honored with a dinner at the Waldorf in New York where he was presented with the Bane Award "for the most important technical achievement in aviation in 1943." Dr. Igor Sikorsky, helicopter inventor, made the presentation.[11] And I haven't yet gotten to see a helicopter! But I'm still hoping! The other flying Gregory, Col. Louis, is still instructing in the Bombardier School in Deming, New Mexico, and on the very day his mother heard about Frank getting the Bane Award, her other son, Owen, got his orders to report for his physical! Owen, married

10. Barrage balloons were hydrogen filled balloons, tethered on long wires, which were designed to protect bases and other strategic areas against low-flying air attack. They resembled miniature blimps, which were manned vehicles. Mrs. Somerville may have confused barrage balloons with blimps. The Navy used blimps to patrol coastal waters and convoy lanes.

11. The Aeronautics Institute awarded Colonel Hollingsworth Frank Gregory the Bane Award for 1943 for his work with helicopters. News coverage of this event appeared in the New York *Times* on January 13, 25, 1944.

and with a family, has been Boy Scout Executive in Clarksdale for some time. "But," he told his brothers, "when Uncle Sam sends me greetings, I'm ready to go. Only I'm not trading on your prestige."

When the Steeds (Shaw) had five sons in the service, they stood alone in our county as the biggest manpower contributor to Uncle Sam's war effort. Now that the sixth son and a son-in-law have gone, I think they merit a letter of thanks from Gen. Marshall![12] The sixth son, James, left on January 11th for Camp Shelby, and with him went his sister Pearl's husband, James Robertson O'Reilly! Like all the rest of you boys, the Steeds have been moving about. Corp. Estel of the Signal Corps is now stationed in Trinidad, and the other day he sent home the cutest pair of handmade shoes, just like a man's, though with queer rounded soles, to his nineteen month old son, Lawrence. He hasn't seen that babe since he was three months old, but he hasn't forgotten he's here! His wife (she was Agnes Floyd—Boyle) also has a couple of brothers in the service, just to bring the family's patriotic average up a bit! Brother James Howard Floyd is with an Ordnance Detachment (Care of Postmaster Miami), while Willie's address is Care of Postmaster New York! The Floyd boys attended Cleveland High School. De Witt Steed is now at Camp Dix, New Jersey, while his wife (Musette Howley) and their ten month old daughter are in Belzoni with her parents. SSGT Edward is at Camp Stewart, Georgia, and writes, "Hope I'll be sent over soon." That's what Sgt. Bernice Steed wanted, too, and it's what has him pining away in Ward A9 of the hospital at Camp Pickett, Virginia. Many of his old pals of the National Guard outfit with whom he left home three years ago have gone over, and there he is left, with nothing more exciting to do than drink milk! His pencil positively wailed as he wrote, "I've been with old E. Company a long time not to get to go with them. It's about to run me crazy! I'd just as soon cut my arm off as see them go without me." Well, Bernice, hurry up and get well and maybe you can catch them before they reach Berlin! This week's wedding is Tech. Sgt. Carlee Steed, married last week to Evelyn Wade of Calhoun City, down at Ft. Benning, where he is in an antitank company, and she is working! Luck to you both!

12. General George C. Marshall (1880-1959) was the top-ranking U.S. Army officer during the war and one of the most influential Allied strategists.

Back from Guadalacanal last week with a bronze service star on his ribbon was Louis Cole.[13] Remember him in C.H.S.? He's just out of Bachnell General Hospital, Brigham City, Utah. No, he wasn't wounded overseas, but he contracted a bad kind of malaria (lots worse than our Delta variety) and he's had seven spells of it, poor dear! However, he looks grand now, is still smiling, and when his leave is up will report to Ft. Douglas, Salt Lake City. Another Cole (James) is now at Ft. Dix, New Jersey. Wife Maurine went up to see him Christmas and had a wonderful trip, but she's back on the job again (Virden Lumber Company). . . .

Guess what—our own Capt. Ringold (Dr.) was present when Harris Wheller finished his basic at Bush Field recently, and wrote Mother Marcia all about it, for he was afraid modest Harris wouldn't tell all the nice things that were said about him and might not do justice to the fact that he was the most outstanding Air Cadet, and for being that was given a $50 War Bond! His cousin, Lt. Edward Bond (Navigator—Air Corps), is now in England. En route his plane had to land, and who should he see but Lt. E.V. Brock! Two Cleveland lads, saying hail and farewell so far from home! Edward, too, by the way, was outstanding in his training days and has a gift watch to attest to his prowess. In England, too, is Lt. "Grover E." Ingram with the 18th Weather Squadron. That "worst fog in forty years" the London broadcast told of the other night must have been quite a revelation to a weather man reared 'neath Mississippi sunshine! Lt. Linwood Ingram is on a bomber out in the South Pacific now. Quinton Carver is in England, too, and I imagine you'll be happy to receive that nice box Sister Sue sent you the other day, Quinton. Here's hoping those sox-without-holes will help you do an even better engineering job, and you'll like the cookies, too, I'm betting!

In Kroger's grocery store the other morning I ran into Fred Cannon, fresh home from a Navy Patrol Squadron down in the Caribbean.[14] My, what a fine looking sailor he is, and how happy he's been making the family with his interesting yarns about Cuba and

13. Service stars are issued by the Army and Navy for specified battles, services, or campaigns. They are worn on the appropriate campaign ribbon.
14. Kroger's grocery store was in Cleveland.

elsewhere. Maybe SSGT James McKnight, a top turret gunner with a bombardier squadron, is in that vicinity too. One never knows. Anyway he writes delightfully of coconuts and palm trees and of having a half interest in a monkey! (Care of Postmaster, New York could mean just anywhere those things abound!)...

Among our colored friends I hear that Corp. Eugene Carter (Mound Bayou) is now in Africa, and Alexander Wilson (also of Mound Bayou) is at Base Headquarter, Portland, Oregon. "Over the waters" are Leon Gidron (Care of Postmaster, San Francisco) and George Gailey (Care of Postmaster, New York). Corp. Amzie Moore of the 553rd Fighter Squadron (an entirely colored fighter group) stopped over at home the other day from a mission to Langley Field, en route back to his base at Selfridge Field, Michigan.[15] He looked every inch a soldier, from his upstanding carriage to his beautifully pressed tan trousers, and is still liking the Army lots! LeRoy Milton, who was wounded in Africa, has recently been discharged and has gotten a job in Jackson. From a U.S.O. in Los Angeles (with very fancy stationery) comes word that SSGT A. Robinson is "back on the job with old Battery B" after a visit here in Memphis. And Sgt. Richard Morrel has returned to Camp Livingston, Louisiana.

Babies? Well, have you heard about the young daughter of the William Stevensons? She was Alleen Pease and he is in the Navy now at Atlantic City. And the young son of Robert Minert? The mother was Nellie McClellan, a sister of those former football stars who are now serving Uncle Sam. Robert is still over at Camp McCain.

That's all for today. Here at home we're rejoicing because the sun is shining again and the war news on all fronts is good.

Best of luck to each of you.

Sincerely,
Keith Frazier Somerville

15. Amzie Moore, the civil rights leader from Cleveland, was mentioned by Mrs. Somerville in her first "Dear Boys" column of July 15, 1943. Moore was one of 10,000 Blacks who was present at an April 3, 1940, gathering at Delta State, organized by the Cotton Council, to discuss racial and economic matters. This meeting was attended by representatives from the U.S. Department of Agriculture and Tuskegee Institute. The agenda included the topics of school accreditation, the concept of "separate but equal," and the coming of electricity to rural areas. In addition to his post-war work with the NAACP and SNCC,

February 25, 1944
Dear Boys:

February 12th (Lincoln's Birthday) was the third anniversary of the
Taborian Hospital at Mound Bayou and they had an all day reception, and T.R.M. Howard, head of the hospital, which is a credit to
the community, made a speech telling of all that has been accomplished since it was opened.[16] Many people from all over the Delta
attended and it was a big day. Naturally, much of the talk there
centered around soldiers—sons who are off at the war, fighting or
getting ready to fight to insure the future of our community and
others like it all over America. Uncle Sam says his colored soldiers
are making fine records, and it is just as true among our colored
friends as among our white that practically every family in Bolivar
County can boast at least one service star. So here's news I've
gleaned about some of Bolivar County's [N]egro service men.

SSGT Eugene Carter writes his father from North Africa that he,
like all the rest of you boys, craves letters from home. Peas Hardy is
down at Camp Stewart, Georgia and Sgt. Peter A. Jones is in
Georgia, too, while Corp. Hernando Farmer is with the Medical
Detachment at the O'Reilly General Hospital, Springfield, Missouri.
Tommie Bramlett is with a quartermaster group out in the Pacific.
Across the Pacific, too, are Corp. Eddie B. Hooper, Robert T. Perris,
and Corp. Robert L. Isaac. Leon Isaac is still in this country, Ft.
Bragg, North Carolina. One of Mound Bayou's Navy sons, Ozie

Moore also helped to form the Mississippi Freedom Democratic Party of the
early 1960s. He was employed by the Cleveland Post Office for thirty years,
retiring in 1968. He attributed his service in the army during World War II with
providing him with the understanding that "people are just people."

16. Taborian Hospital was established in 1942 by the Knights and Daughters
of Tabor, a black lodge founded in Independence, Missouri on August 12, 1872.
The Knights and Daughters was organized to perpetuate the memory of the
Twelve Knights of Liberty, an organization which fought for freedom for the
slaves during the antebellum period. For more than forty years, Taborian
Hospital served a major health center for black Mississippians. For further
information on the Taborian Hospital, see the interview with Minne L. Fisher in
Ruth Edmonds Hill, ed., *Black Women Oral History Project*, Vol. IV (Westport,
Connecticut: Meckler Publishing, 1991), pp. 8, 16. Fisher was the Taborian
Hospital bookkeeper.

Williams, is now on the U.S.S. *Prairie*, also somewhere in the Pacific. Across the Atlantic are Winston Trotter and Pride L. Stuphs. Denny Newell's address is Port Company, Port Battalion, A. P. O. 555, Care of Postmaster, New York, which I take to mean that he's at some port across the Atlantic where they're loading and unloading troops and supplies.

Among those writing to Mound Bayou recently were Cornelius Dillan from McDill Field, Florida; Jimmie Fair from Camp Edwards, Massachusetts; Loran Hawkins and Harry Parker, both with the 337th Aviate Squadron, Yuma, Arizona; Ishman Washington from the Army Air Base at Portland, Oregon; and Daniel Stephs from Ft. Ord, California; Sgt. W. E. Jasper from an amphibian company—also "across."

Johnnie Neal writes his mother in Mound Bayou not to worry about him, for he is getting plenty to eat and having a swell time "somewhere in Great Britain." Also, good son that he is, he writes he's sending her his money as he gets paid off. His address is A.P.O. 516, C/O Postmaster, New York. On maneuvers down in Louisiana is Corp. George Scott whose brother, Henry, expects to be in before long. He is just now helping to print this paper, so after his experience with Mr. Langford, he may one day be helping to print *Yank*, the service paper overseas.[17]

When we hear that one of our boys is "missing in action," the whole community is reduced to tears, but we all refuse to give up hope, and just recently our hopes have been justified in two cases. Frank Wynne (Merigold), "missing" for over a year, is now reported by the War Department as being a prisoner of the Jap[anese]. Carl Bailey (Shelby), whose plane fell, too, out in the Pacific, drifted about in his rubber raft, foodless for thirteen days, was finally located by a flying boat and picked up by a "P. T." on a tropical island. We must remember that, all us people here at home, when we're tempted to fuss because we can't get new tires, or a rubber hot water bag! Rubber can save our boys' lives. . . .

Re Thweatt writes glowing accounts of learning to ice skate in the beautiful mountainous country around Boise, Idaho, where her

17. *Yank* magazine, a U.S. Army publication, was widely read by enlisted personnel during World War II.

husband, Capt. Roger Lambright, is stationed. She's also learning to make cornbread since "the people in Idaho never heard of cornbread, poor things!" Loving the mountains, too, is W.A.C. Josephine Webb, now stationed at Camp Logan, Denver, finding the westerners very friendly and the mountains "magnificent." Remember pretty Edith de Lashment who used to be technician for Drs. Wiggins and Russel? She's now at the Army Nurses Corps for the present at the Foster Hospital, Jackson. Helen Hicks (W.A.V.E.), after her Smith College training, is now taking a radio course at the University of Wisconsin, and W.A.C. Beatrice Waller (Merigold) is now stationed at Roswell, New Mexico. SSGT John W. Harden is at Ft. Francis Warren, Wyoming. That fort, John, is named for an old friend of mine, Senator Warren of Wyoming, whose daughter married Gen. Pershing of World War I fame. He came thru that war unscathed, but she met a tragic death—was burned to death in her own home. Seeing your address brought back a host of memories to me of the handsome Senator, whose sheep ranches enabled him to give such wonderful parties, always "hostess-ed" (I'm coining a word) by his daughter, Mrs. Pershing, who, with "Black Jack", lived with her father in Washington when I knew them, alas, so many years ago.... [18]

A babe all Cleveland is interested in is young "Pinkie" (Crawford) Jones, the young son of "Pinkie" and Lucille Jones. "Pa" Jones is not exactly a service man now (tho' he was in the last war), but he's on our local draft board and has sent a lot of you boys off to this war—which should make him a kind of "associate" service man, and as so many of you know him, I knew you'd be interested to know he was now eligible for the "safety-pin club!" Other "service babies" whose dads are off to war belong to D.C. Dearmans and the Albert Fergusons (both of Boyle) and to the Frank Campbells (Skene).

18. Francis E. Warren (1884-1929) was a U.S. Senator from Wyoming from 1890-1893, 1895-1929. Hew as one of the great cattlemen of the west. His daughter, Helen F. Warren, was married to General John J. Pershing (1860-1948), the commander of the American Expeditionary Force in Europe during World War I. General Pershing's nickname was "Black Jack," a name he derived from his service with a black regiment early in his career. Helen Warren Pershing and three of her four children lost their lives during the burning of the Presidio on August 27, 1915.

From the Merigold *Spot-light* (High School paper), where Betty Sue Rayner is doing a bang-up job of keeping up-to-date records of Merigold's service sons (which I am thankful to say she shares with me!), I learned that James Charles Gregory is at the Great Lakes Training Station. (That's where Alvin Campbell, Shelly Steiger, Truman Beavers, and Alvin Coloman have also been training.) Also, that Horace Craddock (214th Signal Depot) is at Camp Crowder, Missouri and Milton Fink is at Shreveport, Louisiana.

Before I close I want to say thanks again for your letters and cards boys—just measure your delight in mail and gauge by it how much of a thrill we get out of hearing from you! Why, George Woolfolk (Boyle), I practically threw a fit over your writing after reading in one of my letters about Dorothy Shands being with the Red Cross in Sicily, inquiring, finding she was at your base, looking her up, and enjoying a visit with "a girl from home." Norwood Brown is rejoicing in a letter [he received] . . . saying that the matchfolders and cigarettes he sent in large quantities were put into the Christmas stockings of the soldiers in the Near East. I hope some of you boys got some of them! Sorry I can't send you each something as tangible as that, but I do send, in each letter, the thanks of the entire community for what you are doing for us. "May the Lord bless and keep you."

Sincerely,
Keith Frazier Somerville

March 17, 1944

Dear Boys:

A German spoke at Delta State this week and all the Delta turned out to hear him. He was and is the anti-Nazi author, Emil Ludwig, whose interesting biographies and other books were burned by Hitler's orders . . . as he proudly boasted.[19] His subject, "What Kind

---

19. Emil Ludwig (1881-1948) was a German writer who was internationally known for his many popular biographies. He became an outspoken opponent of Nazi oppression. At the Nuremberg rally of 1934, his books, as well as those of H. G. Wells, Thomas Mann, and others, were burned in a large public bonfire. A front page story about Ludwig was published in the March 10, 1944 issue of the *Bolivar Commercial*.

of Peace Shall We Make With Germany," was something in which all of us are interested, so I tho't perhaps you'd like to know what a German thought should be done. Since Dr. Ludwig's arrival in the United States, he's been helping our country by radio broadcasts to Germany, and recently told the Foreign Affairs Committee of the United States Senate just what he told us. In substance, he advocated an army of occupation for at least ten or fifteen years, in which time clear thinking Germans should be employed to teach the children new ideas and try to uproot the war ideas which for hundreds of years have been ground into the Germans, first by the Junkers, and lately by Hitler.[20] Then he urges total disarmament, even down to toy pistols and no sympathy, lest the next generation of our children should have to go thru with another war. Then he feels that the older Germans now fighting this war should be made to help rebuild the Europe they've destroyed. "If you compassionate Americans can't do it, why leave it to the Russians and the English—they'll do the job," he declared. He dwelt at length on the idea that all the Germans understand is force; that our idea of freedom and democracy is so foreign to them, who for centuries have known only to command or to obey, that it is totally misunderstood. "In America," he said, "everything is free but what is specially forbidden; in Germany everything is "verboten", not specifically allowed; children are born in Germany with their hands by their side (in the attitude of a soldier awaiting commands!); in America you obey when it suits you; in France they never obey. (Laughable, says I, but questionable? French children, at any rate, do obey as well as if not better than ours.) He cited an incident of a German who went to see an American officer in command. The colonel smiled and offered him a cigarette. "That can't be the boss," was the German's reaction. "Those in command don't act that way!" They don't understand us and our easy ways. Because we sent no soldiers into Germany proper after World War I, and they saw none, they were convinced they had not lost the war. If they had, where were the conquerors? They fooled themselves by thinking that Americans were not fighters. Mr. Ludwig admitted that he thought so, too, and spoke of his amazement when he saw our peaceful land turned overnight into an armed

20. Junker was the name given to the Prussian landed aristocracy.

camp. "There you have the advantage of every country in the world," he declared. "Will Russia be a menace to the world after the war?" was one question asked him, and he replied in the negative, pointing out that, in his opinion, Russia was passionately nationalistic and tremendously interested in building up its own great land, wanting only to be left in peace to work out its own problems. From his knowledge of the German character, Dr. Ludwig predicts that the Germans will collapse suddenly when they become convinced of eventual defeat, will leave the sinking ship like rats, and all begin protesting vigorously that they were not Nazis and so not responsible. (Of course he, with his wonderful command of language, did not put it that way! That was my own interpretation of what he did say!) As a matter of fact, he commented, there really were originally only a small percentage of real Nazis, compared to the whole population of Germany, but he warns us not to be fooled by that, for all the German people are responsible for the war and its atrocities. Another thing he said which surprised me was that all Hitler's talk about needing elbow room was josh (my interpretation again) and that Germany really was big enough for the Germans. It really was very interesting, and I hope some of you can hear him if he comes your way. The only trouble was that he spoke fast, in a high pitched voice, and with such a decided German accent, that now and then one missed some of his words. Speaking of voices, he said the Germans loved Hitler's blatant voice. And he wondered what might have happened had Hitler had Roosevelt's voice and vice-versa.

Home last week was Lt. (J.G.) Edwin Nunnery from Kingsville, Texas, where he is an instructor in the Naval Air Corps. In Texas, he had acquired a stunning small moustache (very becoming), and in Cleveland he acquired a new car, in which he and "Coach" Bennett (Cleveland High), also stationed at Kingsville and home on leave, returned to their base.

Home, too, is Mary Shands to pack up her summer "duds" preparatory to flying to Panama (Naval Intelligence). Sister Dorothy wrote the other day of an interesting experience in Sicily, attending the wedding of a lovely Sicilian girl to a captain in our Army where the bride (married in an age old chapel on her parents' estate) marched under crossed swords (British, American, and Italian), where champagne flowed like water, and where all the guests were given sacks of sugared almonds, symbolizing the bride's good wishes for her guests. An interesting variant of our custom of giving rice to the wedding guests to throw at the bride and groom to wish them luck. Another of our girls, Fran West (Shaw), paid Cleveland a flying visit last week from her new Red Cross base at Camp Campbell, Kentucky. . . .

In Italy, too, is Machine Gunner T.H. Stout. Because of moving about so, he's been having mail trouble. After weeks with none, he got twenty-five letters and three packages all in one day. On Christmas eve, though, he was the only lucky lad in his outfit to get a letter, so all the boys read the one he got from his mother, written on Thanksgiving day. I wonder if the letter telling that his young brother, Jack, now a senior in Cleveland Hi, is now in Naval Reserve and will leave after graduation in June, and the package containing a shockproof watch he requested (as his old one "couldn't take it") have caught up with him? Here's hoping!

The War Department has notified the J.A. Crawfords that a shortwave broadcast picked up from Germany mentioned that SSGT Carl T. Crawford was a prisoner of war, which is hopeful news for his parents as he has been missing from Italy for some time. His brother, SSGT Louis H., is somewhere in the South Pacific; brother Bertram (Navy Pharmacist Mate) is on a hospital ship somewhere near North Africa; and the fourth brother, James Harold, is now at Camp Shelby (his wife is with her family in Ashland). . . .

Bolivar County wasn't so peaceful itself recently when we were all terrorized by three bandits who had escaped in December from San Quentin prison, were captured, and then escaped from Jackson's "escape proof" jail and went on a rampage, stealing nine cars and kidnapping four people in twenty-four hours! One of the latter was an air pilot, home from the fighting front for a rest in quiet Crystal Springs, only to find himself in the midst of a hectic experience![21] Another was our own Olline McKnight (age fifteen) who, after the bandits shot her father and stole their car, was forced to sit between them while they gaily drove said car through Cleveland to Belzoni,

---

21. Crystal Springs is twenty miles south of Jackson, Mississippi.

where she was held a prisoner all day.[22] Well, all of you fighting McKnights, scattered over the globe, will probably have no more exciting experience to tell your grandchildren! Can you, Maj. Alvie, peacefully teaching at Harvard (where the Lodges speak only to Cabots and the Cabots speak only to God) match that exciting escapade? Edward, with the Air Corps in England, and James, flying in Italy, probably can match thrills with Olline, but Elmo, down at Camp Shelby, can't—yet! Speaking of Cambridge (Harvard) reminds me to tell you that Comos Brocato (Merigold) and Purvey Griffin are there, too, and that Berlin Griffin (Purvey's brother) has been in a hospital out in the Pacific for over a month now—sick, not wounded. I wish I could send you some of my jonquils, Berlin—they are so lovely now. Each year when they bloom, I believe anew in the "immortality of the soul." "And so my heart with rapture thrills and dances with the daffodils."[23]

Best wishes for each of you.
Keith Frazier Somerville

April 7, 1944

Dear Boys:

I had such an interesting train trip to Memphis recently in company with Walter Lopez (Boyle) who, for almost two years, has been employed with the 14th Naval District in Honolulu. When war came he wanted to join the Seabees but was turned down because of his eyes. However, as a civilian employee of the Navy, he has done exactly what he had hoped to do in the service, and for many months has worked at Pearl Harbor, repairing ships, acting as building warden, and lately as instructor on diesel electric cranes. He had with him the most fascinating collection of Kodak pictures depicting every phase of life in the beautiful islands in wartime: Navy pals and sunsets over Waikiki; hula girls and Dorothy Lamour (in sarong) and Jeanette McDonald (looking lovely in a swim suit);[24] public buildings

22. Front page coverage of these events appeared in the Memphis *Commercial Appeal* on January 7, February 25, 1944 and the Jackson *Clarion-Ledger* on February 28, 29, March 1, 1944.

23. This is a line from William Wordworth's (1770-1850) poem, "The Daffodils."

24. Dorothy Lamour (1914-), a popular movie star of the 1940s, often appeared in films wearing a sarong. Jeanette MacDonald (1903-1965) was famous for her voice, not her figure. She and Nelson Eddy (1901-1967) appeared in many musicals together.

and the sign "at the crossroads of the world, advising car drivers how many miles to Tahiti and Tokyo, to New York and Berlin! When the train pulled into Memphis and I was rudely jerked back to reality, I felt I'd been on a journey to another world! I really do get such a big thrill out of your travels!

Walter was telling me that his sister, Kathleen, is now working as a welder in Mobile (helping to build those ships he helps to repair, and others of you help to man) and that Bill Alexander, Jr. (Boyle) has been home, too, from Kessler Field, Biloxi. We talked to five Lamberson boys—Lt. O.B. and Whitfield, Jr. both get their mail now—Care of Postmaster, New York; Bob Frank, a Marine, who was at Bougainville and who for some time has been in a hospital in Oakland, California, being treated for a wound in his foot;[25] E.C., also a Marine, somewhere out in the South Pacific and stationed near Dick Alexander (Boyle), by the way; and Kenneth, the last to go, who left with one of the Burnside boys not long since for a Marine camp in California. Five brothers, all serving Uncle Sam! What a patriotic record! We should ask ourselves here at home, "What have we done today that makes us worthy to have five boys from one family go out to fight our battles for us?" For me, the answer is "nothing", and it makes me humble and filled with gratitude! And by the way, Lt. Ben Spells (Boyle), another of five brothers in the service, has had a leave, too, recently from Claims, New Mexico. I'll tell you about the whereabouts of the Spells boys another day. . . .

Cleveland nowadays is a regular mecca for servicemen's wives. Mrs. Travis Carpenter is here (Travis is still at Camp Shelby) and Mrs. Frank Taft Watson moved here this winter. Before taking his Navy training at Great Lakes, Frank was connected with the Greenwood Country Club. Mrs. Watson was Eulalia Jeffcote (Benoit) and she and her little blonde daughter welcomed "daddy" with open arms when he came recently on a leave after completing his Great Lakes Training.

25. Allied forces landed on Bougainville, an important island in the Solomons chain, on November 1, 1943. Fighting in the dense jungle was fierce, and Bougainville was finally brought under Allied control in the spring of 1944.

Another charming newcomer is Mrs. Arthur Blessett (Virginia Campbell of Boyle). Capt. Blessett (Air Corps), after months in Alaska, is now at Fresno, California, while his wife and two attractive youngsters have an apartment here.

At a recent "Coca Cola" party for Jack Nowell's pretty wife, Willie Ruth (here on a visit from Sewickly, Pennsylvania, where Jack is still stationed), were a bunch of service wives: Dehlia Liddell Hallman (Louis is in New Guinea); Estelle Myers Bedwell (Cullen is in England); Marian Alice Owen Perkins (Ben is paratrooping in North Carolina); Vi Smith Ingram (Cliff is at Camp Forest); Dot Robinson Carpenter (Bunny is on maneuvers in Tennessee; and my Keith (Joe Rice Dockery is still in New Orleans). To join the daily growing group soon will come Eleanette Shands Leake (Hunter is in Panama).

Have you noticed how many men in the public eye have come to Mississippi in the past for their wives? Walter Winchell's wife was a Mississippi girl (which does not alter in any way his feeling about Representative Rankin!), and so was the wife of Gen. Hershey, head of the Selective Service.[26] He's been resting up a bit in our state, so Oscar Johnston promptly got to him with a plea not to take any more of our farm boys, as labor in the Delta was fifteen per cent off.[27] His reply was, "I sympathize, but this is war! You can't convince me that the 67,000 farm deferments in Mississippi are all needed. You've got to have fields to plant crops in before you need to harvest them and

26. John E. Rankin, a Democratic congressman from Mississippi from 1921-1953, was a recalcitrant racist. Walter Winchell (1897-1972) was a journalist and radio personality. In 1923, he married Mississippian, June Magee. Like her husband, she was a former vaudeville performer, the Aster of the Aster and Hill vaudeville team. Lewis B. Hershey (1893-1977) was the director of the Selective Service System, the organization which oversaw the draft and the deployment of men for service during World War II. He was married to his high school sweetheart, Ellen Dygert, who was actually from Indiana. However, the Hersheys were married during World War I at Camp Shelby in Hattiesburg, Mississippi.

27. Oscar Goodbar Johnston (1880-1955) was a Jackson, Mississippi native who became a banker, politician, and Delta planter as well as the chief expert on cotton for New Deal agriculture policymakers. Best known in Delta circles as the president of the Delta and Pine Land Company, the largest cotton plantation in the world, Johnston was the founder in 1939 of the National Cotton Council of America. For additional information on Johnston, see Lawrence J. Nelson, "Oscar Johnston, the New Deal, and the Cotton Subsidy Payments Controversy, 1936-1937," *Journal of Southern History*, 40(August 1974): 399-416.

you've got to fight your battles far enough from these fields to keep them from being destroyed." So he and Uncle Sam sent out forty-six more greetings in Cleveland a few weeks ago!...

Care of Postmaster, San Francisco, would reach a lot of Merigold boys these days! Among those whose letters now reach them through that medium are Gerald Barrentine, Bennie Milligan, Marion Chester Hollis, L.K. Millican, Hubert Mullins, Vernon Springer, James McGarrh, and James O. Thomas. And one of Merigold's Chinese sons with the same address is Lellewyn Chun. He's hoping his pet "Battery B" will get a chance to "blast the blasted Jap[anese] to kingdom come." In fact, that's the deep seated wish of all Bolivar County's sons of Chinese descent. I was talking with Joe Y. Fong, home on leave from a medical detachment at the Station Hospital, Army Air Field, Herington, Kansas. Joe was born in Canton, China and the dearest hope of his life is that he may one day re-enter Canton with a victorious American Army. That they may do the same and help run the Jap[anese] from their birthplaces, Joe tells me, is also the hope for Earnest Joe (now stationed at Roswell, New Mexico), of Kenneth Wong (already overseas with a Parachute Company), of Chester Joe (likewise with A.P.O. 32, Care of Postmaster, San Francisco as his present address), and of Jack Chow, now at Camp Savage, Minnesota. Chung Pang Leung was born in this country, but he is no less anxious than his China-born friends that his present training at Gulfport Field may prepare him to help drive the Jap[anese] from China, which he is hoping one day to see! Well, I notice where the English Lord Louis Mountbatten is sending United States manned gliders and troop transports laden with Indian and American troops back of the enemy lines in the Far East (the first airborne operation of Asiatic war), so maybe they'll get their wish yet![28]

Spring is here in the Delta, but what a wet spring! It has rained and rained, dampening not one whit the ardor of the lovely spring flowers, but making the planters and the early spring gardeners tear their hair! Neither England nor the South Pacific jungles can have had a wetter season than we've had since Christmas this year! Or can

---

28. Admiral Lord Louis Mountbatten (1900-1979) served as Supreme Allied Commander for Southeast Asia from 1943-1946.

they? I wouldn't be knowing from actual experience! Maybe the skies all over the world are weeping over the sad condition of said world and with peace will come sunshiny weather in a sunshiny world. Here's hoping anyway! . . .

Sunshine and cheer to each of you!

Sincerely,
Keith Frazier Somerville

4

We Think of Ourselves as Soldiers on the Home Front

June 1944—December 1944

Dear Boys:

No, indeed, I haven't forgotten you (nor has anyone in Bolivar County), but thanks for your cards of inquiry and for missing my letters. I hate to admit it, but old age got me down and I finally ended up in the Baptist Hospital (Memphis) with an operation, which the doctors assure me will cure all my ills and make a new woman of me. (Here's hoping, but I'm a bit skeptical about surgical "fountains of youth"!) Now I am home again after a month in the hospital, and it's grand to be back and awaken to the singing of the mocking birds and the odor of honeysuckle and cape jasmine instead of hospital noises and odors! Getting home is something you, too, have to look forward to—and truly "be it ever so humble, there's no place like home." *There's No Front Like Home*, by the way, is a new book which has the nation rocking with laughter. The author, Robert Yoder, pokes such amusing fun at all of us that we are compelled to laugh with him at ourselves, though, if the truth be told, it made me, for one, ashamed of myself (which is what it was supposed to do, I imagine).[1]

1. Robert Yoder, *There's No Front Like Home* (Cambridge: Houghton Mifflin, 1944).

So much has happened since I last wrote that I'd never be able to catch up. Rome has fallen, France has been invaded, and Japan bombed with those super bombers, with which one of our own boys, John Wiley Erwin, has been so closely connected since they were a hush-hush secret.[2] He was sent for months to study them "from the ground up" in factories where they were being built, and tested the first one flown by Army pilots at a Kansas airfield near the factory where it was assembled. Then, in Kansas, he helped instruct the first group which trained on those ships, and later was sent to Georgia to do the same work. Then he flew to England (via Newfoundland) and stopped there only long enough to inspect our own R.A.F. and Canadian air bases, (being especially interested in the latter, for you remember he flew with the R.C.A.F. before we entered this war).[3] In England, too, John Wiley attended conferences with Gen. Eisenhower and big-wig British generals, and went to Buckingham Palace.[4] Thence he flew on, via Cairo and India, to China, where for months now he has been with those super Flying Fortresses. (I believe all the young "Superman" comic strip fans will unite with us in proclaiming the men who man those "super planes" to be "supermen" themselves!) Whether John flew with them when they bombed Japan is not yet known, but it is highly probable. Since he's been in China, his Canadian wife, Lenore, has presented him with a young daughter. Karen Ann was born in Detroit, where her mother has been staying with an aunt. John Wiley wanted that youngster born in the U.S.A., but Lenore got as close as possible, to her mother, who, by the way, is a trained nurse. Needless to say that grandmother was present for the young lady's arrival. Grandmother Erwin hasn't seen her yet, but reports tell her she has John's blue eyes and blonde hair. I hope she'll be as beautiful as her mother and have her daddy's' contagious grin! Though the babe is over a month old, it was only a few days ago that a cable from her dad came, announcing that he had gotten news of her arrival. As he sits smoking, six miles up in the air

2. Rome fell on June 5, 1944. The invasion of France began on D-Day, June 6, 1944. Beginning in June 1944, very large bombers, the Boeing Superfortress (B-29), began to attack the Japanese homeland from bases in China.

3. RCAF is the abbreviation for the Royal Canadian Air Force.

4. General Dwight David Eisenhower (1890-1969) was Supreme Allied Commander in Europe during World War II.

on one of the world's "biggest, most potent, and newest bombing planes," doubtless many of his thoughts are with the new daughter he has never seen. I notice from dispatches where the engines of one of the B-29s has been named for the wives and sweethearts of its crew. Perhaps John Wiley, who flew the first B-29, is also flying again on that ship, affectionately called (so A.P. reports tell us) "The First," and perhaps one of the engines may be called Lenore! Anyway, here in Cleveland we all feel we have a very special interest in the new "20th Air Force," the first global bombing force, which is expected to alter history.[5]

Now that it can be told, a foreign correspondent, just home on leave from five years in China, told on the radio the other night of the tremendous work of preparing bases and extra long runways deep in the heart of China for those big ships. He called it the most stupendous job since the building of the Great Wall of China, for like that, it was all done by hand. It seems that when Chiang Kai-Shek was told of the plans and sites had been selected (there are several of them), he sent out a call to all the adjoining provinces for labor. Then the great trek began, some coolies walking for five days from their homes to the places selected—167,000 Chinese men and women have worked for many months for that raid on Japan (not to mention the thousands working here in the U.S.A. to make it possible).[6] The locations selected were flat rice fields, which from time immemorial have been flooded, so the "squashy" soil had to be excavated to the depth of eight feet. That was the first step. Then it was filled in with rock from nearby mountains and river beds—huge boulders at the bottom, the rocks graduating in size till the top layer was tiny pebbles. Remember all this had to be done by hand, as there was no modern machinery available. Somewhere in the interior was found a rusty old steam roller, long discarded, and 500 men pulled it back and forth to smooth the runway! A month or so ago the Generalissimo, swearing them to secrecy, took some of the American correspondents then in Chungking to see one of the then almost completed fields.[7] That day only 60,000 men were at work there, but often,

5. The U.S. Twentieth Air Force, which used the new Boeing Superfortress (B-29), was created for the strategic bombardment of Japan.

6. The word "coolie," now considered patronizing, meant laborer at this time.

7. Chiang Kai-Shek (1887-1975) was usually called the Generalissimo.

they were told, over 100,000 had worked daily on the huge project. . . .

When D-day arrived, Cleveland joined with Roosevelt and the nation in prayers for the success of the invasion, and lots of Cleveland girls sent up special prayers for the safety of their own spouses stationed in England. (Rose Engleburg Sabin, Estelle Myers Bedwell, Maurine McKnight Cole, and Ida Lee Nowell Nance, to mention but a few. I have been told there are many others.)

Here at home things have happened fast, too, since I've been away, but I imagine it's stale news to you that Rowan Thomas's (Boyle) book—*Born in Battle*—is now for sale at the nation's bookstores.[8] It's hard to get a copy, though, for the first edition is about sold out, I'm told. It's fascinating reading. Stale news, too, about so many weddings. Among them Mary Jane Myers to Lt. Carl Nichols of Rosedale. Mary Jane is now learning to cook cornbread and vegetables in Gainesville, Texas. And it was only the other day that she was one of my "kindergarten babies"! Elizabeth Davis, too, was one of them. She married Lt. (J.G.) Bill Carr out in Seattle, Washington, and they are now in Jacksonville, Florida, where Bill is taking some special Naval training. Lt. Norman Hardee (also once one of my "kindergarteners") came home, too, from years of flying in the Pacific, covered with medals and married to a lovely Texas girl. They are now in Miami. And Ann Bedwell married Sgt. Gaddy Wells, an aerial photographer, now at Sioux Falls. I heard the head of that branch, too, talk on the radio recently from London. Asked, "How did the maps of Normandy, made from your aerial photographs, stand up in the invasion?" he replied, "Ninety-nine percent perfect." (Those guys must be good!)

As a number of our boys from Bolivar County have been reported as being prisoners of both the Jap[anese] and the Germans, Mr. Frank Wynne (Merigold) feels that many of you would like to write to them if you only knew how. His son, you recall, has for a long time, been a Jap[anese] prisoner. His address is "SSGT Frank O. Wynne, Jr., American Prisoner of War, Camp Tokyo, Tokyo, Japan via New York City, New York." If the camp where your boy is located is not known, substitute for Camp Tokyo, "Care Japanese (or German) Red Cross—via New York." Your address is to be written upside

8. Rowan Thomas, *Born in Battle* (Philadelphia: John C. Winston Co., 1944).

down on the envelope flap. On the front side—in the corner above address, type—"Prisoner of War—Postage Free..."

Our thoughts, our hopes, and our prayers are with you all, wherever you may be.

Sincerely,
Keith Frazier Somerville

July 14, 1944

Dear Boys:

The other night on the "American Eagle in Britain" program (a goodwill broadcast from the B.B.C.),... after interviewing a paratrooper and flyers about their part in the invasion, [the host] said to a sailor, "Tell us what you did." His reply was, "Well, after those fellows' exciting experiences, mine was nothing. I am just on an L.S.T.". "Listen to the modest lad!" chided the Englishman. "He was JUST on an L.S.T. (Land Ship-Tanks). JUST on one of those marvelous boats the enemy hates so much. JUST on one of those boats whose wonderful success, teaming up with the flyers, the infantry, the paratroopers, have done so much to make this invasion a success!"[9] Well, a number of our home boys are JUST on LST's too! C.P. Brocato and Fay Stanley Livingston (Ruleville) for instance. And Carl Booth Nelson (Coast Guard) has just been ordered from Florida to report at Norfolk for service on one. (Wife Martha Rushing comes next week to join the wives at home group). Speaking of C.P., Mrs. Tony Brocato, his mother, is now a three star mother, with Anthony in the Field Artillery at Ft. Riley, Kansas and Joe at Camp Perry, Virginia. (Camp Perry where so many of the Seabees trained is now a Naval training station.) Jack Stout is there, too, just a mile away from Joe. His uncle, Ens. Holton of Vicksburg, is one of the instructors there. Jack's brother, T.H., who received a shoulder wound months ago in Italy (Anzio beachead), is now convalescing and enjoying—guess what?—sheets! Those in the hospital are the first he's slept on in blows and centuries...

9. Landing Ship Tanks were large, flat-bottomed ships designed to transport tanks, vehicles, and troops across large ocean distances and land them directly on a beach. The men who served on these ships often referred to them as Large Slow Targets.

Lt. Lawson Magruder got as far as the Normandy beaches and was wounded on the fourth day of the Invasion—shrapnel in both legs. He was taken back to England and given such excellent care that he's about ready to return to the scrap—minus the shrapnel.

The wedding bells still continue to ring—Capt. (Dr. Jim) Westerfield (Merigold), home from two years in Alaska, has married Shirley Wynne. "Buck" Lemons (Boyle-Cleveland), former R.A.F. pilot and now a test pilot at the Ford plant, married Henry Ford's niece, Carol Bryant, at Dearborn, Michigan.[10] The wedding pictures and Mrs. Lemons' enthusiastic accounts show it must have been quite an enthusiastic wedding! Well, charming Buck deserves the best! Bobbie Pleasant, also a Ford test pilot, was one of the attendants and the Hytken boys, Robert and Sidney, were among those present. Shelby's handsome Col. Frank Gregory, of helicopter fame, also took unto himself a wife "up North" recently, marrying Sarah Elizabeth Kohr at Dayton, Ohio. Col. Lewis Gregory, Maj. W.W. Denton, and Maj. John W. Thomas, all of Shelby, were among the attendants of that wedding, which was equally lovely.

And W.A.V.E. Madeline Baird, daughter of "Brother Baird," former Methodist preacher here, married Ens. Robert L. Fay (Nanuet, New York) at Ft. Monroe, Virginia. Best wishes for long and happy lives from all your Bolivar County friends! . . .

After two years in Burma and India, SSGT Jack Houston is now an instructor at Savannah, Georgia. But a lot of our boys are still in that theatre of war. Willis Langston, with a hospital unit, service of supplies, was recently promoted to Tech. 4th Grade in New Delhi, India. And Lee Davis writes from Burma that the monsoon season is bad there, and oh, those insects! One especially bad kind he says sticks like ticks and leaves the boys bloody from bites. Lee is looking for relief from them soon when he has a leave, which he expects to spend in India where he'll probably see Raymond Hutchinson. (Both Lee's brothers-in-law—Lilly Veigh's husband, Percy Faulkner, and

10. The Ford plant is a reference to the bomber plant at Willow Run, Michigan, conceived by Charles E. Sorensen, the production chief of the Ford Motor Company. Only eleven months elapsed between the ground-breaking for the plant and the production of the first bomber. It was the site of one of the most important wartime studies about life on the home front: Lowell Juillard Carr and James Edson Stermer, *Willow Run: A Study of Industralization and Cultural Inadequacy* (New York: Harper and Brothers, 1952).

Raymond's brother, Clyde, have recently been called up. Percy has been working for the government down in Puerto Rico, but is now stationed at Butmer, North Carolina. Clyde was making a crop, and what's to become of it, Mother Hutchinson can't figure out while he's away soldiering.)

Writing of India in his book, *Born in Battle*, Capt. Rowan Thomas (Boyle) says, "There are millions of beggars throughout India. They put out clawing hands, positive you are going to backshee them. Great masses of people are homeless and live and sleep in the streets. You step on whole families as you walk thru the large cities at night, the naked babies sucking at the shriveled breasts of their ragged mothers. Here is another war we have got to win after this war is over: the war against misery and poverty. This world cannot long endure dazzling jewels on the perfumed body of one lady, and only sparkling tears in the eyes of hungry millions."

Honestly, boys, I think Rowan's book is one of the best this war has produced. It's the kind of a book that once started can't be put down till finished—a tale of thrilling adventures, interspersed with amusing and heartbreaking incidents and comments like the foregoing, which show that he and many of you other boys are thinking about future world affairs. Having read most of the favorably reviewed of this war's books, I felt I had a good basis of comparison and that my long time fondness for Rowan had not influenced my judgment of his book too much, yet I was pleased to have my judgment confirmed by Sterling North in the *Washington Post....*

Best of luck to all of you, and here's hoping it isn't as hot where you are as it is here. I imagine that's a silly hope, but best of luck anyway.

> Sincerely,
> Keith Frazier Somerville

August 4, 1944

Dear Boys:

Everybody has a hobby, don't they? Remember when you used to collect bird's eggs and hunted for Indian arrow heads? And I expect a lot of you are now collecting curios from far parts, or Jap[anese] swords or German helmets! One of my hobbies has always been collecting descriptions of places I'd like to see, and as I've been a big "fireside traveller," I have note books full of what other people have written about famous places. So now that the papers are full of the Leaning Tower of Pisa, whether or not the Germans have used it as an observation post, whether or not our artillery has destroyed it, I bethought myself of my travel books and brought them out to see what I had on Pisa. And I unearthed an interesting fact. If our boys do have to destroy the leaning tower, there is almost a replica of it (designed by Niccola Pisana, who constructed the campanile at Pisa) at the hill town of Ovieto, Italy. Only this one doesn't lean. . . .

I imagine F.W. Bishop, who is now stationed at Norwich, England, is remembering the Mother Goose rhyme he learned in his childhood—remember it? "The man in the moon, came tumbling down, and asked his way to Norwich, he went by the South and burnt his mouth, Eating cold pease-porridge!" F.W.'s cousin, Leon Wingate (formerly with the Mississippi Power & Light Company), visited him recently at Norwich and was the first Mississippian he'd seen since he'd been in England. Lt. Paul Mulrenin (Shelby) is back now from a long stay in England, and the family staged a reunion in his honor, with James home from the Pacific coast and sister, Betty, a cadet nurse, home from St. Vincent's Hospital, Little Rock.[11] The Cowans, too, had a reunion in Shelby, with "Doc" and George both home. Lt. George is now at Camp Campbell, Kentucky.

In England, too, is John Thomas Greer, serving as a mail clerk. It seems only the other day that I talked to John Thomas, home on a leave, in Denton's, and really it seems only the other day when John Thomas was helping build a post office in my room—Grade One—at the Little School! Veritably this is a young man's war! But then we must remember that great things have always been done by youth. Alexander Hamilton was only nineteen and James Madison only twenty-four, when they helped OLD Thomas Jefferson (age thirty-two) frame the Declaration of Independence!

Also based in England is Lt. George Boozer (Boyle), bombardier

---

11. In order to help alleviate the acute nursing shortage, Congress passed the Bolton Act in 1943, establishing the Cadet Nurse Corps. This act provided federal funds for nursing students who promised, upon the completion of their course of study, to practice essential nursing for the duration of the war.

on a Flying Fortress, who has received the Air Medal for bombing German industries and for attacks on enemy coastal defenses and supply lines in support of the Invasion. (Just as the weddings and babes keep coming, so do the decorations for our Bolivar Countians!)

Speaking of babes, Bobbie Wall (Boyle—F.B.I.) and his wife, Joyce, are rejoicing over the arrival of a young daughter up in Washington. So are the Clayton Wests—Lt. West is stationed at Columbus, Ohio and young Miss West's name is Constance Carolyn— and Lt. and Mrs. Jack Denton (Shelby) have a young son. The Dentons had plenty of excitement in their family lately—a new baby and another bride! Had you heard that David (Air Corps cadet) had married out in Ballinger, Texas? Caroline Brown Ambrose is the lovely name of the lovely bride!

A lot of our boys have gone on over to France. Victor Aguzzi (another of my youngsters) with the Rangers, writes he's finding it very inconvenient not being able to speak French so he can thank the "natives" for the wine they offer him at every turn![12] Lt. Ernest McMurchy (Duncan) is also somewhere in France, having participated in the Invasion with the 329th Infantry.

Speaking of brave youngsters, Sidney Mayo (Boyle) celebrated his nineteenth birthday in a hospital in Hawaii by writing his mother not to mind about him losing a leg; that he didn't, for he felt that he was lucky to be alive, and he wrote, "Now I can go to college"—(Sidney enlisted in the Marines the morning after his Hi School graduation). Isn't that a wonderful spirit!

On the home front, the canners are busy these days. Private Leo Brown of Pace (also somewhere out in the Pacific) has about the most patriotic family I know of. On the morning of July 4th, his father gathered four bushels of green peas, and mother and the girls spent the rest of the day canning them. That's what I call a really patriotic fourth.

But everybody in Pace didn't celebrate the fourth that way. Little Leonard Pace and his small pal, Cedric, took a picnic lunch and fished all day. They caught a lot of fish, too, and Leonard wishes he could have sent some to his dad, Jessie L. Pace, now stationed at San Diego, California.

---

12. The U.S. Army Rangers were specially trained and equipped soldiers who often carried out surprise raids behind enemy lines.

Lt. Revis Westbrook (Duncan) with the 172nd Infantry, writes that he has a captain who is "good at recognizing Southern drawls". Recently, at a picture show somewhere on an island in the South Pacific, his Captain heard a boy behind him talking. "Are you from Mississippi?" he asked. "Yes sir," came the reply, "from Cleveland." His name was Gibson! Now which one of the Gibsons do you "reckon" that was? . . .

That's all for today.

Best of luck to each of you.

Sincerely,
Keith Frazier Somerville

August 25, 1944

Dear Boys:

The other day a battered letter, all the way from Oregon, was handed to an officer on the front line in France. His wife had written, "Well, I guess it's all over but the shouting now. The police here in Portland have been given instructions for handling the armistice crowd and I hear the same is true in New York and Philadelphia." Shaking his head sadly, the colonel handed the letter to a radio newsman with the comment, "The only trouble is that those Germans out there don't know it's all over—not yet they don't."

Well, here at home most of us realize it's not over yet by a long shot, and realize there will be more "blood, sweat, and tears" and, alas, casualties, before total victory comes, but we are more happy than we've been since Pearl Harbor.[13] So hopeful that up in Washington Congress got to work and passed on June 22nd the so-called "G.I. Bill of Rights," providing for that happy day when its over, over there. This bill provides educational aid for those who want it, by way of payment for tuition and maintenance ($50 monthly for unmarried veterans, $75 for those with dependents). You can choose your own college and your own subjects, and the length of time you can spend

---

13. On May 13, 1940, in his first statement as Prime Minister, Winston Churchill (1874-1965) warned the members of the House of Commons of the hard road ahead and said, "I have nothing to offer but blood, toil, tears, and sweat."

in college is from one to three years, depending on the length of service. The allowance for tuition and books is up to $500 a year.[14]

The bill also provides for loans (fifty percent of the purchase price) for those of you wanting to build or purchase homes. It also created a Veteran Employment Bureau, and provides that those of you not immediately able to get work shall be paid $20 a week, for as long as fifty-two weeks. (Lots of people think there will be much abuse of this, and that many soldiers will just take a year's vacation on the nation, but I don't believe so. Some will, of course, but the majority of American soldiers have proven themselves trustworthy!) On being mustered out, each man who has served is country as long as sixty days overseas will receive $300. Those who have served more than 60 days here at home will be given $200. If a man has been in service less than sixty days, he will receive $100. The bill also provides for all kinds of disabilities, the rate ranging from $10 a month for ten percent disability to $100 monthly for total disability. It also provides for hospitalization and special rates for specific losses, such as arms, legs, eyes, etc. Then, in case a service man is killed, his wife will be paid $50 monthly, ($65 if she has one child, and $13 for each additional child).

For years after the Civil War, it used to be said that the sure way to success was to have lost a leg in the war, so cheer up Sidney Mayo and Claude Milstead! Two of the most interesting men I knew in my youth were one-legged Confederate veterans. One was that great Southern orator and statesman, John W. Daniel, who represented Virginia for so long in the United States Senate.[15] The other was a locksmith in my home town. He was the jolliest old man, and we children were fascinated by him and by his wooden leg, on which, in his spare moments, he had carved wondrous figures. He would have scorned one of these new-fangled legs which are so perfect that no one knows one is minus a leg! No, he was proud of that "peg leg,"

14. The G.I. Bill or Servicemen's Readjustment Act of 1944 was signed into law by President Roosevelt on June 22, 1944. This landmark legislation provided veterans with funds for education and training, low-interest loans, unemployment insurance, and job guarantees.

15. John W. Daniel (1842-1910) served as U.S. Senator (Democrat) from Virginia from 1887 until his death in 1910.

which he would wave at us and say "Scat" when he grew tired of our admiration and of spinning yarns for us. To neither of these men was the loss of a leg in the service of his country a handicap. Both were equally successful along their chosen lines. But when did a handicap ever stop an American? Our great President Roosevelt is an example of that. Not even lameness caused by the dread polio stopped him from reaching the top![16]

In a B-29 camp somewhere out in the Burma-China area, a surprise cable reached John Wiley Erwin from Gen. Wolfe (head of the Super-Fortresses) ordering him to report immediately to Wright Field, Ohio.[17] The General had flown back home to see about some changes deemed advisable to be made in those big babies after they had been in action, and he wanted Capt. Erwin to test the planes after the improvements had been added and also to test out the bigger B-32s.[18] John Wiley flew over immediately and was here to see his mother for a few hours. No, he told me, he did not participate in the raid over Japan, but he has been "flying the Hump" between India and China, which Eddie Rickenbacker and many others say is the most perilous flying spot in the world.[19] In order to get over those peaks, one must fly so high that everything freezes up. When that happens, and they have to come down, they have to play tag with Jap[anese] planes between those mountain peaks, some of them so close together that the plane wings often hit the sides. The Hump is in Japanese territory. (John Wiley didn't tell me all this in the few minutes I saw him. I heard a description of a flight over the Hump on the radio given by another of those men

16. Franklin D. Roosevelt was crippled when he was stricken by poliomyelitis in August 1921. Discussion of the extent of his disability was voluntarily withheld by the press.

17. General Kenneth B. Wolfe (1896-1971) supervised the development and testing of the B-29 Superfortress.

18. The B-32 was a prototype bomber developed as a possible alternative to the B-29. It was slow in going into production and only fifteen of the bombers arrived in the Pacific in time to see action against the Japanese.

19. After the Japanese gained control of key portions of the Burma Road in March 1942, a new route to China had to be found. Called the Hump, an air route over the Himalayas between India and China was inaugurated in April 1942. Large shipments of vital supplies were flown over the Hump to China between the spring of 1942 and the war's end in August 1945.

who have been flying that dangerous trip in aid of the hard-pressed Chinese.)

After reporting to Wright Field, Capt. Erwin hopes to run up to Canada and make the acquaintance of his little new daughter. Another of our boys, Lt. Oscar Crutchfield (Boyle) is also home from overseas and getting acquainted for the first time with adorable Patricia, whose mother (Mary Elizabeth House) has taught her to greet the new man in her life as "daddy." Just between us, I don't think men as a rule are as crazy about teensy-weensy babies as we women are, so I imagine a lot of them would really get a bigger thrill in meeting them first when they could sit up, smile, wave, and salute, as for instance cunning Dehlia Hallam can do for Capt. Louis when he gets home from the Pacific! Capt. E. F. Todd (Marie Lewis' husband) is home, too, from two years overseas, and having a grand time playing with his three precious "chillun". . . .

Decorations? Why of course, Capt. Eph McLean (Navy) has gotten another one—the Legion of Merit this time.[20] (Eph and wife, Jan, have been visiting with Mrs. Mac and Louise in California this past week.) And had you heard about Lt. Ralph Long (Skene) getting the Distinguished Flying Cross for extraordinary achievement in aerial flight as pilot of a United States Navy torpedo bombing plane which sunk a German sub in the Atlantic some time ago?

Best of luck to each of you,

Sincerely,
Keith Frazier Somerville

September 8, 1944

Dear Boys:

The whole community is jubilant over the fact that when the 1063 American flyers in prison camps in Romania were recently released, our own Bill Litton, reported missing after an air raid on the Ploesti

20. The Legion of Merit is awarded to personnel of the armed forces of the United States as well as to personnel of the armed forces of friendly nations who have distinguished themselves by exceptionally meritorious conduct in the performance of outstanding services.

oil fields, was among them![21] Col. Bill is one of the most decorated flyers in the Mediterranean theatre, having earned the Legion of Merit, Silver Star with Oakleaf Cluster, Distinguished Flying Cross, and Air Medal with nine Clusters. He led the daring raid on the Romano-American refinery at Ploesti. . . . His wife and two babies are with the Littons in Shaw, and is that a happy family now that their "famed lightning fighter group commander" (as Associated Press calls Bill) is safe in Rome![22]

Our boys have certainly distinguished themselves in the Mediterranean area (as well as elsewhere!). Sgt. James McKnight (Cleveland), of the 15th Army Air Force Liberator "Craven Raven," has flown twenty-five combat sorties there, flying over strategic targets in Italy and Romania (including Bucharest and Ploesti). He, too, holds the Air Medal and Oakleaf Cluster "for meritorious achievements in sustained combat fight." And Lt. Col. Bernice S. Barr (Boyle) is now commanding a B-17 squadron in that area. He, too, has covered himself with glory and medals, being a veteran of fifty missions in the Pacific, and holding the Silver Star, Distinguished Flying Cross, and Air Medal with Oakleaf Clusters. And Lyda Murrell's husband (Remember her? She lives out from Boyle) as waist gunner on a B-24, Italy based, has just been awarded the Air Medal, too. SSGT Tranquilino Ancheta is not a Bolivar Countian, but we can lay claim to him by virtue of his wife! He once lived in Manila and joined the Air Corps in California.

It's wonderful, isn't it, to know that we now have so many planes and such air supremacy everywhere? I read that in the early days of the war, planes were getting so low that they figured that at the rate they were losing Flying Fortresses they'd all be done in six weeks. They told Gen. Eaker that, and asked if he

21. A raid on the German-controlled oil refineries at Ploesti, Rumania, was conducted on August 1, 1943. Ploesti was not an easy target, for the flight from North Africa to Rumania was long and difficult. The August 1 raid dealt a savage blow to German petroleum production, and subsequent air raids inflicted further damage. However, Ploesti did not stop functioning until the end of August 1944. In September 1944, the Russians occupied the ruins.

22. Lightning was the name of a fast fighter aircraft, the P-38.

intended continuing daylight raids.[23] "Yes," he replied, "down to the last plane. I will then climb aboard that one and go over with you boys!" Fortunately, reinforcement began to come in about that time and now the general can send out thousands daily. . . .

Mind if I confide in you some very personal things? The first is good news. I now have a little G.I. of my very own, for my first grandson, whose initials are G.I. (George Ingram), arrived on September 1st. (He's Ashton's babe.) The second is bad news—I fear I'm growing old. (Naturally, with four grandchildren, I hear you dryly comment). But it's worse than that; I've always said I hoped I'd pass out of the picture before I began living in the past as so many old people do, but I've done just that and been just eighteen (in my mind) for the past week! It all began when last week's *Time* arrived, featuring my old friend Gen. "Sandy" Patch on the cover. I rushed to dig out an old scrapbook I kept in my youth and there I was, in kodak pictures taken with Sandy at West Point! Am I funny looking, and I thought then I was very chic, in a white suit, white furs, and a huge blue velvet hat! But Sandy, a six footer in his big cadet overcoat against the snowy background of Cullum Hall, is still definitely glamorous looking! Now only his blue, blue eyes and his sandy hair seem to remain of the youngster I knew thirty odd years ago![24] That night the radio blared out the news that Gen. John Courtney Hodges's 1st American Army was knocking at the Belgian border, and I was back again to my dancing days! And capping the climax, last week's *Post* had to feature "Johnie Lee" (Gen. J.C.H.), announcing that, in addition to being Eisenhower's right hand general, "he had, and has, an irresistible gift for caricature." Out came the same scrapbook again (buried for years in a back closet), and there was proof that he, too, was an old friend, in a caricature he had done of me, and a wonderful calvary man—with the caption, "Nix on the Calvary" (he being an Engineer). And by the way, in the foreground was he himself on one

---

23. General Ira C. Eaker (1896-1987) served as the Commanding General of the U. S. Army Air Forces in the United Kingdom and was a strong proponent of daylight precision bombing.

24. General Alexander Patch (1889-1945) commanded the Seventh Army, which invaded southern France in August 1944. The young Keith Somerville met "Sandy" Patch while a student at the Castle.

knee at my feet! Just to think I once had a general at my feet—if only on paper![25]

I got such a thrill out of my old friends being headliners that I just had to tell you about it! You can laugh if you want to, but I'll wager that now and then when you're my age, you, too, will go back in memory to the days you're now living through! I hope in thirty years we won't again be in the midst of another war, but if (by sad chance or the wrong kind of peace) we should be, then I'm sure that many of your friends will be generals too! The way you're acting now, some of you will be generals yourselves... Had you heard about Annie Tutwiler (who lives between Mound Bayou and Merigold) who has six sons in the service? David Tutwiler writes from Marfa Field, Texas for his mother not to worry now that the Army has all her boys, "Just pray for us all to get back safe," and they'll all send her help, "to show we really love you." Robert and Eddie, two of the brothers, are together in the Navy and getting alone fine. John, also in the Navy, is now at Bainbridge, Maryland, and thinking all the time of his baby and wishing he could see it. Lewis is with an engineer regiment and writes he, too, is well and happy, and sends instructions for one of his bonds to be sold to buy and send him a watch... A salute to our six star [N]egro mother and her six American soldier-sons, each writing longingly of the day when they'll return to their homes in the deep South and each probably today grinning in the face of difficulties and showing their white teeth, as they show to the world, that all races, creeds, and colors in America are in there fighting for that victory, which today seems almost in sight!

Till that happy day when each of you returns to Bolivar County, God bless and keep you all.

Sincerely,
Keith Frazier Somerville

25. In the spring of 1944, General Courtney Hodges (1887-1966) was appointed Commander of the U.S. First Army in Europe. The First Army achieved a remarkable number of "firsts," including first ashore on D-Day, first to break out of the beachhead, first into Paris, first across the German border, first across the Rhine, and first to contact the Germans in central Germany. Mrs. Somerville evidently confused General Courtney Hodges with General John Clifford Hodges Lee (1887-1958), who was featured in the September 2, 1944, issue of the *Saturday Evening Post*. See Martin Sommers, "Lee—Batting for Eisenhower," *Saturday Evening Post*, September 1944, pp. 9-11, 37, 39-40, 42. Lee served as the deputy commander of the ETO. The *Saturday Evening Post* described him as "the least known of the key figures of this war" (p. 9). Lee was a graduate of West Point, and Mrs. Somerville had met him while a student at the Castle.

September 22, 1944

Dear Boys:

As some of you are now able to hang your washing on the vanted Siegfried and Gothic lines and as bombs fall on the Philippines, or other Pacific isles, and all over Europe, our thoughts are marching and flying with you![26] For instance, little Kathie Jane Walton (aged 4) is a bit too young to wonder if that B-24 which is named for her, has dropped any bombs on Mindanao, but the rest of us have wondered![27] Her uncle, Charles Renfro, wrote from out in the Pacific that he and his pilot had named their plane for his niece and the pilot's young daughter. Happy landings to the "K-Lucy" and her crew!

Out in New Guinea is John B. Murray Jr., with the 391st Engineers. Johnnie, I saw your pretty wife the other morning wearing the loveliest jewelled engineers's towers.[28] She told me she wore that pin all the time, even riding uptown on her bike in a gingham dress, with her lovely eyes all covered up with dark glasses! So you're always with her. Too bad you and her uncle (Sgt. Ray Lewis, Air Corps), also in New Guinea, haven't contacted each other yet. Maybe you have by now. Anyway, your wife and Jane Lewis... are hoping you two will get together and talk of them as here at home they talk of you!

Erline Hanson Lusk and Sue Griffin Sims get together often, too, and compare letters from their husbands, also now in New Guinea. Sue and Erline, with their babes, followed those boys to camps all over the U.S. since they left home together with the National Guard, and now those gals have houses not far apart in Cleveland....

My, what a job the Army branch of the Telephone Company must be doing! The Bell Telephone News for August tells us there's no shortage of telephone equipment on the fighting fronts.[29] For the Army and Navy,

26. The Seigfried Line was the name given to the German frontier fortifications in Europe. The song, "We're Going to Hang Out the Washing on the Siegfried Line," was a popular British music hall tune. The Gothic Line was the name given to the German defensive outpost in Italy.

27. Mindanao is a large island in the Philippines archipelago.

28. The engineer insignia for the U.S. Army was a lapel pin with small towers, signifying construction.

29. The Bell Telephone Company carried numerous full-page advertisements in the popular press urging citizens to "Clear the Lines for the War," and to "please give a clear track to the war effort by confining... Long Distance calls to those that are really necessary."

there's plenty and on time. As our Armies roll and new victories against the enemy come, more and more equipment is required, and that's why there's so little for normal civilian use. The home front reserves are about exhausted, but the demand continues. For its part in the overseas communication on D-Day, the Bell system received congratulations from the Chief of Army Communications for their splendid cooperation. Twelve exciting minutes many operators will never forget were those between 3:20 and 3:32 A. M. on D-Day, as the prearranged plans for carrying Invasion news across sea and land were thrown into high gear. Lloyd Sims wrote of a one night session in his hut when they put on a concert and used the phone as a mike to broadcast all over the company area. George Kelly (Pace) was one of the performers. They had guitars and a sax and Lloyd himself joined in on his twenty-five cent harp, regardless of the fact that it didn't have enough notes. Also, he had to stop now and then, as he was acting announcer! The hut was crammed full of boys coaching from the side lines, and wrote Lloyd, "It was one hell of a jam session!" (Sez I, thank heaven they can think of something to relieve their hard life and lighten the tedium!)...

Had you heard about the narrow escape Lt. James Boozer (Boyle) had recently? He was in that big Army bomber which crashed near Shiprock, New Mexico. James and four others parachuted to safety before the ship crashed and burned. . . .

David Joseph (Merchant Marine) recently married in New York, a lovely Spanish girl, and brought her home with him when he came to his father's funeral. Queer thing—David dreamed Mr. Joseph was going to die, called home and found it was true. Sometimes the occult is right, and it makes one believe in the supernatural. And though soothsayers and prognosticators are oftener wrong than right, I've found, I continue to watch and hope when they foretell the end of Hitler and the war with Germany. . . .

Sincerely,
Keith Frazier Somerville

November 10, 1944

Dear Boys:

There are a lot of happy grandmothers hereabouts, for the fortunes of war have sent home a bunch of our daughters with their babies.

Mrs. Thweatt has Re and beautiful little Susan (aged one month) with her while Capt. Lambright is at the Greenville Air Base; Mrs. Ward has Marjorie Johnson and baby, Judy; Mrs. Shands has Eleanette Leake and her three boys (Lt. Leake is in Panama); and I have Ashton, with little Ashton and baby George (two months old) with me (Ens. Ingram is stationed in Washington). And to mention but two other doting grandmothers there are Mrs. Kelso, who thinks Carol Ann, the month old daughter of Richard and Jeanette, is a wonder child; and Mrs. Nowell, who is equally enthusiastic over Jack's small son (Jack is stationed in Pennsylvania with the Coast Guard, while his wife and babe are in Clarksdale with her mother). These are but a few of the three score and ten of us grandmothers, and I fear we're all alike and all, like proverbial grandmothers, are prone to baby-spoiling! But anyway, we're all enjoying those babes a lot and we see safety for the future of America in them.

I stayed with Ashton six weeks before bringing her and her small family home with me.[30] While I was away, many of our boys have come and gone and I missed seeing a lot of them. Col. Bill Litton (Shaw) was home and I hear got a big ovation as one of our returned heroes. He's now in a Georgia Hospital undergoing treatment after his months in a Rumanian prison camp. Lt. Jimmie T. Robinson, who got his wings at Moore Field, Mission, Texas, after a visit home has returned to that base. T.D. Wodd (Marine who served quite a spell at Midway—'nough said!) and a bunch of others have gladdened the hearts of the home folk. I saw Floyd Dill on the street the day I got home, on leave while his ship, the U.S.S. *Hermitage*, is being worked on in New York. The *Hermitage*, by the way, was formerly a Jap[anese] ship captured and converted to our use. Floyd has spent a year in the Navy, and once he spent a year in my room, Grade One!

Had you heard that Bolivar County has another author in the person of the celebrated Col. Franklin Gregory (Shelby) whose new book, *Anything a Horse Can Do—A History of the Helicopter*, is just off the press?[31] Col. Gregory, you may recall, last year received a package of mail from Speaker Rayburn of the House of Representa-

30. Ashton and her husband, George Ingram, and their two children lived in Norris, Tennessee, during the early years of the war. In 1944, George entered the Navy, and Ashton and the two children returned to Cleveland to live.

31. Franklin Gregory, *Anything A Horse Can Do: The Story of the Helicopter* (New York: Reynal & Hitchcock, 1944).

tives on the steps of the Capitol, and flew it to a mail plane, thus being the first person to carry mail by helicopter.[32] Col. Gregory also scored another first, much earlier, in being the first to talk by phone to the ground from a heavier-than-air craft. Last year, you will recall, he was awarded the Bane Award for having made the greatest contribution to air advancement during the year. He is still at Wright Field, Ohio. His brother, Col. Lewis Gregory, has recently been made "Chief of the Specialized Air Crew Training Section in Command Headquarters," and as such, now has charge of all bombardier and navigation training conducted in the Air Forces. He is stationed at Deming, New Mexico. Many thousands of you boys taking these courses will be interested to know that the chief of that branch is one of our own Bolivar Countians. Another of the Gregory boys, Owen, is now a Lt. (J.G.) in the Navy and stationed at Asbury Park, N. J. . . .

"We think of ourselves as soldiers on the home front," writes Rachel Reed Dunn, whose husband, Sam, has been doing defense work for the past three years in powder and ammonia plants building ships, and now doesn't know what he's doing in this immense government project near Knoxville. But from the G.I. appearance of the 60,000 acres, guards at every entrance, and the wearing of a badge as an absolute necessity to enter any of the gates, we are assured this work is vitally important to the war effort. This "Project X," as the War Department calls it at Oak Ridge, is really an amazing place. Eighteen months ago the place was a barren, woody hillside adjoining the tiny town of Clinton, Tennessee—a town then not as big as Boyle. Today, it has grown into a city larger than Knoxville, with every kind of store and dwelling. The houses are a preview of what our after-the-war homes will be, having every modern convenience: heating systems that heat in winter and cool in summer, and every known electrical device. They are built of a compost material which makes both the outside and inner walls. The inside walls are painted in pastel shades, have huge windows, and are really lovely. Just what is being done at Oak Ridge, as Rachel writes, nobody knows. Only five men in the United States really know, I've been told. Some think it is an after-the-war project which is to revolution-

32. Sam Rayburn (1882-1961), a Democratic member of the House of Representatives from Texas from 1913 until death in 1961, was first elected Speaker of the House in September 1940.

ize our living; others, that they're manufacturing a secret war weapon with which to administer the knock out Axis blow. Of the thousands working there, each knows only his own little job. But anyway, "Project X" is something tremendous. . . . [33]

Well, election day has come and gone and it looks now like our great Commander-in-Chief F.D.R. is to remain at the helm to guide in Peace when it comes. [34] I, for one, am jubilant, for tho' I assert (as he did in a recent speech, stressing the "assert" and hoping the papers wouldn't say "admit") that he has made mistakes, I do think he's done a marvelous job and I couldn't see where Dewey would be an improvement. I got all hot and bothered over this race in Mississippi (though I was reared in politics up in Tennessee) this past summer. For the first time in my life, I got enough aroused over politics to write protesting letters to all those bolting electors, who, like obnoxious small boys who refuse to play when they can't have their way, refused to vote for the party nominee. Of course, it did no good, but I wanted to vote for Roosevelt, and I didn't think it fair for them to prevent me doing so. Fortunately, the legislature stepped in, elected another group of electors, and gave us . . . who wanted Roosevelt a chance to show . . . [those] who didn't, just what we thought of them! And I was pleased that so many Mississippians agreed with me![35] . . . . Well, anyway, it looks like most of us didn't want a change! And when this war is over, the only change most of you want is to get out of uniform and come home to good jobs in the U.S.A. God grant they'll be waiting for you. If F.D.R. has his way, they will be our way of saying "Thanks to the Yanks."

Sincerely,
Keith Frazier Somerville

33. It is astounding that Mrs. Somerville knew so much about the construction at Oak Ridge, Tennessee, where the components of the atomic bombs were manufactured and assembled. Project X was, as she surmised, of major importance. Clearly the censors did not read the *Bolivar Commercial*, for they would have had this paragraph excised.

34. In November 1944, Franklin D. Roosevelt defeated his Republican opponent, Governor Thomas E. Dewey (1902-1971) of New York, and won a fourth term as president.

35. During the presidential election of 1944, a small group of dissatisfied Democrats, mostly from the south, mounted an ineffective campaign to elect

December 8, 1944

Dear Boys:

How is the cigarette situation with you? . . . You'll smile, boys, when I tell you I've tried "rollin' my own." The only person who has gotten any satisfaction out of my make of cigarettes is my wee granddaughter, who beseeches me hourly, "make a cigawett, ganmarna!" Mine won't stay lit, will yours? And the tobacco spills out, no matter how hard I lick! This is doubtless the time for all grandmothers to stop smoking! I notice where a disgusted Cincinnati tobacco purveyor put on his locked door: "Out of cigars! Out of cigarettes! Out of gum! Out of cokes! Out of town!"[36]

Evidently they've heard of the cigarette shortage way out in the Pacific, too, for Ray Vowell (Shaw) sent this one, which he read in some guy's home paper and tho't was good: "A lady in Portland, Oregon, saw people standing in line, so she got in line, too. Hours later she asked someone what they were waiting for. 'Cigarettes,' was the reply. 'Oh, I don't smoke,' she cried and hurried along." Which story is in line with Fibber McGee's broadcast the other night when he got all excited over discovering a cigarette black market, only to be cruelly reminded by Molly that "neither of us smoke, dearie!" I wish I didn't!

Speaking of Ray Vowell reminds me to tell you about those Vowell boys. There are four of them in the service, you know, and their

---

anti-F.D.R. electors. The issues included the New Deal's support for blacks, federal election laws, and Roosevelt's fourth bid for the presidency. Discussion of the prospective revolt occurred throughout the late summer and early fall of 1944. Although Mrs. Somerville was upset by the "revolt," it had little chance of success in the wartime atmosphere. In Mississippi, three of the selected electors on the Democratic ticket did announce that they might vote for Senator Harry Byrd of Virginia. A fourth elector was undecided. The Mississippi legislature then passed a bill creating, if necessary, a special supplementary list of "loyal" electors. The governor signed the bill into law on November 3, three days before the general election. The measure was never needed as the original slate of electors remained loyal to Roosevelt and Truman. Mississippians voted overwhelmingly for Roosevelt in the general election of November 1944.

36. The cigarette shortage which plagued Mrs. Somerville was not experienced, to any great extent, among the troops overseas. In fact, approximately 30 percent of all cigarettes made went to the armed forces. At home, however, the shortage was real, and many smokers tried "rollin' their own" in an effort to make scarce tobacco last longer.

mother is very proud that none of her family are slackers. (Besides the four in uniform, she has another son working in a shipyard, and two brothers and a son-in-law in the service!) Ray is on the U.S.S. *Shasta* out in the Pacific and writes amusingly of boiling water and using the steam to boil more water and then starting all over again. He fears he'll never get anywhere like that, but despite his routine job, he has gained three pounds and he "feels like a million." Pete (SSGT Earl of the Infantry) has been overseas two years, going through the African, Sicilian, Italian, and French campaigns, and has been wounded three times. (Naturally his mother treasures his Purple Heart and the medals he's sent home). He is now in a hospital in France recuperating again!...

This business of pacing the floor in lieu of absent service daddies is a bit nerve racking on the grandmothers of this era! But we're coming through with flying colors! My latest floor-walking was for Keith Dockery (age two weeks), the youngest daughter of Lt. and Mrs. Joe Rice Dockery. Joe is stationed down in the Gulf (Grande Isle, Louisiana), and like so many of the rest of you dads, was not home for the young lady's arrival. Jane Gaines and Lt. Fernie Wood have a young son, Fernie, Jr., born at Columbus, Mississippi, where Fernie is taking advanced air training....

Today is a real Delta-Christmas-y-looking day—damp and cold and gloomy outside—but inside by the glow of the fires, people are pressing last year's wrappings, repainting old toys, baking fruit cakes (with a lot of ingredients left out this year), picking out pecans, making cookies, and preparing for another War Christmas. By the time this paper reaches some of you, you will be hearing "Silent Night" and thinking of the folks back home, whose best Christmas present this year will be a letter from you! How your letters are prized! The ones I've been privileged to read are all worn out from much refolding!

This year there isn't a lighted Christmas tree on the Court House porch—instead there's a big thermometer registering our War Bond purchases in the Sixth War Loan Drive. And the little lighted Christmas trees, which made our Main Streets so gay in other years, will be absent again—to be relighted only when you boys are home again. But there'll be Christmas in our hearts just the same, and memories of bygone days when all was gaiety when we listened to the radio only to hear "Carols" and a good jazz band, and the only worry we had was whether the fudge would turn out creamy! The cotton is about all in (prisoners of war picked some of it) and it is selling for a good price.[37] There's lots of fruit in the stores, but oysters are selling for eighty cents a pint (the oyster pickers and their boats, like the cotton pickers, have gone to war).

And there are no roller skates, wagons, or bicycles available for your little brothers (the ball bearings have gone to war, too), but they don't care, for they want commando suits and jeeps, anyway! (Little sisters want W.A.V.E. bags and W.A.C. uniforms, but big sisters still want permanents so they'll look glamorous when their pet beaus come home on leave!)

To some of your pals from other parts of the U.S.A., "picking the goose" means snow, but to many of you, it literally means picking the goose for Christmas dinner. There are still geese and hens and turkeys hereabouts, so you can picture the home folk sitting down to a table laden with all those good eats. "Mom" cooks so well, and wishing each of you was here to enjoy it, too. The service stars in our windows (1, 2, 3, 4, 5, or 6!) will have a sprig of greenery in your honor, and when the blessing is asked, there will be added clause— "God bless our boys and keep them safe." . . .

To each of you, wherever you may be, every good wish for Christmas, and though Old Santa may have trouble finding some of you this year, please know that there is not a home in Bolivar County, in the State of Mississippi, that is not sending you thought waves of loving remembrance.

Sincerely,
Keith Frazier Somerville

37. For information on the use of German prisoners of war as cotton pickers, see Merrill R. Pritchett and William L. Shea, "The Enemy in Mississippi (1943-1946)," *The Journal of Mississippi History,* 41(November 1979): 351-371.

5

Peace Has Come Again
to the World

January 1945—August 1945

January 12, 1945

Dear Boys:

Christmas has come and gone and the new year of 1945 has started. January 1 was a lovely, sunshiny day here, giving promise of good weather, but the radio news from the Western Front did not give us much promise of an early peace.[1] The bowl games on the radio sounded exciting, especially Duke and Alabama in the Sugar Bowl, where they seesawed back and forth (first one ahead, then the other) till Duke finally won out. In New Orleans, where that game was played, they tell me it is the custom to leave Christmas trees up till "Twelfth Night" (January 12th), which is a custom I wish I'd been reared in, for I always hate to see the Christmas decorations go, especially so this year, for they were a symbol of the happy times my lucky, little Santa-age granddaughters (two, three, and four years old) had with their gifts and their service daddies home for a few days). . . .

---

1. Mrs. Somerville is referring to the Battle of the Bulge, the German counteroffensive which took place in the Ardennes region of Belgium and Luxembourg in December 1944 and early January 1945.

I come of the school of thought which says it's bad luck to leave the red candles, the holly, and the tree up over into the New Year. So on New Year's Eve, as I heard the whistles blow in Times Square (radio) and a lovely voice raised in "The Star Spangled Banner," I took everything down at my house and carefully packed the few remaining lights and unbroken ornaments away for another year. As I burned the greenery in my fireplace, I tho't of you boys. No, I didn't make any resolutions to break; I just said prayers for your safety and for the peace of this war worn world.

Before closing the books on 1944, I'd like right here to say thanks to each of you who remembered me. I loved your cards, and the knowledge that so many of you, far from home, remembered me gave me a tremendous thrill. I loved those notes some of you wrote on the cards, too, and I am writing each of you personally. A stack of V-mail letters is going out to you today.

One of the loveliest Christmas presents that arrived in Cleveland this year was some beautiful English china which Lt. (J.G.) C.P. Brocato sent his mother. C.P., still on that L.S.T. in which he crossed and re-crossed the Channel on D-Day, is based in England, about forty miles from London. He has acquired a delightful English friend, Col. Eustes Harrison, an old bachelor of Coome, England, who has him down to his beautiful home often for weekend leaves. His brother, Sgt. Anthony, is with a Field Artillery Battalion and has been at Camp Hood, Texas, but he has already stood his overseas exams and may be "on the way" here now. Tony is a "computer" —sets the big guns which shoot over the infantry and computes the target. (That probably isn't G.I. talk, but anyway it takes a good mathematician to do it, and Tony always has had that bent since two plus two days!)

Their brother, Joe, is on the U.S.S. *Trego*, a very new type of ship only recently commissioned at Newport, Rhode Island. While awaiting his ship, Joe lived for a while in Cambridge and enjoyed the environs of historic Boston.

Remember Charles Sutherland who lived with Mrs. R.E. Johnson for awhile and went to C.H.S.? After three years in the Pacific (he was out there when the Jap[anese] struck at Pearl Harbor), he is just in the States from Australia. For years he was a private, but he went up the hard way thru jungle fighting and is now Lt. Sutherland. His first act on returning home was to marry his college sweetheart, Marjorie Rowlett of Mt. Home, Idaho, a classmate at the University of Idaho. En route to his new station at Spartanburg, South Carolina, he called his foster mother (Mrs. Johnson) from Memphis. His father, Col. Finn Sutherland, is now at Camp Bowie, Texas. Just before the holidays, Jessaly Johnson joined her husband, Air Cadet Charles B. Harrison, at Douglas, Arizona. She had Christmas dinner with a Mexican family there (hot stuff!) and couldn't wait to get down "south of the border" where she'd been told nylon hose were available. Her trip to Mexico was fun, but alas—she found nylons priced at seven dollars a pair![2]

The years roll back for me when I think of the Langston boys, now scattered around the world and sailing the seven seas. They probably won't like me saying so, but they were such NICE little first-graders— smiling, smart, clean, and happy. "Sailor Bill," as brother Alton calls him, writes that he's still nice when he's broke! (I refuse to believe that's the only time!) But I'm terribly sorry to know he was broke when he shipped in to Shoemaker, California. And it was tough luck that "Santa didn't find him, even to leave ashes in his stocking" and that he slept through his Christmas dinner and missed it! Brother Alton is at Assam, out in India, where he has service for a long time. I was intrigued by your letterhead, Alton. It looked like a United States Shield plus a rising sun, with the initials C.B.I. under it. Do those letters mean "China-Burma-India"? I'm all bogged up in the alphabet again! Those ABC's I taught you so long ago are all mixed up these days!

The third brother, J.T. "Jake," is now an ensign in the Navy somewhere out in the Pacific. At one time he was up in the Aleutians, but our Navy is the moving-est thing. He may be in the China Sea by now!

The fourth brother, Calvin (Sgt. R.C. to the Army' "Lemon" to his

---

2. Silk and nylon stockings were scarce during the war years. Silk had become scare in 1941 when the U.S. government instituted an embargo on the Japanese product. Nylon, which was used to make parachutes, resulted in nylon hose becoming as scarce as silk ones. It was estimated that one parachute consumed the equivalent of thirty-six pairs of nylons. Rayon and cotton lisle hose were both scarce and unpopular. As a last resort, some women painted their legs with makeup to give the illusion of wearing hosiery.

family) is in the Signal Corps—Care of Postmaster, New York. Well, wherever they are and whatever they're called on to do, I know those Langstons are doing a good job of it and taking it with a grin!...

James Hilton, who wrote the delightful *Good-bye, Mr. Chips* and originated "Shangri-La", says that in this year of destiny, 1945, none of us can afford the luxury of an armchair.[3] (You boys don't have them in barracks or foxholes and even we grandmothers don't have time to use ours, except now and then when we sit down to give the baby its bottle!) He thinks 1945 will be a year of destiny like 1919, and that to make it so, we must not only fight and work, but believe passionately in certain things (like true peace and fairness) and stand up and express our opinions—not sit back as people did in 1919 when so many believed in and approved of the League of Nations, yet it died because so few stood up for it.[4] That we are already, ere the war is won, at cross purposes with our Allies on some points, and here at home some people (like Senator Wheeler) are agin' "unconditional surrender" scares us, but hope for the future comes with the news that the Allied leaders are to meet again soon to talk things over.[5] Let's hope they'll iron out their differences—for all people everywhere want Peace (even in Berlin and Tokyo, I imagine!)

To each of you, and to the world, best wishes for 1945.

Sincerely your friend,
Keith Frazier Somerville

February 9, 1945

Dear Boys:

Hurrah for the Stars and Stripes, again unfurled over Manila after

3. James Hilton (1900-1954).

4. The League of Nations was founded by the victorious powers of World War I. It was seriously weakened by the nonadherence of the U.S. During the 1930s, the League was discredited when it failed to prevent the Japanese expansion in Manchuria and China, Italy's conquest of Ethiopia, and Hitler's repudiation of the Treaty of Versailles. The League ceased activities during World War II. In 1945, it was replaced by the United Nations.

5. Burton K. Wheeler (1882-1975), a well-known isolationist, was a Democratic Senator from Montana from 1923 until 1947.

three years![6] And hurrah for our boys, wading thru deep snow to break thru the Siegfried line into Germany! And hurrah for the Russians moving hourly closer to the heart of the "Vaterland"![7] That they, who have suffered so much from the Germans, will show no pity as they go about avenging their ten million war casualties is a foregone conclusion and personally, I can't help being glad they are getting there "firstest with the mostest men!" We Americans are so tenderhearted and so apt to let our pity for the individual make us forget the overall picture! Perhaps after a Russian invasion, the Germans may have the desire for war (inbred in them since the days of the ruthless Attila, the Hun) knocked out of them! That might insure a few hundred years of peace as effectively as a dozen Dumbarton Oaks conferences![8] . . .

From the Philippines, Bruno Sandrani (Shaw) wrote of how happy the Filipinos were when the Americans landed: "They had a hard time under Jap[anese] control and know now they will have it easier. The Jap[anese] took their clothes and food, destroyed their homes, and paid them with Jap[anese] invasion money, which they couldn't spend. Now they are giving it to American soldiers for souvenirs. It isn't good for anything else. They are pitifully poor—half starved and many with no clothes. We feed them. Some are well educated, attended colleges and universities. They are all good workers and will do anything for Americans."

Pretty blackhaired Bernice Grable (Boyle) is proud indeed of husband John Curtis Grable (Navy)! She treasures a letter and citation from Admiral Halsey to Lt. Commander J.B. Duffy, "for outstanding achievement on a Naval salvage vessel in a combat area in the western Pacific which resulted in getting two damaged war-

6. The Japanese entered Manila in January 1942. The reconquest of Manila, under the direction of General Douglas MacArthur, began in early February 1945. For the next month, fighting was fierce. On March 3, 1945, Japanese resistance collapsed. Casualties were extremely high among both military and civilian personnel, and much of the city was destroyed.

7. Soviet and U.S. troops met at the German town of Torgau on the Elbe River on April 25, 1945.

8. Between August 21 and October 7, 1944, representatives of the United States, Great Britain, the Soviet Union, and China met at Dumbarton Oaks in Washington D.C. to discuss the structure and composition of the proposed United Nations organization.

ships out of the area into a safe port, under constant danger from enemy aircraft and submarines known to be operating along the route. The highly efficient work done by your men under difficult and trying circumstances is in keeping with the highest traditions of the United States Naval service."[9] Commander Duffey sent this letter to Curtis with the notation, "Your fine efforts contributed." Bernice (nee Mallett) and their two small daughters are living on Route 1, Boyle, while Seaman Grable is doing such commendable work at sea. Her brother, Charles Mallett (Army) is stationed at the same place out in the Netherlands East Indies, where SSGT Louis Kaplan is now serving. Louis says they have Jap[anese] bombs falling most every night, but now and then the enemy skips a night and they get a good night's rest. His wife is working in Greenwood. His brother, Abe Kaplan, is now in Germany (91st Chemical Battalion). His last letter was written in a snowy foxhole by the light of a small flashlight. (Your dad is justifiably proud of those pictures of you boys he carries about in his pocket! I don't blame him, for they are grand likenesses of two fine looking soldiers!)

No wonder all your letters are so treasured, for many of them are written under just as trying situations as Abe wrote under. For instance, Harry Campbell (Boyle) with the Third Marine Division somewhere out in the Pacific battle area, wrote his mother from a hot spot by the light of a flickering old lantern! (She promptly sent him a modern lantern! Hope you got it, Harry!)...

New babes? Henry Taft Watson, Jr., age one month, has never seen his Navy dad, now out in the Pacific. His mother (Eulalie Jeffcote) and his little sister know his dad would be proud of Junior! Decorations? Technician Elma L. Reynolds (Merigold) is, I believe, the first of our boys to receive the newly authorized Bronze Medal for outstanding bravery of noncombatants. Elma got his for repairing tanks and half tracks under fire—some job! Dan B. Fulwood (Shaw) writes he's hauling vital ammunition to the battle front under fire—so he's another who may be eligible for that decoration!...

Dot Robinson Carpenter had one of those "get-togethers" the other night—the kind you all used to enjoy in hi school days. Only

9. Admiral William F. Halsey, Jr. (1882-1959) was a U.S. naval commander who led a number of important campaigns in the Pacific during World War II.

this time there were no boys! It was an all-girl affair! Among those present were Marian Denton (Joe is at Camp Fannin, Texas); Margaret Thomas Thompson (Elijah J. is with the 124th Infantry in the Pacific); Dehlia Ray Liddell Hallam (Louis is in the Philippines—so, by the way are Bunny Carpenter, Frank Aderholt, Ernest Fondren and John Ward); Ida Lee Nowell Nance and Catherine Carpenter, (both Dick Nance and Travis Carpenter are in England); "Happy" Smith (Milton is attending the Commanding Officers' General Staff School at Ft. Leavenworth, Kansas, from which he graduates on March 16); Eleanette Shands Leake (all in a dither because Hunter has been ordered home from Panama and is to be stationed at the Great Lakes Training Camp); Corinna Adams (Dr. Jerry "Junior" is in England); Joyce Wall (Robert is off F.B.I-ing in "furrin" parts); the two Ingrams, Viola Smith and Ashton Somerville (Cliff is in Normandy and George in Washington); Dimetri Cole (Luper is in Ordnance Department in France); Evelyn Hand (Ben is in New Guinea); and Peggy Lyon (whose husband, Tedlow Johnson, is a Marine out in the Pacific). Those gals had a nice gabby evening, but it lacked something! In fact, if each had been questioned, they'd have all admitted that this little verse expressed their sentiments exactly!

> "Come strew your clothes around
> the house
> While dressing and undressing.
> I'll pick them up and never
> grouse,
> Nor find such chores depress-
> ing.
> For I am lamentably bored
> With female company my lord."

Yes, the wives and sweethearts of Bolivar County will be good and glad when you guys come home!

Here's to that happy day and best of luck to each of you.

Sincerely,

Keith Frazier Somerville

February 23, 1945

Dear Boys:

I sort of have a hankering to have someone carry one of my "letters about in his pocket till it is frayed at the edges and smudged beyond recognition", and William Fitzgibbon, in a recent article in *Liberty*, gives the prescription for a letter which will achieve just that![10] Lt. Fitzgibbon, home from several years overseas, is out to wage a one man campaign to liven up V-Mail letters. Says he, "The old home town is damned hazy after a year or more overseas, and any letter that takes a walk down Main Street, pointing out Mason's Shoe Store and Carter's Drug Store and the civilian clothes in the Men's Shop, is a letter your soldier will read and reread till it's worn out. We got a lot of general information, so what we want is an estimate of the home town situation. Tell us what the restaurants have to eat; how many bonds our town bought; the price of things; about the girls working and how they're taking the manpower shortage. In fact, tell us how war is affecting our town."

So I decided if that was what you wanted, I'd send it to you. Parking my five year old Ford in front of Pik-Nik, I started out.[11] (Sure we all still have cars. No shiny new ones, but the garages have done a swell job of keeping most of the old ones running. You still have trouble finding a parking place anywhere, even though sometimes all of us run out of gas before the next coupon is due and have to rest the car a few days.) Did anyone tell you that Nick Feduccia had sold Pik-Nik to Mr. Ashford and Mr. Saliba who used to be at Kroger's? Mr. Saliba (also an ex-Kroger man) presides at the meat counter and generally has fresh Graneda butter (twenty-four red points and fifty-five cents a pound) and cheese. I like butter and cheese, so more of my ration points go for them than for meat. We eat liver and pork chops and sausage. There aren't many beef steaks, anyway, for ninety percent of the beef supply is going to the service. I heard the other night where one and one-half million pounds of

10. *Liberty* was a sprightly magazine of the 1930s and 1940s which was widely read. It contained short articles and listed the average time it should take to read each article.

11. Pik-Nik was a Cleveland grocery store.

hamburger meat had been delivered to the boys in France and Germany. But I "hear-tell" you can get a really good steak at the Post Office Cafe for $1.25 (when they have them).

Next door, Mike Carouso, after three years as a cook in the Navy, is home again with a medical discharge and running the pool room. I went in there the other day in my wild search for cigarettes and it was full up. (The men looked a bit startled to see a female barging in, but gray hair can go anywhere!) P.S. I didn't find any.

Ward-Ellis, Owens, Finks, and Bobbs that day still had boxes of candy left from the Valentine supply.[12] Why, of course, they had those red satin, heart shaped boxes you used to send your best girl. They're an American institution, aren't they? No more expensive than usual either ($1.10 and $1.50). Lt. Fitzgibbon said what he couldn't get enough of was candy and magazines. Plenty of the latter and generally some kind of candy. (Always some kind at Camise's and the "5 and 10": Hershey bars and Milky Ways, along with chewing gum, have been off the counter for years.[13]) Checking up on the candy situation, I heard at Owen's about Marian Alice's husband, Lt. Ben Perkins. You probably remember that he is a paratrooper—but did you know he was at Bastogne, called the "Gettysburg of World War II," where surrounded by Rundstedt's elite German divisions the besieged airborne troops stood with storybook courage? In the February 17th issue of the *Post* is an article called "Bastogne— American Epic," which tells of the heroic stand made there. Yes, she has heard from her husband since. He is well and in Belgium now. Those airborne troops are certainly making history in this war.[14] Did you know that Gen. "Charlie" Hall, whose paratroopers landed atop

12. Ward-Ellis, Owens, and Finks were drug stores in Cleveland. Bobbs was a newsstand which also sold candy and tobacco.

13. Camise's was a five-and-ten-cent store in Cleveland.

14. Bastogne, a Belgian town, was the site of an epic stand during the Battle of the Bulge in December 1944. The U.S. 101st Airborne Division refused to surrender even though the town was surrounded by German forces. The article mentioned by Mrs. Somerville is C. Small, "Bastogne: American Epic," *Saturday Evening Post*, February 17, 1945, pp. 18-19. German field marshall Gerd von Rundstedt (1875-1953) was one of Hitler's ablest leaders during World War II. He held commands on both the Eastern and Western fronts.

Corregidor the other day, is a Greenville man? (Was an Ole Miss Phi, in case that interests any of you.)[15]

At Camise's I heard that J.A. has just had a raise and been made an instructor down at Jacksonville, Florida. (He's an Aviation Electrical Mate.) Charles, who has had a medical discharge, is now working as an inspector at the Ford Motor Company in Memphis. He is just one of the many of you boys who are back in civilian clothes again. Tobe Kaplan tells me almost one a day comes in now. Hunter Jones (Merigold), home from England and France, was in the other day— and strangely enough he was at General Hospital 297 in England where Mrs. Kaplan's uncle, Maj. (Dr.) Max Kaplan of Chicago is administrative head. Hunter said he was eight days on the boat coming home and all that time without an American cigarette. How ashamed that makes me, griping over the shortage here! Toby's and Escue's seem to have plenty to outfit the returning heroes— woolen suits, priced from $25 to $45; Knox hats ($6 to $10); Arrow shirts ($2.25 and $3); sox, three for a dollar; and shoes (from $4.95 to $9.50). Almost the same price as when you left, aren't they? That's "ceiling prices."[16]

I was in Memphis a few weeks ago and vainly searched every where for size 40 cotton house dresses, only to come home and find Shoenholz has plenty of them—pretty too, and in all sizes (price $3.50 to $6)[17] Airplane Stamps, numbers 1, 2, and 3, are what we use now for shoes, and if you go to every store in town, you can eventually get your size, tho' I doubt if any of them are half as good as your G.I. issue.[18] Another ration free period for dealers to get rid of odds and ends has been declared from now till March 3rd.[19]

Several of the grocery stores have recently been featuring a chart

---

15. On February 16, 1945, the Army 503rd Parachute Regimental Combat Team landed on Corregidor, a heavily fortified island dominating the entrance to Manila Bay. After ten days of heavy fighting, on February 26, Corregidor was secured. General Charles P. Hall of Greenville, Mississippi, commanded the XI Corps. He joined Phi Delta Theta fraternity while a student at the University of Mississippi.

16. Ceiling prices, determined by the Office of Price Administration, were the highest prices for which specified items could be sold. Ceiling prices were established in an effort to cut down inflation.

17. Shoenholz was a dry good's store in Cleveland.

18. Shoe ration stamps carried the engraving of an airplane.

19. Many goods were rationed during the war. As Mrs. Somerville suggests, rationing was sometimes lifted in order to enable dealers to sell odd sizes and styles.

showing the comparative purchasing power of a dollar, in this war and the last. In World War I, ten pounds of sugar cost $2.65—today, in World War II, $2.65 will buy not only ten pounds of sugar but one pound of cheese (40c), one pound of coffee (21c), one package of macaroni (11c), one can of tomatoes (11c), one pound of butter (50c), one bar of soap (4c), one box of washing powder (23c), one package of spaghetti (11c), and one pound of shortening (18c).

Yes, ceiling prices and rationing have helped tremendously. None of us have suffered at all, for there has been an abundance of fresh fruit (a bag of twelve Texas grapefruit at Kroger's for 49 cents) and plenty of vegetables. We housewives have learned we can't go to town with our menus planned—we just have to take what they have that day—but it's always adequate.

Behind the meat counter in the Modern Store is a regular picture gallery of all the Chinese who used to work there, taken in their uniforms. A fine looking group of soldiers they are, too. Two of them are in New Guinea, Ernest S. and Chester Joe. Chester was wounded there and has the Purple Heart. Joe Y. Sing is in Arizona; Kenneth Gong is with those wonder paratroopers, too, in Belgium; and wonder of wonders, Joe M. Kee is with the Signal Corps in China. None of them, I hear, are related to Yen Quong of Greenville, who found MacArthur's silver in Manila.[20] But there are some of his Quong relatives in Merigold.

Billy Lowry (home with a medical discharge—his Navy clothes and his service ribbons with all those stars, carefully packed away) is at work in the jewelry store. (Sure, there'll be a job for you, too, when you get home. Every store, farm, gin, bank, and garage is understaffed. Some of you won't want to come back. You'll want to use those skills Uncle Sam has taught you elsewhere in the big world, but for those who do, you'll find plenty to do.)

Another thing that Lt. Fitzgibbon said worried you boys was

20. Following the Allied retreat from the Philippines during the early months of 1942, General MacArthur's personal silver, which dated from his days as Chief of Staff, was buried in a garden by a Filipino. When Allied forces, under the command of General MacArthur, returned to Manila in early 1945, this silver was recovered. In addition, a silver tea service belonging to the General was recovered from a warehouse in Manila. For additional information about the recovery of MacArthur's silver, see William Manchester, *American Caesar: Douglas MacArthur, 1880-1964* (Boston: Little Brown, 1978), pp. 423-424.

whether we, here at home, were wholeheartedly behind the war effort. Said that you heard about strikes but nothing of the millions who never miss a day's work. Well, there's hardly a family in Bolivar County who hasn't someone in the service and scarcely a family who isn't helping in some way. We've gone over the top in every bond drive and Red Cross quota and accepted rationing without a murmur. And you'd get a kick out of seeing your little brothers and sisters collecting paper. . . .

As for your big "little sisters," they're helping too—making hospital supplies in home science for the Junior Red Cross. I was up at Cleveland Hi the other day and had a wonderful time seeing my erst-while babes all grown-up and as pretty and vivacious as hi school girls should be! It was a club meeting and just as of yore, they discussed first how best to make sandwiches to sell for ten cents apiece at a coming basketball game. (That's quite a problem with rationing. Someone suggested tuna fish sandwiches, but they were out when someone remembered that a tiny can, which would make only about four sandwiches, sold for $.25 and three ration points.) Their fingers went as fast as their tongues as they worked on memorandum pads and tally cards. They're making "Buddy bags," too, in sewing class, under the direction of home science teacher, Mrs. Mack T. Blackwood, whose husband is a Marine Captain, now on Bougainville. . . .

You see, boys, this war touches us all so closely that we ARE all wholeheartedly behind it! As Lt. Fitzgibbon found in travels all over the United States, there aren't many young men left at home. Said he, "I think if I had a penny for every draft age civilian I saw, I would have had enough to buy a forty-nine cent necktie! And those I did see looked mighty peaked." Take the Monroe Steeds (Boyle) for our biggest example. Their seventh son, William P., has just entered the Navy! Then there are Mrs. W.W. Blaylock and her sister, Mrs. B.J. Keith, who live together, and each has three sons in the service. Howard Blaylock has made five trips back and forth across the Atlantic as an Armored Guard on an ammunition ship loaded with high octane gas and T.N.T. Otis is a Marine in the Pacific and Lloyd (Shorty) is now at Norfolk. Of Mrs. Keith's boys—Raymond is in the East Indies, Gordon in northern France, and Albert in the Marshall Islands.

Wrote Lt. Fitzgibbon—"We all wondered what the hell when our friends failed to write us from the states. We knew it wasn't carelessness. They must be sparing us ugly truths, we thought. Something must be wrong at home."

"But the U.S. is all right. I know that now, but I had to come home to find out why the men who came home failed to write back about it. I know now it was the task of describing how it felt to get home that proved too much for our friends. The answer is so simple it will sound unconvincing to the overseas soldier who has thought and dreamed so much of home that he is prepared only for drama and surpassing emotion. It's not that way. Suddenly you are home. You belong. You are a part of it. You feel like you have never been gone. You only experience a surge of contentment to find things as you left them. That's the way it is."

And that's the way I hope it is for you already home and will be for each of you others when you come home to stay. We'll be glad to see you all!

Sincerely,
Keith Frazier Somerville

March 30, 1945

Dear Boys:

Easter greetings to you! Remember the Easter egg hunts you used to have in the tall grass when you were six? The colored dyes are still in evidence in the stores, and the small fry will again, this year, be seeking for the golden egg, but you are off hunting for intact Rhine bridges and Jap[anese] snipers. The redbud trees in Boyle and the gay Easter bonnets (all flowery) in the store windows attest the season's approach here at home. All our little towns are ablaze with jonquils, iris, wisteria, and flowering shrubs. Isn't it wonderful that our blaze is not caused by incendiary bombs! It's just the yearly reminder that "He is risen." How anyone could see spring's beauty and not believe in immortality is a mystery to me. Each year after months when the flowers are apparently dead, comes the wonder of the resurrection. Reverently, at this time of year, I go out for my early morning worship of my flowers, convinced anew that "death is but a sleep" and that we, too, will rise again in renewed splendor.

Have you been keeping up with all that is being written in the papers and magazines these days about our relations with France? It has interested me a lot, and I feel that perhaps you'd like to hear of a letter I received from France a few days ago which gave me a tremendous thrill. Following World War I, many people in the United States (myself included) were filled with a deep sympathy for the thousands of French war orphans, and "adopted" many of them by sending a certain sum of money to help in their upkeep and education.[21] When a letter addressed in beautiful flowing script and postmarked "Le Havre" arrived, I wondered who could it be from. None of you boys, I was sure, for it carried a French stamp and lacked the familiar "Free" of your letters.[22] But who else did I know in France? Amazingly, it was from my French war orphan. That he and his mother had kept my address for a quarter of a century certainly shows that the French are an appreciative people! My rusty college French, to my surprise, was still good enough to enable me to read his letter, which began: "Dear Benefactor, do not know that you will remember me, but now that I am a man, I wish to thank you for the generosity which you extended to my mother when I was a boy." He went on to say that he was now thirty-one years old, had served in the French army, and after being demobilized had "continued the battle with the Marquis. Now, as in 1917, Americans are fighting for us, and thanks to them I am alive and a free man, and not a tragic, hunted beast." He is now "Controlleur des Contributions Indirect" at Havre, which sounds to me like some kind of tax collector. Havre, he writes, is almost destroyed, but despite their misfortunes, they are able to laugh because Hitler and the Germans were not able to stand up against the imposing masses of the Allies.

But the crux of the letter, and the part which warmed the cockles of my heart, was this: "Today I would be very happy to prove to you

21. Over 100 French orphans were supported by citizens of Bolivar County during and after World War I. See Wirt A. Williams, ed., *History of Bolivar County, Mississippi* (Spartanburg, S.C.: The Reprint Co., 1976), p. 224.

22. Beginning in March 1942, all ordinary mail, that is V-Mail and surface letters, sent by members of the armed forces was accorded free transmission. Civilians paid three cents for V-Mail postage and six cents per half ounce for air mail letters. This uniform postage rate was established to insure the secrecy of troop locations around the world as well as to be fair to those who had loved ones stationed in remote areas.

my appreciation for your kindness to me when I was a poor orphan. If you have a son, friend, or protege serving in the American Army who would be stationed or passing through Havre and would send me his address, it would be a great pleasure for me to receive him and treat him as a member of my family." Now isn't that nice? Please, some of you, "my boys," look up Jean Duclos for me! His address is 84 Rue Ernest Renan, Le Havre. I am writing him that I am sending his address to a lot of my friends in the hope that one, at least, may happen to be in Havre and can bring me news of him. He must be a very nice person indeed, and I'd like for some of you Bolivar County boys to know my "adopted son." I'd like to know him myself!

Many of you have already rushed across France and are now in Germany, but maybe you'll ship home from Havre. Lots of boys did in the last war. Carmen Epton Valentine, after his long service in the Pacific theatre, is now with Patton's Army, which staged the spectacular break across the Rhine last week, and Velma Sims's husband, Cpl. L.B. Williams, is with the 9th Army in Germany, to mention but a few who have already crossed despite "The Watch on the Rhine."[23] They tell me those Army Engineers of ours can put a bridge across the river in nothing flat. One, 1400 feet long, was built in nine hours and eleven minutes and the span can stand up under a load of forty tons.[24] Perhaps Howard Reid (Shaw), Howard Nelson (Cleveland—recently arrived in France), and Robert L. Buford (Shelby) helped build some of them, as all are in engineering outfits. . . .

Tal Williford ran up from New Orleans (where his ship put in) for Sunday dinner at home last week. Joy Somerville, who recently saw him in the Crescent City, said she almost had to throw old shoes at the gals who whistled at him on Canal Street. And no wonder, for he's one fine looking guy in his Navy blues! Joy, by the way, is leaving April sixth to resume her flying. This time as airline hostess from Houston to Chicago.

I ran into Mrs. Griffin at the grocery store the other morning and

23. General George S. Patton (1885-1945) commanded the Third Army as it swept across Europe in 1944 and 1945. His troops often referred to him as "Old Blood-and-Guts." The Allies first crossed the Rhine River on March 7, 1945. Max Schneckenburger wrote "The Watch on the Rhine" in 1840. The concept of "The Watch on the Rhine" was revived during World War I and World War II.

24. Utilizing assembly line methods and standardized parts, Army Engineers could construct bridges very quickly.

she tells me Roy is now in China and Purvey in Washington. Roxy was with her! And believe me, fellows, she is a little beauty!...

Alvie McKnight (chaplain who served on Guadalacanal) is now in Washington, too, a Lt. Col. with the Office of Chief of Chaplains. And had you heard that James Wiggins has been serving as chaplain's assistant out in the India-Burma Theatre? The jeep he's been jostling about in is called "Sweet Chariot"!...

Weddings? Sure! Seaman William Edward Henry (Pace) arrived home from the Pacific and married Sylvia Smith.

Babes? Sure! Want to meet two young ladies who haven't met their daddies yet? Meet Patricia Nelson, daughter of Carl Reid Nelson (Coast Guard in the Pacific) and Martha Rushing; and Shirley West (Shaw-Boyle) daughter of Alex West (Navy) and Ruth Garrett. Both lassies come from fighting families. Pat's uncle, Howard Nelson, is now in France (or Germany, as is her great uncle, Clifton Lee Rushing). Her uncle, Ronald Craft, is in San Antonio, Texas; her great uncle, Sutherland Rushing, is at Camp Bowie, Texas; and her great uncle, Edgar Rushing (Lt. Col.) is in the Philippines....

Two of Mississippi's sons (tho' not from Bolivar County) have been headline news recently. I mention them just in case you didn't know they're Mississippians: Gen. Dan Sultan of Oxford, who took Gen. Stilwell's place in China, and Admiral John S. McCain of Carrollton, recently deputy chief of Naval Operations for the Air and now commanding a carrier unit in the Pacific.[25]

Sincerely,

Keith Frazier Somerville

25. General Joseph W. Stilwell (1883-1946) served as commanding general of U.S. forces in China, Burma, and India during much of World War II. He was relieved of this post in the autumn of 1944. The standard sources are Theodore H. White, ed., *The Stilwell Papers* (New York: William Sloane Associates, 1948) and Barbara Tuchman, *Stilwell and the American Experience in China* (New York: MacMillan, 1970). Daniel Isom Sultan (1885-1947) was a 1907 graduate of the U.S. Military Academy. An army engineer by training, he was the engineering commissioner for the District of Columbia (1934-1938) and later the commanding general of Camp Shelby in Hattiesburg, Mississippi (1941-1942). In November 1944, Lieutenant-General Sultan became the commander of the U.S. forces in the China-Burma-Indian Theatre. John Sidney McCain (1884-1945) was a 1906 graduate of the Naval Academy and an early Navy pilot. During 1942-1943 he was Chief, Bureau of Aeronautics. In July 1943 he became a Vice Admiral and deputy chief of naval operations for the air. He witnessed the surrender of the Japanese on board the U.S.S. *Missouri* in September 1945.

April 27, 1945

Dear Boys:

"There's a gold star in the world's window"! That is the phrase that impressed me most in listening to the seventy-two hours of wonderful tributes to our fallen chief. I sat beside my radio for hours on end, listening and grieving. Many were the eloquent tributes paid him by the world's great and near great—yet those words were uttered not by any of them, but by one of the "little people" like you and me. He was the unheard of editor of a small newspaper in the, to most of us, unheard of small town of London, Kentucky in the foothills of the Allegheny mountains. I don't even remember his name. Yet he coined the phrase that struck me most. Probably, like us, he only knew Franklin Delano Roosevelt through his silver-tongued voice on the radio, but he paid him the greatest tribute I heard! A friend came in Sunday morning and found me in tears, having just listened in at Hyde Park (both London and New York).[26] I was arranging, on my dining table, my tribute to the greatest man of our era—a red, white, and blue flower arrangement. F.D.R. would never know I made it, anymore than he knew that I was one of his greatest admirers, or that I had ever raised my voice in his behalf. (I grew up in politics up in Tennessee and it has always interested me, but until last fall I never got upset enough about it to write protesting letters. But I was so furious over the bolting Mississippi electors who, like small boys who refused to play when they didn't get their way, would not agree to vote for the party nominee, that I wrote each of them a hot letter telling them that I, and thousands like me, wanted to vote for Roosevelt, and I didn't think it fair for them to prevent us doing so! Of course, it did no good as far as they were concerned, but Governor Bailey, to whom I sent a copy, said that it and the hundreds like it helped him to make the decision to appoint, at the eleventh hour, a new set of electors who would, and did, vote for the man selected as the standard bearer of the Democratic party.)[27]

Well, he's gone and never again will we turn on our radios in our

26. Mrs. Somerville had listened to radio broadcasts from Hyde Park, New York, the home of Franklin D. Roosevelt, and from Hyde Park, London, where a ceremony honoring him had taken place.

27. Thomas L. Bailey (1888-1946) of Meridian, Mississippi, served as governor of Mississippi from 1944 until his death in 1946.

small homes all over this big land and hear Roosevelt's mellow voice greet us as "fellow Americans," take us into his confidence, and reassure us that "there is nothing to fear but fear."[28] But he laid the framework for victory in battle, and for Victory in Peace. We'll all pray that a lasting structure to his honor may be erected at San Francisco.[29]

But even now with the sounds of muffled drums still in our ears, I heard a man sowing dissension and distrust of our ally Russia by intimating that the only reason Stalin was sending Molotov to the Conference was because he was afraid England would rule unless they sent a super diplomat.[30] Now I think Stalin is sending him as a gesture of friendship to assure us and the world that Russia stands ready to abide by her agreement with our late President and would be our ally in peace as in war. If we can't accept even our friendly allies in good faith, then the future of the world is doomed, and it makes me fearful. But I mustn't say that word. We must all try to remember that truly "there is nothing to fear but fear." What a comforting thought that is! Years hence, when some yet unborn "Dr. I.Q." on some future quiz program offers $1000 for its author's name, perhaps someone will have forgotten who said it, but the phrase itself will never die.[31] Did you hear that stupid person, offered $1200 in war bonds the other night for the author of "Life, Liberty, and the Pursuit of Happiness," lost, wailing "I know the phrase but I don't know who wrote it"? Shades of Thomas Jefferson! Such is fame. But there's one comforting thought. Even though the name of the man whose brain conceived it is forgotten, the idea, once planted, lives

28. The quotation comes from F.D.R.'s first inaugural address of March 4, 1933. The President told the nation: 'The only thing we have to fear is fear itself."

29. The San Francisco Conference, which convened on April 25, 1945, was an international meeting which established the United Nations.

30. Vyacheslav Molotov (1890-1986) was a major spokesman for the Soviet Union at international conferences during and immediately after World War II. He was also felt to be the person who best understood the Soviet leader Joseph Stalin (1879-1953). Molotov's arrival at the San Francisco Conference was viewed as a sign that the Soviet Union was serious about the United Nations.

31. Dr. I.Q. was a popular radio quiz show which was broadcast from local theatres from around the nation. Contestants, introduced from their location in the theatre, won silver dollars if they gave the correct answer. Losers were rewarded with theatre tickets and candy bars from the program's sponsor.

on. And F.D.R., like Jefferson, has planted for us many great ideas which will flourish and help enrich America for hundreds of years to come.

The Howell girls, Julia Lynn and Josephine, are very happy this week, even though the world is in mourning. For Julia Lynn's husband, Jack Steele (Jackson), is home again! He was a linesman in communications with the 3rd Division of Gen. Patch's Seventh Army—associated with the French about whose bravery he can't say enough. After eighty-four days in combat, he was wounded and finally sent home, arriving in New York two weeks ago. From there he was sent to La Garde Hospital in New Orleans, where later he is to undergo another operation. But now he's here on leave with his wife and cunning, curly headed Jackie (age twenty-seven months). And Josephine is out in San Antonio visiting her husband, Lt. Elbert R. Alford (Shaw) of the Supply Department of the Air Corps. She left wee Bobbie (seven months old) with her mother and is enjoying a second honeymoon with the eyes of Texas upon her!

From the papers I heard that a North Carolina paratrooper, one of the capturers of von Papen, erstwhile Fuehrer advisor, after listening to him talk could stand it no longer when von Papen expressed the pious hope he "wished the war was over." His reply, "You and eleven million other guys." That's the way it is, isn't it? Well, here's hoping![32]

Best of luck to each of you.

Sincerely,
Keith Frazier Somerville

May 11, 1945

Dear Boys:

Well, V-E Day has come and gone—that day of Germany's complete downfall for which we have waited and prayed since they marched into Warsaw almost six years ago, starting the bloodiest war in all history and beginning their triumphal march to overrun all

32. Franz von Papen (1879-1969) was an aristocratic supporter of Hitler. For a brief time in 1932, he served as the German Chancellor. After he was deposed, he served in a number of advisory positions to Hitler. He was often given more credence for power than he actually had.

Europe.[33] But there wasn't the wild jubilation which followed the supposedly end of Germany in World War I. There are many of us who recall the celebrations of November 11, 1918, when people went crazy with happiness. Twice in my generation have "the bugle calls of freedom sounded the end of war with Germany." But this time our joy was tinctured with the knowledge that the War Department thinks it must send six million of you boys to the Pacific to wipe out Japan and finish the job. We're quietly thankful that Hitler has got his (how or by what method we may never know) and oh, how happy we are to know there is an end to those awful concentration camps where men, women, and children were slaughtered like cattle, many of them merely for the crime of daring to speak against the sacred Fuehrer, the dreaded Gestapo, or simply because they happened to have been born Jews.... [We] have lived to see Nazism with its stupid idea of race superiority crushed, and to revenge the mass murder of millions, to see all Europe freed, to see Democracy triumphant over Hitler's dream of world domination and the "Fatherland" laid waste.

But just as our flags fly at half mast, so we are only just half happy. For total jubilation we must await the complete surrender of Japan, the coming home of all you boys, and to see whether the United Nations Conference in San Francisco is able to set up a real structure on which to build an enduring peace.

This was the attitude I found in practically everyone to whom I talked, and especially so in the mothers and wives of servicemen. Said Mrs. Tony Brocato, "Yes, its grand, almost too good to be true, but we have a long road ahead of us before the real end comes. But we're this much further along the way." You see, two of her boys are out in the Pacific. C.P., on a newly commissioned transport ship, which he says is a beauty with all modern conveniences, and Joe, on a new type cargo ship with his base on a small Pacific island. (He called his family not long ago at 6 a.m. from San Francisco where they were picking up a cargo. Joe had one wonderful day there with "Wacky" Riley, a "medic" on a troop ship who, by the way, is home

33. V-E Day, Victory-in-Europe Day, formally marking the end of the war in Europe, occurred on May 8, 1945. The German assault on Poland had begun almost six years earlier, on September 1, 1939.

now on leave.) The third Brocato son, Anthony, is in O.C.S. at Ft. Sill, with only eight more weeks to go before he can wear his lieutenant's bars.

Mrs. L.B. Fondren also tho't the news "grand", but with Ernest on Mindanao, she couldn't be too happy.[34] Her son, George, after his years of Marine service in the Pacific, is now still at Camp Le Jeune, North Carolina and son, Billy, is in Italy. I talked with Billy's wife, Evelyn, and she was very, very happy because she had just had a letter from him written on Sunday, April 30th, telling her all about the Italian surrender accomplished that day. Lt. Col. Fondren is attached to the Headquarters of the Mediterranean Theatre and for a year now has been living on the palace grounds at Caserta, where the surrender was signed.[35] He wrote he'd been terribly busy and had had no sleep for two nights, but was looking forward to it on that, their first night of peace in Italy. Evelyn's parents, Rev. and Mrs. Baird, are here visiting her from Booneville (where Brother Baird is now preaching), and so is her pretty sister, Madeline, a former W.A.V.E.—Madeline is en route to New York to visit the parents of her Navy husband, Robert L. Fay, now in the Pacific.

I imagine Col. Bill Litton (Shaw), in an Alabama hospital, feels happier over that Italian campaign that he aided so nobly being over than he does over all those decorations, which continue to be heaped upon him! Our other wounded boys in hospitals probably feel the same way. To mention a couple—there is Russ Brewer (Boyle) and Johnnie Allegrezza (Shaw).

Another only half happy family were the Norwoods. Happy because Forest, now back on duty in Germany (after being wounded and hospitalized) and carrying food to troops in eight German towns and helping to keep order in them, may follow his Purple Heart home before too long. But there's still Bryson, a radio operator, sick

34. A series of landings on Mindanao, the southernmost island in the Philippines chain, began on April 17, 1945. By mid-July, the Japanese had been forced to retreat into isolated pockets in the mountains. Sporadic fighting continued until the end of the war.

35. German forces in Italy surrendered at Caserta on April 29, 1945. This occurred the day after Mussolini and his mistress, Clara Petaccii, were murdered just outside Milan.

with malaria on Luzon, and Clovis, still attached to the giant "Mars," but now in a hospital at Pearl Harbor. . . .

Anyway, there's one man who'll probably want to stay in radio when peace finally comes, and that is Dr. and Mrs. Byrd's grandson, John Tillman. (His parents live in Alabama but we claim a bit of him!) He was sent to Oklahoma to help put on the Sixth War Loan Drive and did such a bang-up job of it that he was immediately transferred to the Army Forces Radio Service, sent first to Hollywood, and is now located for the duration in San Francisco where he daily broadcasts news overseas.[36] Perhaps some of you out in the Pacific have heard his voice. His wife, too, is interested in radio, a script writer for C.B.S. She, a New York girl, Patricia Voils, is now studying at New York University where she will get her degree in a few weeks, after which she expects to join her husband in California. Mrs. Byrd's oldest son, Maj. Herbert, is also stationed in San Francisco, and Col. Carol Byrd is at "Gen. Ike's" (Eisenhower) headquarters in Paris. Mrs. B. is now wondering if the General and his staff will stay on in Europe with the Army of Occupation, be transferred to the Pacific, or be sent home. Anyway, Carol sent them four bottles of wonderful French perfume recently which delighted her heart. The third Byrd son, Lorenz, is down at Pensacola, repairing Navy bombers.

Judge and Mrs. Jackson were more than half happy, too, over V-E Day, though not completely so. "If we could only hear from Charles!" said Mrs. Jackson. Charles, you know, has been reported to be a prisoner of the Germans, and we hope is among those thousands of war prisoners now liberated. But they were very, very happy because Bobbie is home! He was flown from France to New York last Tuesday, reported to Hattiesburg, and is here for leave before rejoining his outfit wherever it may be.

Like Mrs. Jackson, Mrs. Emma Smith voiced the wish, echoed in so many American hearts, "If I could only hear from Robert, now that the fighting is over." Lt. Robert, after serving with Patton's tanks in the Saar basin, was when last heard from with those racing tanks

36. In total, eight war loan drives were conducted. The eighth one is generally described as the Victory War Loan. The amount of money raised by these drives was quite prodigious.

of the 3rd Army down in Czechoslovakia where the last pocket of resistance has been holding out. Maj. Milton Smith is now liaison officer from our Air Corps to the English R.A.F. and is stationed in England. But there's still Clarence, and he's at Okinawa! So she was glad "it's over, over there" (from the song we used to sing in World War I) because it's a milestone on the road home for her boys, but she felt more like praying than celebrating. I saw her at the huge Union Thanksgiving service we had here in Cleveland on the nite of V-E day. With her was her sister, Mrs. Eva Chiles, none too happy either, because her son, Lt. Jimmie, who has been in the Air Corps almost three years, much of the time as instructor, is now finishing up his combat training and expecting to head toward the land of the rising sun soon. The Thanksgiving service was an impressive one, conducted by local ministers, with a huge standing audience inside, on the Methodist church porch, steps, and in the yard. Multiply our meeting by the hundreds of thousands of hamlets and cities in America and you can see how many prayers went up on V-E day. Yes, most of us felt more like praying for the early end of the Japanese war and for an abiding peace than like celebrating. . . .

Now, all our eyes are turned toward the Pacific and to San Francisco where "the hope and fears of all the years are met in you tonight." With the horrors of war so close, I believe all nations honestly desire peace more than anything else, and despite differences of opinions, a start has been made. If the nations (our own as well as the rest) can only realize that a union of countries, like marriage, must be a give and take affair, and often a compromise!

With a prayer for each of you, for the day of total victory and enduring peace.

Sincerely,
Keith Frazier Somerville

June 29, 1945

Dear Boys:

Our own "Boo" Ferris (Shaw) has made headlines on the nation's sport pages lately and been given almost as much publicity as that other Mississippian, Sgt. Jake Lindsey of Lucedale, the 100th Infantryman to win the Congressional Medal of Honor![37] Well, we Americans do love our heroes, war or baseball! When a new baseball star looms on the horizon, he "jes natcherly" gets the limelight, even in war times, particularly, as has happened in this case, when the star is a recently released soldier and the hero of what the papers call "a Cinderella story." Boo (David M.) played ball at Mississippi State and then for awhile at Greensboro, North Carolina, before entering the Army where he was an athletic instructor at Randolph Field, Texas. It was there, he says, that he perfected his pitching under the tutelage of a former White Sox hurler, Bibb Falk, who coached the Air Corps team and gave him "some big league pointers."[38] Because of asthma, he was given a medical discharge in February and joined the Boston Red Sox, where he pitched seven straight victories for them—three of them "shut outs"—pitching thirty-four scoreless innings in thirty-six pitched! Some record.[39]

Well, even in Germany the boys are beginning to think again in terms of sports. Lt. Lawson Magruder has written home for his golf clubs to be sent him there. But other of you boys say those so-called "recreation centers" they're setting up in Europe "aren't so hot" —more like the toughest G.I. training—mile runs and strenuous exercises rather than sports. Lt. Robert Smith, also stationed in Germany, doesn't talk of sports, but he did send home some lovely pictures of the Bavarian Alps near Salzburg where, in happier times, were held the great Wagnerian music festivals—the scenery was beautiful, but he found the nearby concentration camp anything but beautiful!

As news of our boys in Europe trickles in, we are all very happy, particularly over the five recently released from German prison camps.

The first heard from was Charlie Jackson, taken prisoner near

37. The Congressional Medal of Honor is the highest decoration awarded in the armed forces. The award, made in the name of Congress, is granted to any person who has distinguished himself in conflict with the enemy by gallantry and courage, at the risk of his life and above and beyond the call of duty.

38. Bibb Falk played the outfield for the Chicago White Sox from 1920-1928 and for the Cleveland Indians from 1929-1931.

39. "Boo" Ferriss was the leading pitcher for the 1946 Boston Red Sox team which lost the World Series to the St. Louis Cardinals in seven games.

Munich, and he was the first to get home, too—slipping in from Camp Shelby on Sunday. He was flown to New York, then reported to Hattiesburg, and then home! Judge and Mrs. Jackson are undoubtedly the happiest couple in Bolivar County—what with W.A.V.E. Jean, flyer Bob, and ex-German prisoner Charles, all once more around their dinner table! Then came news that June Cummings (Pace), taken prisoner during the Battle of the Bulge, had been freed.

June, you may or may not have heard, married a very beautiful South Carolina girl—Mary Ferguson of Gray Falls, South Carolina. He met her while training at Camp McCall and she's the kind of a blonde gentlemen are said to prefer—and with reason! She is in Pace now, making friends on every side, and they have a little eight weeks old son, James Allaway, Jr., about whose arrival June knew nothing when he wrote after being freed. Since then, Mary has been keeping the cables hot! If he's gotten the news by now, I'm betting he thinks that boat he's coming home on is crawling and the eighteen days till he gets here will seem a lifetime!

Gradually you boys are getting home, and there are many smiling happy people amongst us. Kyle Kestner (Air Corps) arrived Sunday from Selma, Alabama, with a medical discharge—"Home to stay," he says happily.

You fellows keep on getting married, too! Did you see that appalling note on international relations, released the other day? It stated that . . . in Northamptonshire, England, 1150 American airmen have married English girls! Good thing for our girls the war in Europe is over.[40] Maj. Raymond Litton (Shaw) did it recently, but he didn't marry an English girl. He found himself a charming American, red-headed Red Cross girl (Marjorie McKensie from Long Island), flew to Paris (now her headquarters), and flew her back to London with him where they had 'em some wedding! All the post turned out and rode to the wedding in decorated cars, the chief cook made a super-wedding cake, and then the happy couple each had a ten day honeymoon leave.

---

40. For additional information on British war brides of World War II, see Elfrieda Shukert and Barbara Scibetta, *War Brides of World War II* (Novato, California: Presidio Press, 1988).

Down at Boyle, William Turner Poe (Navy—formerly with Missis-sippi Power & Light Company) married, too—an old Delta State girl, Marta Ruthel Turner of Memphis. And over at Sumner the other day, Lester Eavenson also married another "Delta Stater"—Charlene Webb.... And two other Clevelanders who took the fatal step not long ago, Lt. Ray Ruscoe and Ann Bishop, are now at Victorville, California, where Ray is studying radar.

Buck Lemons (Cleveland-Boyle) has been home lately with the delightful wife he acquired up Detroit way while testing planes for Mr. Ford. Remember when Buck was our only R.A.F. pilot and how proud we all were of him? He's still tops to my way of thinking.

Norman Lampard and his wife have been here, too, from his base at Mariana, Florida. His wife, you probably remember, was Marjorie Fikes, who lived here before moving to Florida. The other Lampard brother, William (pharmacist mate-Navy), was due on a leave recently while his wife and babe were here visiting. But alas, the leave was cancelled and K. (Nee Piatt), knowing what that probably meant, shortened her stay and rushed to San Diego to be with him. Col. Bill Litton (Shaw) is also visiting the home folk, and another airman, Lt. Rufus Walt, flew in... for twenty-four hours at home, from Moor Field, Mission, Texas, where he is now an instructor. With fighting over in Europe, a lot of our boys are en route home. F.W. Bishop, with the 8th Air Force, who has been in England two years, is expected home soon, and every day brings news of others who will probably get that thirty day leave before being shipped to the Pacific. All our eyes are turning that way these days....

I read where they've found in Germany a place making rocket bombs which would shoot accurately 3000 miles—the distance across the Atlantic![41] We are told that if the Nazis had had six more months, some of them would have hit New York and Washington. If we are so unfortunate as to have a "next war," I suppose they'll start with those and go till civilization is destroyed. Let's all pray for cooperation in peace, as in war, among the United Nations!

Remember when Roosevelt told the world that the first attack on Tokyo came from "Shangri-La," and we all smiled, remembering the

---

41. The location of the German rocket experiments was Peenemunde, a town located on the Pomeranian coast.

fascinating story of the mythical land, shut away where people lived in no contact at all with the world?[42] It's the kind of place many people have dreamed of when life pressed down too hard on them; the kind of place men seeking surcease from the world's problem's thought, some years ago, they were getting when they settled on lonely atolls in the South Pacific. And just see what THEY got! Listening to an account of the squabbles a the Golden Gate Conference one night recently, I heard someone say: "The future scares me! I'd like to settle on some far away mountain top." So even now, when it has been proven that isolation can't ever exist anywhere anymore, people still dream of a Shangri-La! And now they've a true Shangri-La out in Dutch New Guinea—only now that it's been found, it is no longer Shangri-La! Already, American planes are circling overhead, dropping supplies and paratroopers who are building a landing site for a glider, which is to be sent in. The A.P. tell us, "A wartime tragedy has unlocked in a dramatic fashion, the mysterious hidden valley of Shangri-La." It seems that a transport plane, with twenty-four passengers, on May 24th crashed against the mountain walls surrounding this unexplored valley where 50,000 people have lived entirely cut off from the world. Now their peace is being disturbed by the effort to rescue the three survivors (a W.A.C. and two air men). They have been given salt, candy bars, and American cigarettes! Will they, I wonder, want to renounce their isolation after this, and get out and see the world beyond their mountains? Well, Shangri-La is "opened up"; if they ever want peace again, they'll have to join the United Nations.[43] The news from San Francisco seems encouraging, but sometimes I can't figure out the whys of all their arguments. To me, a bystander, it seems such a simple matter

42. Shangri-La was the name of the mythical country in James Hilton's novel, *Lost Horizon* (New York: Morrow, 1933). When President Roosevelt was asked where the bombers came from that attacked Japan in the April 1942 raid, he answered "Shangri-La."

43. In the early summer of 1945, many Americans became interested in the location and rescue of several American survivors of a military aircraft crash in a remote section of Dutch New Guinea. The area where the crash occurred was described in the press as "Shangri-La." Many goods were parachuted to the survivors. This and other largesse from the skies led to the development of "cargo cults" among the aboriginal people. These events were reported in the New York *Times* on June 9, 10, 14, 23, 25, 30, July 3, 8, 10, 1945.

to realize that we MUST have peace—or else! Why can't all the delegates see that and stop jowering over unimportant details? . . .

With hopes that the world's thinking may clarify and the true road to future peace and happiness may open by the time you reach Tokyo.

Sincerely, your friend,
Keith Frazier Somerville

August 31, 1945

Dear Boys:

It seems almost unbelievable, doesn't it, that Peace has come again to the world? We have lived with war so long—it almost seems forever! It's even hard to remember a time when we weren't hanging over the radio waiting for "the news." I heard the glad tidings atop a Tennessee mountain where I've been spending the summer helping nurse the five grandbabies.[44] (Someone said we'd win the war if the grandmothers could only hold out! Well, we did.) Compared to the wild celebrations the radio recorded all over the United States, ours was a quiet celebration. We all went over and each took a hand at ringing the big bell which calls people to church services and picture shows here. I even held up the tiny granddaughters and let them pull the rope, so that in later years they might recall that they had a hand in the jubilation of ushering in peace in our time. "God grant that peace may at least last out their life times!" Then we went to a big rock on the edge of the mountain and sang "Praise God From Whom All Blessings Flow" and "America the Beautiful" and wept some happy tears and said some prayers—just as people were doing all over the world. My prayers were of thankfulness for you boys who will return and thanks for the bravery of those who have given their lives that freedom might live and the forces of evil be crushed. This has been such a horrible war, and so far flung that even we noncombatants, who have suffered not at all, are exhausted emotionally and mentally trying to keep up with it, do our small parts, and try not to worry. We've lived on a tension for so long that it's going to be

---

44. Mrs. Somerville usually spent part of each summer at Monteagle, the residential Chautauqua grounds near Sewanee, Tennessee. She was at Monteagle when World War II ended.

hard for all of us to relax. They tell us that in this postwar world we're entering the atoms will help give us leisure when it is geared to peace, as it now is to war.

I got a tremendous thrill over being here in Tennessee for the unveiling of "Project X" (the Clinton Oak Ridge atom bomb project) on which so many people I know (including many Bolivar Countians) have worked and which has been a mystery for so long. Wasn't it wonderful the way the secret was kept? They say we're a garrulous nation, but no one can say again that we tell all we know! The implication of the split atom being discovered and harnessed is awe-inspiring and terrifying, isn't it? I almost felt, for a moment, like some of the people interviewed on the radio, that it should have been buried and forgotten. Perhaps we have unloosed a Frankenstein which may eventually destroy us, but it's here, and we should only be thankful its secrets were discovered first by a peace loving nation! What if Germany had beaten us to it? It did shorten the war, and with proper handling may help preserve the peace and bring to the world undreamed of luxuries. "The atomic age," someone said, "may well be the golden age of civilization." Let us hope it will be.

Yesterday I got another thrill, even though a minor one: I drove into a filling station and said once more, "Fill her up!" We didn't half appreciate cars 'till we had to think twice before using them! I suppose we'll take them for granted again one of these days, but for me it will be a long time. Did you hear about the filling station attendant who replied to a customer's wonder over getting all the gas he wanted, his windshield wiped, and a coke and package of cigarettes in the bargain, with, "Say Mister, didn't you know there's a war off?" Wonderful thought!

I haven't any news today for you about any of your friends, for I've been away, but I just HAD to tell you how happy I am that you'll be coming home one of these days, and how grand it will be to see young faces everywhere again. We've missed your smiles and collectively we've worried so much about you! It will be good to have you home!...

In 1918 a friend of mine, Corinne Roosevelt Robinson, (a sister of President Teddy Roosevelt), wrote some lines which are just as applicable today, so I'll give them to you in closing—

Once more comes "Peace—Goodwill."
Once more hope unstifled springs,
And hearts are glad because it seems that still
We heard the rustle of the Angels' wings.

As, long ago, the men who watched their sheep
Welcomed the radiant messengers of light,
So we who walked in darkness, woke to weep,—
No longer dream of slaughter in the night.

Ring out oh! bells of Peace, and let your voice
Be the new pledge of brotherhood in truth—
The valiant Dead would bid us to rejoice,
For this they gave their ardor and their youth.

That all the anguish, all the mortal pain
Shall bring new vision to a world once blind;
The booming guns, though silenced, call again
Not now to die, but live for all mankind![45]

Sincerely, your friend,
Keith Frazier Somerville

45. Mrs. Somerville had met Corinne Roosevelt Robinson (1861-1933) during her Washington years, 1905-1911. During World War I, Corinne Roosevelt Robinson was active in Red Cross work and a frequent speaker at Liberty Loan campaigns. She was also the founder of the New York City Committee for the "Fatherless Children of France." She published several books of poetry including *The Poems of Corinne Roosevelt Robinson* (New York: Charles Scribner's Sons, 1924). The poem quoted by Mrs. Somerville is a slight paraphrase of "Christmas, 1918."

INDEX

www.ingramcontent.com/pod-product-compliance
Lightning Source LLC
Chambersburg PA
CBHW051146030726
47504CB00004B/1065